THE GREAT
CLIMBING
ADVENTURE

John Barry

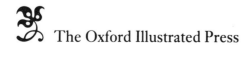
The Oxford Illustrated Press

© 1985, John Barry

Printed in England by J.H.Haynes & Co Limited,
Sparkford, Near Yeovil, Somerset.

ISBN 0 946609 07 1

Distributed in North America by Interbook Inc.,
14895 E. 14th Street, Suite 370, San Leandro, CA 94577 USA

The Oxford Illustrated Press, Sparkford, Yeovil, Somerset

Front Cover

Guy Neithardt climbing on West Ridge of Gauri Sankar.

Back Cover (left to right)

1. Deborah. Climbing to the Col. East Ridge in the background.

2. Gauri Sankar. Looking back at Camp II.

3. Gauri Sankar. The Ridge above Camp III.

CONTENTS

DEDICATION

For Dad who taught me about climbing and writing.

And for Mum who worried.

ACKNOWLEDGEMENTS

Dotti, Val and Kathy for typing.
Guy Sheridan for loan of diary and maps.
Famille Egal for house and help.
DVN, Sam and Tulip Bemrose for loan of their memory.
All my Royal Marine Friends for the good times.
Nigel Shepherd, Malcolm Campbell and Rob Collister for loan of their slides.
Diagrams by Steve Ashton.
(Photos by author unless otherwise stated.)

Other books by the author:
Cold Climbs A selection of great British winter climbs, with Ken Wilson and David Alcock.

Introduction

'Daffed the world aside and bid it pass'
Henry IV: Shakespeare

The most common question all climbers are asked is 'why?' 'why do you climb?' It is the most common and the most reasonable question, yet it is also the most futile — you'll never get a good, or even a truthful answer. A question asked so often that it's become a cliché, it brings embarrassed or indulgent smiles to the faces of the *cognoscente*. Yet, it remains a perfectly legitimate question; the only question about climbing that needs to be answered; the question that is still *the* question.

I have never heard a half-convincing reply — nor been able to essay one myself — beyond the easy one: the excitement, the danger (and that provokes the same question all over again so that it is more question than answer, more enigma than explanation), the pleasure (more questions), the views (a glimmer of understanding), the friendship, comradeship (a nod) and a dozen other easy-to-spot ingredients of this most arcane of recipes. It is more for those unspecified ingredients that we climb — for that something which is greater than the sum of all those glib replies. And yet no-one can say it clearly, or speak its name.

Perhaps there are no words to convey the truthful answer — but that is unlikely, given that climbers come from the four corners of the earth, scour another four corners for their climbs, and would explore the four corners of hell too if it offered hope of a hill. Unlikely too, given that the climbing game embraces a goodly portion of the world's best languages; tongues that have enabled Shakespeare, Proust and Goethe to reach the upper-most slopes, if not the summits of their consuming passion. It can hardly be that the words just aren't there.

1

And certainly climbers try to explain. We try to explain verbally but that allows little time for reflection, so we write; reams of the stuff. Few sports can have generated such a welter of literature; far, far more than is needed merely to explain or answer. Why then, these reams? After all when a runner turns in a good mile he doesn't trot home, grab a pen and write the story of it — so why do climbers?

Articles, stories, reviews, profiles, confessions, thoughts, interviews, photographs, photomontages, pictorial essays, diagrams — they fall like perennial snow and, snow-like, most settle in a soft veil, vaguely appealing. Others obfuscate. Some hide altogether. A few (too few), like some snows, enhance, shine, reflect, frame, accentuate — or try to do too many of these things at once. Then the truth avalanches. Some of this writing is marvellously mundane, some spectacularly awful; some though is magnificent. And some of it is funny, some sad — tearful sad — and lots plain daft; but it's been spewing out for a century or more and shows no sign of slackening. Is it merely boast? I think not. A hope to entertain? Maybe. A genuine desire to pass on useful information? Perhaps. A need to share? Possibly. Or some strange catharsis? Probably it's all of these things in varying proportions according to individual taste — and to the story that is being told.

So we do try to explain even if we only scribble a mumble and even if we fail. Perhaps it can't be done, truly just can't be done. Or perhaps mountaineering awaits its Shakespeare. It could be that the climbing effort drains the writing effort from us (writing is the greater effort in any case), or maybe, just maybe, we tread softly on the truth lest we squeeze it out and surprise or disturb ourselves; for once it has been revealed we'll have no more reason, no excuse, no desire to climb again. The game — and it is only a game — hardly bears rational examination after all. The dozens of questions got up as answers to the big question 'why do you play this game?' are proof of that, not refutation.

Here then are my ninety thousand words on why I climb. I doubt that they will advance the quest for the answer one jot as all I can tell you for sure is that I find it fun; that I love it. Love it right down to the bottom-most moment of it when the morale is at its lowest, the heart in the pub and the soul elsewhere — anywhere elsewhere. I love the anticipation, thrill to it still; love the execution, the doing of it; and the reflection. (Indeed, sometimes

2

the pleasure is exclusively retrospective — and even then it may need a few pints to get it started.)

But, if in these pages you perceive some reason for it all, I will be pleased; if you do not — well then at least I join an eminent team of failures.

1
New Zealand

THE SOUTHERN ALPS AND
NOT TO REASON WHY

'Oh, our manhood's prime vigour!
No spirit feels waste,
Not a muscle is stopped in its playing,
Nor sinew unbraced.
Oh, the wild joys of living!
The leaping from rock up to rock—'

Saul: Robert Browning

We went to New Zealand at the charge; full tilt. It was the only way to do it; the only way we stood a chance. We knew nothing, absolutely nothing about alpinism; had not so much as sipped at mountains' Pierian spring. Yet here we were, off half way round the world to good-sized chunks of wild mountains — mountains with a big reputation — with nothing much more between us than a pile of mostly duff gear, a colossal ignorance, and a seemingly inexhaustible supply of enthusiasm. But I'm rushing; charging at New Zealand again. It's difficult to go there any other way — to go slowly is very hard work — for even after a fifteen-year pause the memory of the heady, joyous, crazy, carefree, full-tilted charge of that first foray fires me fullblast still.

To begin at the beginning. In 1969 I was posted to Singapore to join 40 Commando, Royal Marines, a unit languishing, like all the others on that island, in end-of-Empire lethargy. We worked a thing called 'tropical routine': 7.30 am to 1.30 pm. The remainder of the day and most of the night we played. Just once in a while we'd be galvanised into action by General Percival's Ghost and storm off across the Straits and into the Malayan jungle, there to tackle some imaginary 'Red' host. (To begin with we always fought against 'Red Forces'. They were later watered-down to 'Orange Forces' — a diplomatic dilution. I cannot

4

believe it fooled anyone, 'Red Forces' included. We always won which was fun, but fooled no-one either).

On one such bout I recall going without sleep for more than sixty hours; good training for stemming the Red tide maybe, or for mountaineering, but a rude shock to de-tuned fighting men idling at tropical routine. Mostly then it was seven-thirty to one-thirty at a barely audible tick-over, followed by an afternoon of lazing at the pool or water skiing and then a turbo-charged riot of a night. In between we squeezed parties. There were plenty to choose from: formal parties, balls, fancy-dress parties, shipwreck parties, come-as-you-are parties, white-tie parties, planters' parties, satay parties, scruff-rig parties and, if you ran out of ideas, just plain ordinary parties. One enterprising friend threw a *soixante-neuf* party, it being 1969, but no-one had any clear idea of what he had in mind so that it was surprisingly poorly attended — and then only by mates — not what anyone had in mind. There was even a wild rumour or two of wife-swapping parties but since we bachelors lacked the currency needed to qualify for attendance, the rumours remained rumours — which is probably all they were anyway.

Looking back it was the sheer waste of time that I regret. That, and, apart from some high moments of huge fun and two terrific climbing adventures, the mindless, stultifying, interminable boredom of it all. The old hands loved it of course. Next-to-no-work and generous overseas allowances allowed a sybaritic life-style and an *amah* to clear up afterwards. Few of us ever had it so good; fewer, if any at all, were going to have it so good ever again. An easy, decent going-on-decadent, cruise to nowhere in particular; a slow boat to December 1971, the British withdrawal from the Far East and the end of a great chunk of history. A last hedonistic hurrah flung down the final flank of Empire.

But, that waste of time excepted (and there must have been a time when it wasn't wasted), I saw nothing in Singapore that explains why it is now so fashionable to apologise for our colonial past. Grown-ups playing grown-up games and playing them pretty well and fairly honestly. Consenting adults right down to the most virgin soldier, we were generally happily tolerated by the other much larger consenting adult populations of Chinese, Malays and Indians. They liked each other a lot less than they liked the British whom they all, cheerfully and with much good

5

grace, exploited and to which exploitation the British, with equal good grace and just as cheerfully, submitted. What a bunch we must have seemed, expecially to the serious-minded, industrious Chinese; these Brits who lived as if the tomorrow of Britain was a long way off, and to be postponed if at all possible; as if the rest of the world was farther away still and better, cancelled altogether. And all this was fine and dandy for the old hands.

But for us — we subalterns, the young Turks of 40 Commando — for us, with atrophying brains, with no thought in the primary jungle of our minds for the life of an island that manifested the energy of at least four major cultures; nor with hardly any care for tomorrow and certainly none for the day after that; for whom only a hunger for the morning staved off a thirst for the afternoon; for whom the amok of a full today was everything; for us it was *not* all fine and dandy. Once the novelty of Wanchai Burburys, of haggling over prices (a two-dollar saving cost a lot of time), of transvestites and Bugis Street, of 'you wan' short-time John?', of noodles at 'Fatties' as the sun came up Sunday morning, of sabotaging the Naval Officers' Club pool with piranhas, of smuggling LP's into Johore, of Saturday afternoon Plate-Throwing Olympics at Ceyion Sam's, of chuppati-eating competitions, of ferocious rugby against the New Zealand Regiment and of a near endless series of drunken binges; once the philistine novelty of all that wore off, we were bored; even to the veriest Goth or Visi-Goth or Hun amongst us. Few of us wrote a word beyond the odd letter home or a placatory note to the Bank Manager. Few read. Few did anything but what the day demanded, though *that* we did with interest. Looking back I bitterly regret my indolence. If only I could have those years to wrestle with again.

Now four or five of us were climbers, rock climbers and not bad by the standard of the time, leading what would now be graded E2/5b or so, and as keen about the game as anyone before or since. We searched Singapore high and low, though mostly low, for the trace of climbable rock; found none, not a crag nor the least boulder. So we invaded Malaya, fast as the Japanese but in the other direction, determined to circumnavigate the entire country if necessary in our quest; up the East Coast, across the top as close to the Thai border as we could get and down the West. There were rumours of some sort of rock at Ipoh and at

Kuala Lumpur, both miles to the north-west, and of limestone at Kuantan 200 miles up the east coast. We looked at that first, sped north undeterred by an all-enveloping jungle that could have easily hidden a 'Cloggy' in its humid embrace — sniffing and poking and prodding, following our noses and every local rumour until, indeed at Kuantan, we found what we needed — a 1000-foot-high dollop of limestone that rose vertically clean out of the jungle to a lost world on its summit; a real boredom break-er. Had we been able to muster one whit of intellectual curiosity between us we might have wondered how this mighty edifice arrived there; but we couldn't and we didn't. It was the climb we were after, the geology could wait. (It is still waiting. I have no idea what caused this 1000-foot by 5-mile calcarious wart.)

It was said in the local bazaar that the monolith, full of tunnels and enormous caves, had served as a hospital and a headquarters for Communist terrorists during the Malayan Emergency of the 'Fifties. We found nothing to give that rumour credence but we did find our climb. Parking the Land Rover at a *Kampong* we left the sweet-sour smell of tropical habitation to the indiscriminate pig, and set out for the crag. The walk was pleasant at first, through the open lines of a rubber plantation, then less easy in a push through secondary jungle to a narrow band of primary jungle that fringed the base of the monolith. The limestone wall rose, nowhere less than vertical — or so my recollection has it — clean to the roof of the jungle 200 feet above. Though we couldn't see through the canopy of thick green foliage, we knew from our binoculared view from the road that the rock soared on above for perhaps another 800 feet.

A brief reconnaissance, conducted in great excitement, found the beginnings of a crack-and-chimney system that led as far as the canopy — and which looked as if it might continue above. It did; at roughly VS. A few hours and many pints of water later — we carried water bottles slung about us, jungle-patrol style, to combat the 95° heat and enervating humidity — we stood on top in a Doyleanesque lost world of limestone pinnacles and stunted shrubs, incongruously set above a tumbling sea of luxuriant green that flooded to every horizon.

It was 6 pm. The quick equatorial dusk meant that it would be dark by seven: dark up here and pitch black below the canopy. Spotting new lines as we abseiled off pegs and trees, whooping down. Our great discovery had sparked off a whole new enthusiasm, had kindled imaginations unbridled by sense of gravity, realism or anything much besides.

But a swarm of hornets put paid to all that. We were searching for an anchor for what we hoped would be our last abseil, about level or just above the jungle canopy, when we heard a helicopter buzzing somewhere round a corner. Now we knew all about helicopters — we worked ᴡith them daily and in the jungle too. Indeed, one of our number had earned enormous notoriety by colliding with a helicopter and writing-off the thing completely — they're fragile beasts. He'd been driving back to camp one morning, late for work after some strenuous social duty, when, rounding a bend on the wrong side of the road (common enough practice in Singapore), he found himself square in the path of a low-loader that was slowly bearing a helicopter. The helicopter was swathed in soft protection and was presumably poorly or it would have been flying. Well the low-loader swerved violently to avoid our mate and ended up portside in a monsoon drain. Both drivers were unhurt but unfortunately the helicopter had rolled off the now awry low-loader and taken a short but terminal tumble down a grass bank. And even as we climbed the entire resources of the Department of Army Legal Services, the mecca of military law, were being mobilised to discover what was the name of the crime that had surely been so heinously committed. But the arm of military law was not long enough. Either that or a sense of humour, for which there was ample precedent, prevailed over the statute book; our mate got off scott free, a folk-hero to boot, and the taxpayer footed the bill.

So we knew all about helicopters — and this buzzing, a mild curiosity so far from Singapore — was assuredly a helicopter. Probably a Sioux, someone said, and we agreed. Then a black cloud of hornets buzzed angrily by and froze us to our ledge — not the one of us tied to anything so carefree had the whole enterprise seemed — transfixed now in fear and loathing. The helicopter buzzed on showing us no mind. Our whole new enthusiasm flew with it.

'Some chopper', one said, unconsciously Churchillian.

'Bugger this', another said, consciously populist.

In some anonymous bar in Kuantan that night a new realism dawned. After all, wasn't it ridiculously steep? It was. And didn't

8

the humidity get you? It did. You climbed in a waterfall of per-spiration and a single strenuous move sprung an instant new Niagara. It was hopelessly humid, like climbing in a sauna. And there must be better fun to be had somewhere else and, and, and... The realism rolled on and for the moment the bar girls looked a more attractive and less challenging proposition than the 'Kuantan Jump' as one of us and some Tiger beer had labelled the dollop. Yes, a new realism had dawned and the night looked good.

'How about New Zealand', someone said, Stu I think it was. And that was it. New Zealand it was, those four words represent-ing about 50% of the preparation and planning.

'Not sure how far it is.'

'Nearest map's Singers.' So Singers it was. That same night. Helter skelter down the East coast road, hootin' and hollerin' to the four winds and the nine gods like the idiots we were, an even newer enthusiasm fired with this latest idea, hell bent on New Zealand wherever it might be and whatever it might hold, the world and a crate of Tiger beer at our feet and not a care that couldn't be whooped away into the warm tropical night, nor any hope that couldn't be enlarged with a guzzle.

There were four of us in the team, although this had swelled to six or seven by the time we embarked on the adventure. Stu Ray, Dave Nicholls and myself were all three Lieutenants, Paul Liddell was a Corporal. Naturally he did most of the work and all of the thinking. Stu was easily the most enthusiastic man I have ever met; not just about climbing, that was to be expected, but about everything — in fact he was enthusiastic about being enthusiastic. Stu enthused so much about chasing girls, about parties, about climbing, about soldiering — in roughly that order — you wondered how he could spread it so far and so thick; it just kept coming. For life and all in it, he had energy for the lot. Now he planned with enthusiasm, though with nothing much else to be sure; without system or continuity and certainly with-out geography. To Stu's hair-brained haphazardness Paul Liddell lent some good north-country common-sense. The scheme grew. Dave and I did things differently — which is to say that we did nothing at all except to enquire once in a while, bet-ween games of rugby or parties, how the trip was shaping-up. All

9

we knew and cared was that the four of us were going to climb in New Zealand. How or what, mattered little, if at all. A mountain was a mountain and any mountain would do. Anyway since none of us had ever climbed on anything but British crags, Kuantan excepted, we were hardly discerning judges.

Looking back — and our best moments often pass unremarked and so quickly that as we grow older we spend more and more time in reflection — looking back I find it hard to believe or to understand that we could have been so utterly carefree, so hugely ignorant, so monstrously stupid, so wildly irresponsible and so wonderfully innocent. Experience, life and age have weathered away the corners of those shortcomings now and filled with dust some of the holes between, but the shame of it is that innocence is always the first casualty. Oh for that innocence now! These days I plan, research, study records and accounts, maps and photographs, spend hours in libraries ferreting amongst indexes; and dream and ponder and consider — but mostly dream. In those days dreams and action were closer relatives. Sometimes they were twins born only seconds apart. Oh for that lost innocence and the profligate energy that burnt for it. It was a great combustion; a fine fire that took us places no planning ever could. Why did we climb then? I'm not sure, any more than I am now; but it was almost certainly for the excitement, nothing more. It would be ten years before any of us uttered the word 'philosophy' — and I hope it will be twenty more before we stop to think whether we have one. Life then was about squeezing as much into 24 hours as could be packed tight; we knew that it was not a rehearsal; quality mattered much less than quantity. We thought it better to be greedy and to take big bites, and that anything less than full-tilt was a betrayal of the gift. And that was about it. Not much for Freud to go on. We were probably boors, certainly not nihilists; just young fools who had gone off a bit quick in life's run and, not knowing what the distance was, thought it better to collapse before the end than to finish with something to spare. Today I'm glad that I didn't waste my time trying to work out why I climbed; gladder still that I never wasted another's time in trying to explain. For now I know that there is no explanation; it will not be rationalised; indeed doesn't bear rational examination for much more than a minute. Like life itself, it is untranslatable, an unfathomable question — and there

10

are times when climbing is bigger and better. If you know the answer to one then you know it to both. Few of us, it seems, know either. So we 'daffed the world aside and let it pass'.

We were going to go in November simply because we had been advised that that was the beginning of the New Zealand summer and as early as we could expect to have any chance of getting high. It was August and we, impatient, would have gone sooner if we could.

Alpine gear is not the normal stuff of tropical islands but by September we had imported a modest collection of alpinists' kit and clothing: ice-axes designed in the early 1800s for Swiss guides to cut steps by the score for clients; hammers that only Thor could have wielded (and then with difficulty); crampons with quick release straps so anxious to please that they were on and off more often than a whore's drawers (Stu's lovely phrase that); and clothing to match — match the kit that is, not the whore or her drawers. Nevertheless we had great sport trying it all on, parading it about and thought ourselves to be as well equipped as any other alpinist — and that's what counts. It's morale that keeps you warm in a cold bivouac and morale that gets you up that 5000 feet of mountain; morale and not all the thermal efficiency or power-to-weight ratio in the world.

Early October we had most things but still no lift. The 8000 miles were looming wide, wider even than our enthusiasm could bridge. Then Ray and Liddell pulled off some logistical coups that would have flattered a Chief-of-Staff, let alone a lowly corporal and a lowlier lieutenant. In a month, thanks largely to Stu's stunning ignorance of the 'normal military channels' we had a free flight to Auckland (admittedly in a draughty Hercules transport plane at 300mph or in 2 days — whichever came first) as well as a free train ride from Auckland to Christchurch, the loan of a New Zealand Regiment Land Rover (it may have been *the* Land Rover) and enough food to feed an army; any army.

With things progressing apace I thought it was time to ask of Stu what it was we might be climbing.

'Mt. Cook 12,326 feet', he recited without hesitation. 'First climbed by a bloke called Green in 1882 though there seems to be some doubt about that now, probably less than 100 ascents to date and none earlier in the year than December.'

'I wonder what it looks like?'

11

We had not a single photograph of it but the challenge was no match for Stu's enthusiasm. Three days later he produced eight sets of matching stereo pairs of aerial photographs covering the half of Mt. Cook National Park. Somehow he'd persuaded a pilot friend to fly his Canberra bomber the round trip from Singapore to take them for him. Unbelievable I know, but it's true and I have some of the photographs still. Quite how he pulled that one he wouldn't reveal but I know generals who'd be pleased to think they could command such a feat.

Dave and I still did little, perhaps nothing. Then I flew back to England, bought a pair of boots, got married and drove with Kathy the day after to Brize Norton where we discovered that she, as the wife of an officer serving abroad was entitled to a flight to join her husband, but that I didn't qualify for a flight since there was nothing in the regulations that allowed husbands, who were already serving abroad to join their wives, who were in any case flying out in the very near future, to join their husbands. 'In other words', said a helpful but perplexed Movements Corporal, 'you've blown it. Try hitching.' Even to one as irresponsible as myself it seemed hard luck that Kathy might arrive in Singapore, not know a soul and with no home to go to, before I did. I set about the business of scrounging a lift in a VIP aircraft.

I arrived in Singapore a few hours ahead of Kathy who stepped off her plane into 95° heat and 99 per cent humidity wearing most of my climbing clothing as well as my new boots. I hadn't been allowed any baggage with my VIP's and as most of her 40-lb allowance had, not unreasonably, been taken up with the wherewithal of a two-year stay she had to wear the surplus — my surplus really.

I had spent my few hours alone shopping for a car and looking for a home. The second was easy; a telephone call to a very good mate fixed it. Jonno Thomson lived with his wife Liz in Johore Bahru, the first town on the Malayan side of the causeway that linked the island of Singapore to the Malay peninsula. 'No probs, stay as long as you like.' The car was not quite so straightforward. I had a lover's desire to impress Kathy and a romantic notion that I wanted to drive my new bride across this tropical island to Malaya in some style. I secured the services of a taxi to help me find one. It was a 'Fast Black', service slang for pirate taxis. These were uniformly black diesel Mercedes, long on miles, short on servicing, heavy on pollution but light on the pocket and as a consequence, very popular; economics triumphing over moral and safety considerations — not that the average Fast Black fare went in much for moralising; or safety either.

'You want short time John, nice girl?' It was the standard opening to negotiations between a Fast Black driver and a British serviceman — a sad reflection perhaps on the degeneration of a species that Kipling had described as his 'country's best ambassador'. And it wasn't that he knew my name. No, all Chinese traders addressed all British troops, unless they were evidently senior by age or rank — and I was transparently neither — as 'John'. And all British soldiers addressed all Chinese traders by the same name. On my first visit to Singapore four years earlier, I had been amazed that half the population of the island seemed to know my name. Why it should be 'John' and why that name should be bandied so universally and indiscriminately, I have no idea, but that's the way it was.

'Nice girl, clean girl, John, all night? You wan all night? Exhibish John; you wan exhibish?'

'No thanks John not today. I want to buy a car, nice car, clean car, very fast car; very quickly.'

'OK John, I take you.'

Which was why I'd flagged him down in the first place. He took me alright, through red lights, through swarming pedestrian crossings to one second-hand car salesman after another until at last I saw it, a little red MGA with wire wheels and a tonneau-cover. No salesmanship was necessary: I'd have bought that car from Richard Nixon. An inspection and test drive were equally superfluous; this was love, not mechanics. Earlier that morning I'd gone to see my Unit's Imprest Holder, 'Cookie'. Cookie knew the regulations inside out and was of the enlightened opinion that they were there to be made to work for us, not against us, as the Civil Service are wont to interpret them. 'Make sure you come and see me when you get back from UK', he'd advised when I told him I was shooting off to get married, 'You'll be entitled to all sorts of goodies.' The biggest goody was a lump sum of £120 for 'removal expenses'.

'But I haven't borne any removal expenses, I haven't moved anywhere yet.'

'Rubbish, you've just moved 8000 miles. Don't argue. Then

there's a Settling-in Allowance, the Amah's Allowance, the Service Form 542 for the train fare from Brize Norton to the Church. . . .' There were a few other things too but by this time I'd given up trying to fathom Service regulations. We were lucky we had Cookie. He was good news for us, bad news for the taxpayer. I'd left the Imprest Office with pockets crammed with Singapore dollars and now I unhooked them from my trousers, counted them none too carefully, thrust them upon a delighted car salesman, jumped in (over the door, of course) and sped away leaving the pirate haggling for his cut, and the niceties of tax and insurance to another day.

Kathy stepped from the aeroplane into that heat and sopping humidity and was instantly at home. It took most Europeans weeks to acclimatize but Kathy had been born in Barbados and bred in Trinidad (indeed she was travelling on a Barbados passport); she was a creature of the sun — perhaps the years in the West Indies had left her residually acclimatized to the tropics for life. It certainly seemed so.

I relieved her of my boots and duvet and waved an arm in a big gesture at the car park.

'Whichever one you fancy is yours.'

'That one.' She pointed at the MG; she knew me well.

We drove off, happy as larks. Kathy remarked how like Trinidad it all was. She was clearly at ease in this new world and I was relieved, for despite my *cavaliero*, I had been anxious lest she found the change too sudden or too great, the land strange or Service ways foreign. But I needn't have worried, she was at home; a duck to water.

A couple of days later, about a week before we were due to leave for New Zealand, Stu asked me if I'd remembered to ask the Commanding Officer if we could go. I hadn't. Apparently I had been allocated this task some months earlier; why even Nicholls had done something administrative towards the trip though, significantly, no-one could remember exactly what. It meant a formal letter to our CO, which in turn meant some delving into a manual, JSP101, which gives the arcane format. This was the first service deterrent to young officers and hairbrained schemes. I hurried out a draft and Kath typed it:

14

Lieutenant Colonel J.J. Alexander Royal Marines
Headquarters
40 Commando Royal Marines
BFPO

Sir,
I have the honour to request that Lieutenants John Barry,
David Nicholls and Stewart Ray and Corporal Paul Liddell
are granted six weeks leave for the purpose of climbing Mt.
Cook.
I have the honour to be
Sir
Your Obedient Servant
John Barry
Lieutenant Royal Marines

Fortunately the CO was a genial fellow and blessed, like the
best of that warrior/landowning class, with immense tolerance,
great humour and a deal of plain common-sense. The Adjutant
summoned me by telephone. I knocked on the door of his office,
marched in and saluted smartly. He eyed me with suspicion. An
Adjutant's job is to make a unit work. They rightly regard young
officers as an only just necessary evil.
'The CO wishes to see you.'
It was a statement and a question too. I knew my chances were
better with the CO who had got to the state in his career where
he had learnt to love young officers as a master loves his puppies.
I had no wish to play my cards at this table where I would
certainly lose and likely incur a brace of extra duties in the
process.
'Yes Sir,' it was the least I could get away with by way of reply:
no substance but no offence either.
'Mm.'
The phone rang.
'40 Commando. Adjutant speaking.'
'It's me darling.' I was saved. He waved at me.
'In you go.'
'What's that darling?'
'Nothing darling, just a young officer.'
I moved across to the CO's office and waited outside, rigidly

'at ease'. He looked up, saw me through the open door, and nodded me in.

I marched in, halted, and saluted very smartly.

'Now, tell me John, what's all this about?'

'Well Sir, it's like this. . .' I told him.

'Mm, don't see why not. There's no war on and if one starts while you're away, I dare say we'll hold the fort 'till you get back.'

I assured him that if such a contingency arose we'd be back, 'soon as we could'.

And that was it. New Zealand. Auckland via Alice Springs. Take the Blue Streak from Auckland down the length of the North Island to Wellington, a ferry across to Picton Sound and a flat-board slow train to Christchurch. From there in the loaned Land Rover to Mt. Cook village. Simple. We reckoned that we had most of what we needed and it never occurred to us that some might consider us short on experience. Experience was not a word to be found in our collective vocabulary; if it was essential we'd grab some while we were there. If not, we'd do without. One of the advantages of launching the enterprise from Singapore rather than from Britain was, apart from the obvious geographical one, that there were no other mountaineers around from whom to seek advice. Had we been embarking from the UK I doubt if we'd have left its shores. Wise counsel would have cautioned us away, in our own best interests you understand. Experienced alpinists would have shaken sage heads sadly and steered us elsewhere and as like as not Mums would have had something to say: all in all we would have been persuaded that our energies were better directed elsewhere. They would have been right; but see what we would have missed.

At the appointed hour a New Zealand Airforce C130 Hercules trundled onto the tarmac, 'incoming' from Hong Kong. We were welcomed into its cavernous hold by a friendly uniformed lass who, with an expansive wave, showed us to anyone of about sixty temporary canvas seats. They were designed for parachutists short-stay backsides rather than for long-haul rumps, but for buckshee you could hardly chaff.

As the plane lumbered down the runway we were abuzz with childlike excitement — and very smug. We threw our kit into a net toward the stern and settled into three seats each. Not long after the off Nicholls nudged me and in that confidential way we use when we want everyone to notice he pointed to a plain, brown paper-wrapped carton, the size of a kleenex tissue box, that sat on his knee.

'A gross,' he announced in a shout above the engine noise — from the inside the Hercules looks like a giant piece of Meccano and being designed for carrying equipment, rather than personnel, it wears little or no sound insulation.

'A gross?'

'Yes, a gross,' adding helpfully, 'one hundred and forty four.'

'144 what?'

'Prophylactics.'

'Prophylactics?'

'Yes Prophylactics — condoms, you know FL's, french letters, Johnnies; got 'em at the sick bay on the way out of the camp.'

'What are you going to do with them?'

'What do you think?'

'But we're going climbing and that for about four weeks at most. Anyway there's less than three million people in New Zealand so that lot'll account for a good percentage of the willing females in the entire population. Any spare?'

'Apparently they're all ravers, so I've heard. Not likely.'

I could but wonder if Nicholls, his proven charm, those blue eyes, his blandishment, notwithstanding wasn't something of an optimist. (He was, as it turned out, by a factor of precisely 144.)

Alice Springs came and went, which with the exception of Neville Shute, is about all anyone could say about the place. Rising early for a 4 am breakfast and a 5 am departure we discovered the Hercules crew, every last one of them, on the lawn, toasting the sun with tail-end party seriousness. It was an unsteady and uncertain plane that lurched into the Eastern sky that morning and Charlie, the automatic pilot did the work of several men and a woman all that day. Then Auckland. The day after, the Blue Streak, a railbus whose name owed more to colour than speed and which, it was said, had been handed to the New Zealanders by the Italians as War Reparation. As it 'streaked' south, never faster than 25 mph it was clear that the Italians had got the better part of the bargain. Stu suggested, unkindly, that being Italian it almost certainly went faster in reverse. We all laughed uproariously at that; this was no cerebral trip. Wellington at last. A night ferry to

Picton Sound arrived on the South Island just after dawn. Picton was asleep, we tired, dishevelled and hungry. We found a dairy and drank milk, so cheap it was almost given away, until a café opened and breakfast could be procured.

The train from Picton to Christchurch was even slower than the Blue Streak and consisted of flat-beds interspersed with quaint wood-furnished carriages through which one half-expected an ambling Eastwood.

Christchurch and two days of ferocious New Zealand hospitality. A kind citizen lent us his Rover 90 *circa* 1960, a smart limmo by the Bonnie and Clyde standards of cars in New Zealand then. In a pub we got wind of a party and hurtled off to find it, Stu at the wheel. On the way Stu spotted a couple of girls standing outside a café and hove-to convinced that his English accent and the limousine would prove an irresistible combination.

'I say,' he said a shade plummier than true, 'you girls fancy coming to a party?'

A moment's hesitation, pause for effect, then,

'Bugger off you pommie bastard.'

Stu was hurt, we were hysterical. No cerebral trip this. The party was traced to a house in a smartish residential area that was surrounded by a dense privet hedge, through which no entrance was immediately apparent. Stu did the obvious thing, set the one ton car at the hedge and with a great crash cleaved his own entrance, skidded to a halt athwart a flower bed and we tumbled into the party where we drank as if tomorrow was prohibition. Hours later we piled out (Nicholls clutching his intacto gross) removed the car, repaired the hedge, exchanged car and privet festoon for a Land Rover and revved off into the remainder of the night towards the Canterbury Plain, Mt. Cook and whatever the day might bring. What unrelieved boors we were; not a 'redeeming social value' to be found amongst us!

The day brought Mt. Cook. I will never forget my first sight of it. We were speeding, figuratively and technically, across the Canterbury Plain when we came round a corner and there was Lake Pukaki — the subject of a goodly proportion of New Zealand's postcards. The lake was an uncanny pastel blue and behind it Mt. Cook stood high and wonderous white, the three summit peaks linked in a mile of 'arrested grace'. It was some-

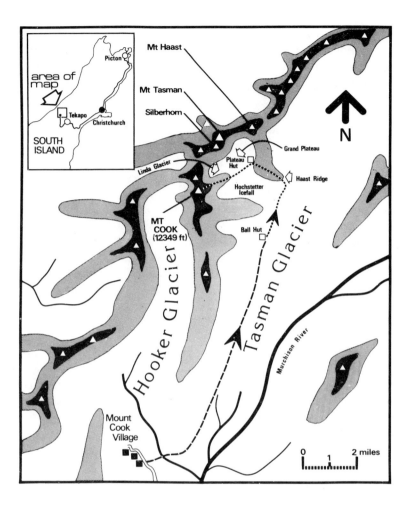

thing to behold and behold it we did for a full minute before
crashing back up four much abused gears, to Mt. Cook village,
an hour distant.

Our plan, if one of our hairbrained schemes could be fairly described as one, was to provision in Mt. Cook village and then
barrel on to the Ball Hut, another ten miles up a track that
followed precariously along the top of the lateral moraine of the
right bank of the Tasman Glacier, a mighty fourteen-mile glacier

19

fed by the snows of Mt. Cook, Tasman and a dozen other hills★.

We shopped and afterwards went to the only bar, the Hermitage, for a beer where we discovered, to our considerable distress, that here in egalitarian New Zealand, they served drinks only to those wearing ties.

'Sorry mate.'

'Not as sorry as we are.'

How long our open necks would have stood between us and our beer is fortunately only matter for conjecture. Fact is that Stu, quarter-master extraordinaire, conjured up a rack of ties worthy of a dandy. It's true that they inelegantly mis-matched our hair-shirt tartan — hair-shirt tartan was still *de rigueur* for mountaineers in the Sixties so that we were all uniformly and itchingly clad in Hunting Stewart or some such. My tie in particular was a sartorial monument to bad taste, sporting a voluptuous nude of the variety that can be seen reclining on verdant pastures, attended by nymphs, shepherds, and cloven-hoofed and hornéd devils in a certain period of oil painting (ignorance precludes greater accuracy); a nude that occupied five of six inches of the tie's width.

We were served, only just, but it gave us time and place for the triumph that followed.

'Who was that bloke you were talking to?' I asked Stu who had been chatting to a friendly couple while we had squabbled over the ties; it was the same man who had raided his wardrobe for our rescue.

'Apparently he's a pilot. Flies folk up to huts. And kit and stuff. He's a good hand. Was explaining the tie routine.'

'His bird's smiling at me,' said Nicholls.

'Probably too polite to laugh,' said Paul.

But Nicholls was off and not half a spiel later, the girl tripped to his silver-tongued tune and persuaded her pilot boyfriend to air-drop all our food and as much of our kit as he could fly at the Plateau Hut. Some boy for blandishment, Nicholls.

The Plateau Hut is the chief start point for climbs on the east side of Cook, the side we aimed to try. It is a tedious 4000 feet

---

★*So precariously did the track follow along that I'm told that neither its last few miles, nor the Ball Hut now exist, both having tumbled down 100ft of moraine into the glacier.*

above the Ball Hut and as we hoped to occupy the Plateau for at least ten days, the promised air-drop represented a big energy saver. It never occurred to us that snow might conceal our supplies before we got there; or that the pilot, for all his undoubted flying skills, might drop the lot into a hidden crevasse (indeed it was doubtful if we had more than a vague idea what a crevasse was) and if either possibility occurred to the pilot or his girl they weren't saying. As a reward we left Nicholls with the girl, the figure 143 uppermost in his mind, while Stu, Paul and I went with the pilot to the airstrip where we wrapped all our food and some of the kit in bits and pieces of hessian, rags and newspaper as protection against the impact, and loaded it into the aircraft to be dropped the next day.

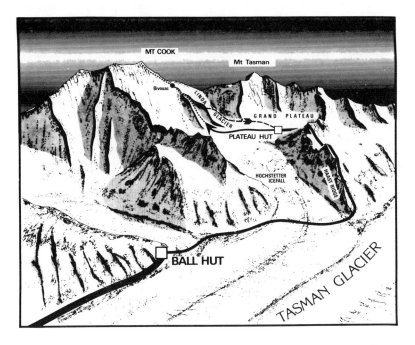

We'd saved a half sheep's carcass, bought on the road from Christchurch, for that night's meal at the Ball Hut where we were met on late-night arrival by the guardian Lyn Crawford. He chatted helpfully as we burnt, then ate our sheep. Brim full of sheep and Lyn's information we slept soundly.

'I say fellas, come and get a load of this!' It was Nicholls. We rushed out to where he was standing. We chorused a profane and wide-eyed wonderment.

Above us towered Mt. Cook, the stuff of glossy climbing books, until that moment the stuff we had only seen in books; the stuff we had only dreamt of, the stuff indeed of dreams. We scrambled, small boys now, to the top of a moraine, stood, head back, squinting, in summit gaze, impressed, excited but knowing too little of the game we had come to play to be awed. And even now when I have other experiences to measure against that first gaze, I think I would still be awed.

We stood still for ten minutes, our longest pause since Kuantan. Mt. Cook has a mighty summit ridge a mile long running roughly south to north through two subsidiary peaks to the main and north-most summit at 12,349 feet. Lyn told us that we were looking at the Caroline Face (most of Mt. Cook's features and flanks are given female names), that it was 7000 feet high, that it had not been climbed. Seven thousand feet is a big face by any standards, though we didn't know that then. Our unwitting imagination enabled us to trace half a dozen lines up its steep snow slopes, through its serac walls. In the years since that day ice climbing technology (and perhaps nerve) has overtaken our ignorance and two routes lie up that face (it would be a couple of years before the front-pointed ice climbing revolution was imported from far off Scotland).

Lyn continued to avalanche us with information as we sprinted through a porridge breakfast. He told us the best way to the Plateau Hut, what to watch out for, about routes on Cook, ways off, ways down. There was no such thing as a guide book to Cook then. Information was passed in conversation or gleaned from articles, magazine cuttings or New Zealand Alpine Club Journals. At best a route had a name which referred to a feature on the mountain. If you could identify the feature you'd found your route. A map would show its length, the rest was yours. No grade, no pitch descriptions, not even the sparsest general description, no hints, advice, nothing. Take it or leave it. The result was that more routes were left than taken, there being far more for the climber to do than just climb the thing. All this is a distinct contrast to the European Alps where guide books and Information Centres provide details of every inch of every route.

22

There the most important mountaineering skill is the ability to read. If you can do that there are few good excuses for not getting up. The Southern Alps are poorly documented and the climbing more serious, crueller, fairer — and, paradoxically perhaps — safer. There's no description to lead you on, no *téléphérique* to tempt you where faint heart and foot alone might retreat; no easy access to hearts of mountains.

But none of this did we know then. These were mountains, pure and simple. What happened in the rest of the world we had no idea, nor did we give a damn. To get to Cook and to get on top of it, that was the thing.

'Let's get packed.'

From a mountain of random kit, sleeping bags were freed and stuffed, punched, the down never so compressed, to the bottom of climbing 'sacks. Spare clothing, ropes, sunglasses, chocolate and all sorts suffered the same fate. Despite the air drop our 'sacks bulged too big, too heavy. We had little idea of what were the essentials so that the rule became, 'if in doubt don't leave it out'. We shouldered the 'sacks, young backs bending eagerly to the weight and scrambled a hundred feet down the moraine, racing to get to our very first glacier. Lyn shouted 'good luck'.

We fair pelted up the Tasman glacier feasting our eyes as we went and, because our eyes spent most of their time miles above or beyond our feet, we frequently tripped and fell. It was of no matter.

'Hey, there must be crevasses, do you think we should rope up?'

'Nah, this is a dry glacier, only an idiot would fall into one of these, they're too obvious.' Paul had been doing his homework. A minute later there was a cry, and splash. Paul had fallen into a fortunately shallow crevasse and his landing had been softened by a small reservoir of very nearly ice cold water. Lesson One. After an hour (or two) we paused beneath a gigantic tumble of chaotic ice: the Hochstetter Ice Fall. It came off the eastern flank of Cook and appeared to lead much more directly to the Plateau than the route Lyn had advised. We toyed with the idea of a direct route to the hut, only taking the caution of discussing it because we felt that had it been quicker, or easier, Lyn would have mentioned it. In the end we gave Lyn's advice the benefit of our considerable doubt. It was as well. The Hochstetter is the biggest ice fall, at temperate latitudes, in the world. There is nothing quite like it in the European Alps and had we attempted it this would certainly have been a very short book.

Nor were we the first to have been impressed with the scenery hereabouts. As long ago as 1962 Julius Haart, an infinitely more travelled and experienced alpinist than any of us, had written:

> 'It is impossible for me to describe in adequate words the majestic scenery by which we were surrounded; the weird mountain chains with their crowning peaks in stately forms, and numerous tributary glaciers on their flanks, often broken into innumerable seracs, of which the glorious ice cascade of the Hochstetter glacier was the most conspicuous, and the wide ice-stream itself carrying slowly its enormous load of debris to its terminal face, crevassed and with deep ponds all around us — all this impressed our minds with deep admiration. But the magnificent pyramid of Mt. Cook, or Aorangi, stood high above all, towering into the sky. As far as the eye could reach everywhere snow and ice and rock appeared around us, and in such gigantic proportions that I sometimes thought I was dreaming, and instead of being in New Zealand I found myself in the Arctic or Antarctic mountain regions.'

'Where ignorance is bliss 'tis folly to be wise?'

At last we gained the toe of the spur that reaches down from the plateau to the Tasman glacier — this was the Haast Ridge. Our first glacier gamble was over and though we'd been enthralled by every second of it — minus just a second or two on Paul's part — we wasted no time dwelling on it. There'd be more of them tomorrow, next week, sometime. Meanwhile we still had to find the Plateau Hut.

'Hey it must be up here.'

'Round here looks better.'

'Come on you buggers.'

'Jeeze it's loose.'

It was loose, looser than any rock I'd seen before or since, but it deterred us not at all. Steadily we gained height, slowly on the steep bits and then in great wanton swoops to the next pinnacle, ridge or crest, always anxious to see the next beyond, and too excited to think of economy of effort, splashed our strength (we had it to spare we thought); spilled our energy as young pups. Having never been exhausted we could not countenance that we ever would be.

It was late when we reached the Plateau Hut and we were tired, but not so tired that we couldn't sit on the roof and stare with wonder at what we beheld. Here were mountains, real ones. Mt. Cook, a huge bulk, sovereign and mighty. Mt. Tasman, a symmetry of graceful sweeps of snow, more beautiful than I imagined a mountain could be; and Siblerhorn, Teichelmann, Dampier, each a shining star that cluttered the kaleidescope of our vision, each a chord resounding in the clamour of our thought. We may not have come onto that plateau on 'soft foot, breath held like a cap in the hand,' we may have been unlovely boors in the valley, but we qualified for a seat on that roof by our hearts; they were in exactly the right place and we — we were in love. In love with it all.

Spellbound. For a long while no-one spoke. We gazed, dreamed, gaze on dream, dream on gaze. Our fancies flighted free fled ridges, flew crests, up, up to dwell on summits then they tumbled gaze and dream and flight and fancy, one upon the other and we were lost in the joyous welter of it all. Silence...

'Fuck me,' Stu said at last, softly. Stu a minimalist now. For once they were *the* words, fit words, spot on, no idle profanity but a perfectly poised breath of wonder; a soft shout from the soul.

The spell broken, we set to work. Two dug out the door of the hut, then a window. It was early in the season, the winter snow still lay thick. Two trudged knee deep in search of the air drop. The pilot had done his job well. Our kit was scattered over a smaller area than we'd feared. There had been casualties though. A sack of sugar had burst on impact icing the snow over several square yards, crystal to inseparable crystal; a pot of jam, a jar of honey broken, but on the whole it had been a good plan.

We settled in, ate a huge meal, talked excitedly, like schoolboys on an outing and made a dozen half plans.

In the week that followed we did everything wrong that is possible for alpinists, even novice alpinists — and more than a few things that might reasonably be considered impossible. The nearest bit of Mt. Cook proper was a mile across the plateau, a

25

friendly sounding name for what was really a huge glacier. We decided to climb Cook immediately. No thought of warming-up or acclimatizing on something lower and easier. Fortunately, it took us four attempts to get at it and when at last we did we were so exhausted from our mid-day wallow across a mile of deep soft snow that we gave up after 500 feet of climbing. We couldn't work out what to do about the soft snow that sapped our energies in minutes. We tried making skis from bits of wood, snow shoes from cardboard, but nothing worked very well. Because the plateau was flat, featureless and apparently uncrevassed — camouflaged as it was by a thick blanket of snow — we didn't think to rope up to cross it and for three days we floundered around in blissful ignorance criss-crossing heaven knows how many crevasses until, on the third day, Dave and I dropped into a crevasse together as we stood chatting. It was a providentially small slot, too narrow to fall into for more than a few feet. We scrambled out shaken. After that we roped up. But we still hadn't solved this soft snow business.

One night at about 1 am Stu got up for a pee. It was a clear moonlit night and it drew him outside well beyond the normal tip-toe peeing spot by the door. There was a shout, 'Yippee. That's it by Christ, that's it,' and he re-appeared at the door in a state of wild excitement.

'Hey fellas, come and see this, come on, come on.'

Sleepily we shuffled out. The moonlit panorama was certainly stunning but Stu wasn't looking at the view, he was jumping up and down on the snow, then dropping to his knees and pummelling the frozen surface like a thing demented. The frozen surface!

'It's hard, it's hard, it's bone-bloody-hard!'

And we all joined in the dance, leaping about in our stocking feet. We had discovered the 'alpine start'. Had we read anything at all about mountains we would have known, but we hadn't and didn't. Had there been anyone else in the hut we would have found out, but there wasn't. It seems hardly credible that we didn't know that since the dawn of alpinism men and women in their hundreds have been struggling from their slumbers at 2 and 3 in the morning and acting out that benighted purgatory known the mountain world over as the 'alpine start'. Now we knew. And what a difference it made.

An hour later, all girded and loined, we skittered across the

26

plateau, bettering all previous times to the foot of the Bowie Ridge of Cook by several hours. We had decided on the Bowie because it had more obvious rock than any of the other routes on this side of Cook — and because it was the nearest to the hut. But it was a bad choice. It had only been climbed once, maybe twice, so that information on it was scant, even by New Zealand standards. It was long, one of the longest on the mountain and the route finding (casting my minds eye back) couldn't have been straightforward. That morning, the morning of the great alpine-start discovery, we reached it at 3.30 am, too early by far to start on a rock climb, another lesson learnt (No.4 I think). As we shivered for dawn the weather turned bad, then fierce. We scuttled back to the hut — instinct telling us that it's a good rule not to begin big routes in bad weather. Or perhaps that is so obvious.

Back at the hut we held a council-of-war. What to do? Stu and Paul were for going down for a rest and some more food — we'd been floundering round for six days, our young appetites growing daily, and now demanding a gluttony of food. Dave and I were for staying up, for making do on food — there was a fair bit left about from the previous season — and for going for a route. Which is what happened. Stu and Paul went down, Dave and I stayed up.

But which route? One of the positive effects of floundering so fecklessly around the plateau for so long, in addition to the wondrous instruction, was that we'd had plenty of time to study the place and work out what was what. And though great inroads had been made in our ignorance, our arrogance was intact. A plan was hatched in the blazing sun on the hut roof where we lay naked (Mazeaud would have loved it).

'What route do you reckon mate?'

'Bowie or Zurbriggen, I reckon.' (The Zurbriggen was an easier angled ridge that started some 500 yards south of the Bowie before joining it about three quarters of the way up the mountain.)

'Bugger the Bowie, I'm browned off with the mention of it. Maybe the Zurbriggen. What a poxy name. Look at that snow gully affair between them, what about that bastard?'

'Mm, got no info on that. Must be a new line.'

And that was it. First alpine season, first mountain route; talk of a new line. I shudder still.

Two very burnt backsides later we retreated inside the hut to prepare. We set out at 2 am, Dave and I, and by 3 had reached a little ice fall just left of the start of the Bowie Ridge. This barred the way to a snow basin that led to the foot of our gully which ran up between the Bowie and Zurbriggen Ridges ending where they joined. It was snow and ice as far as we could see which afforded us the advantage of being able to climb by torch light instead of having to waste time awaiting daylight. With 4000 feet of climbing ahead this was a happy advantage. (4000 feet makes a long alpine route — but like much else we were still ignorant of that.)

We yomped the ice fall and stormed the slope of the snow basin above to the foot of the gully. It was now just light enough to see. It looked steep. Steeper than all our snow and ice experience combined — which would not have been hard.

'What d'you reckon Horse?' Dave's grotesquely bandy legs had earned him this sobriquet.

'Give it a go eh?'

Dave was the classic product of a minor public school and was all that is good about the British upper-middle class, and little of what is bad. He was polite to a fault — to the infuriation of his less mannered friends, of whom Stu, Paul and I were prime examples. He was solicitous for the welfare of others beyond anything asked of saints. He was utterly selfless, incapable of voicing complaint about anything as trivial as physical discomfort or tiredness or hunger. He was as brave, physically brave, as a lion, as near fearless as I think it possible for a man to be; and he was scarce of imagination and scant of education; short on education, shorter on imagination — considerable advantages that day. A real Waterloo man. A real, 'My God sir, I've lost an arm. My God sir, so you have,' man. The sort that made the Empire and kept it and enjoyed it and will never be forgiven for it. The sort whose day has gone, who is hopelessly unfashionable, but who will survive for ever. He was about the best alpine partner anyone could wish for — even if he'd never done a single alpine route.

We went at it; steadily for once. A tentative pitch, a tentative belay. A nervous pitch, a nervous belay. A trembly pitch; no belay. A few hundred feet gained, a few more lessons learned. Our axes were useless, and we soon found it better to use balance and hands than to rely on them. They both had picks exactly at right angles to the shaft and with the encouragement of the slightest pull positively ejected from the snow. After four pitches

Dave found a good belay in the right wall which was by now rock. Beyond, the gully narrowed and steepened. I would guess the grade at Scottish 3 but my memory is an enlarging instrument, it may have been easier.

'Watch it mate, your right crampon strap's come loose.'

I had wobbled up about 20 feet, far enough to see that around a rightwards curve the angle eased.

I looked. To my dismay it had. They were hopeless these straps, too shiny and too soft to work in the quick release buckles we were using. This lesson had been learnt days before but we had failed to improve on the system, perhaps lacking the inventiveness, certainly lacking the experience that would have told us how important was this failure.

In precarious balance, though not for long, I gingered down a hand. Precarious and precariouser. Finger and thumb to the strap, tried to thread it. Precariouser... whang. 40 feet. Dave held on a waist belay. The crampon tinkled on down to the foot of the mountain.

'I say mate, do you realise that's our first alpine peel. What a whazzer. You OK?' See what I mean about Dave?

'You'll have to lead all the ice. I'll do the rock.' No question of retreat. I doubt that the word is in Dave's vocabulary but I might have raised it. Today, it would be home and no hesitation. Instead we struck that bargain; the rock was mine, the ice Dave's. Some bargain — in the 3000 feet that followed there were two rock pitches!

'I wonder why no-one has climbed this gully before?' Dave mused, 'Seems obvious.' A crash of falling stones, funnelled inescapably to the bed of the gully, whistled close by. 'Seems obvious,' I said.

Dave forged on. The belays improved. The angle eased. I hop-skipped on a tight rope. A rock-pitch, quite hard, brought us to the junction of the two containing ridges, two thirds of the way up the mountain.

The summit looked tantalisingly close, a short easy rock band and a snow slope away. We were about to get the fore-shortening lesson.

'Cracked it mate.'

'Good as. Let's leave the 'sacks here, travel light.'

The rock band, the second pitch of my bargain, was straightforward, but the snow slope was ice, hard green ice and 1500 feet long. And still Nicholl's vocabulary let him down and still it didn't occur to me.

It wasn't a conscious decision. It was that there was no decision; not a single thought was given to the matter beyond the getting up with one crampon. No question this of courage, or foolhardiness either — it just plain did not occur to either of us.

Dave would lead a pitch, easy angled, maybe 40° but bone-hard ice. An ice-screw, our first shot with them and they did us proud. 'Tight rope, Dave' — hoppity, hop — 'Cheers mate, off you go — I'll bring the screw.' 1500 feet to the top, where for reasons I can't attempt to explain, we unroped. It's a precipitous summit, corniced on one side and fall-able on all the others but we unroped all the same and scrambled about it taking it in turns to stand well out on the cornice for a snap-shot.

The view was magnificent. That fact I remember well. The details are less sharp now and the colours, once bright, are fading too — as if from kodachrome to watercolour — though recollection brings warm enough pleasure yet. Whatever happens to mind and memory I think that for all my time I will always be able to summon to the inward eye a sepia-tinted image that will bring bliss to my solitude when other things have faded beyond recall.

To the west, close enough at 25 miles to dip a toe, the sea — and from how many alpine tops can the sea be seen? To the distant south, Mt. Sefton. Immediately south, the mighty summit ridge of Cook running a full mile from our feet through two only slightly lesser peaks; to the north the vistaed summits of the giant spine of the Southern Alps with the big bones of Hicks, Tasman and Haast. To the east the rolling Canterbury Plain across which we had rattled all virgin innocence, all exuberance, a week before. Already we were wiser men, and by more than a week. Some week.

All this and not a single soul in sight, not just the summit to ourselves but the whole mountain — which was all of the world that mattered at that moment.

We were happy. Indescribably happy, and pretty damned pleased with ourselves too. It was an hour before we turned our attention to the descent. I would take the ice screws — both of them — sit on my backside on the ice, be lowered by Dave for

150 feet, place a screw and clip in. Dave would descend to that point and lower his burden, from the first screw a further 150 feet, where I would place the second screw. Then Dave to me, recovering the screw and so on for the 1500 feet of the summit ice field; 10 lowers and a terrible toll on the seat of my pants. It was an unnerving business. The summit slopes were spectacularly exposed, running away to huge drops. Even we couldn't fail to spot the almost certainly fatal consequence of a slip. The rock band was a relief and we scrambled cheerfully through to the shoulder, the junction of the Bowie and Zurbriggen ridges, where we had left our 'sacks six hours before. Six hours! Neither of us had noticed the time. The day was nearly gone.

The way down from the shoulder was by the Linda Glacier route, the easiest, though not the safest way up Mt. Cook. But before we could reach the easy ground of the Linda Glacier itself, we had to cross a long ramp of snow that ran from the shoulder to the glacier. This was the Linda Shelf, technically easy but poised, like a roof of a house, about a 500 foot drop. No place for two novices, with only three crampons and Lyn's briefing, half remembered, between them, to cavort in the dark.

'Looks like a bivvy mate,' Dave said with a casualness perfected by generations of selective breeding.

'Jeeze we'll freeze,' I whinged with a querulousness forgivable in one of my stock.

'Oh shouldn't be too bad.' Even for Nicholls this was a touch flippant, I was suspicious, and as events shortly revealed, with good reason. A quick reconnaissance found a good bivouac spot, three sides of a box, the open side to the east — not that it appeared to matter; the weather was perfectly still. Settling in to our first bivouac (the alpine syllabus was nearly complete) was an undemanding task. We simply sat down. We had long since lost the sun, which was now setting somewhere way over the other side of Cook. It grew cold, very cold and we with it. The full effects were postponed by a slow-to-arrive wet of tea and a sunset that awed for full fifteen minutes.

'Just like that Rebuffat Book.'

Dave was referring to *Between Heaven and Earth*, vogue at the time and the only mountaineering book we had seriously studied; it had lots of pictures.

'Yes, except old Gaston didn't say a lot about the temperature

31

did he.' It wasn't a question — more a complaint.

'Time to don duvets,' Dave said wresting from his 'sack an enormous garment straining with Michelin-man down.

'Duvet? Where d'you get that bastard?' Complaint and question too.

'You've got one, Kath brought it out to Singers, I remember. Where is it?'

'It's in the scrofulating hut, that's where it is. Where we agreed to leave them to save weight.'

'Sorry mate, just that it seemed like a soldier-like precaution. Doesn't weigh much. Anyway, there was nothing else in the 'sack.'

Everything he said was true — and so patently obvious.

'Sorry I can't share it with you.' The altruistic bit; damn the man and all his class. 'Tell you what I'll use it 'till midnight, you can have it from then on. He was asleep before I could comment or agree. I climbed into an agricultural poly bag and shivered my way to midnight — the incongruous smell of fertilizer rising on feeble body heat to freeze in the nostrils.

The hour of the swap, for me an eternity of shivering muscles and chattering teeth, a blissful snore for him, came and went. I got up, by now soaked with condensation, and vented my considerable ire in a stockinged kick at the lumpen Nicholls. The kick illicited a grunt, then more snores after which I had not the heart to wake him — it's infectious this stiff upper-lip business — and in any case I was well beyond the warming of a duvet. A stiff east wind got up. This was the bivouac lesson.

At the first hint, the merest suggestion of dawn, I woke Nicholls with a couple of powerful nudges.

'Cheers mate. Sleep well? I slept like a log. Give us a couple of ticks to wake up and I'll be with you. I say what are you doing?'

It was what our PT Instructor in Young Officer Training years before had termed calinisthetics; I was shadow boxing ferociously to try to warm up. I could not think that it was possible to be colder.

'I'm trying to get warm,' I said, tossing in a couple of tasty right hooks at the nearest star. 'Good job Marciano's not here.'

'Marciano? She a climber? What's she done to you?'

'Come on you idle bugger, get up.'

'Fancy a wet.'

32

'Bugger the wet, let's get going, I'm COLD.'

We got going in no time at all and had only moved a few yards when we spotted a perfect natural snow cave between the upper slopes of the Linda Shelf and the rocks of the bivouac.

'Time spent in reconnaissance...' I began, '... is seldom wasted,' Dave said completing the well worn military adage.

'You'd better go first John; like yesterday. Same routine, eh!'

I tried but though the trend was generally downwards it was much more across; an only slightly less-than-horizontal traverse. I wobbled ten feet out from Dave before slipping to a point ten feet below him. It was hopeless.

We thought for a while until a plan emerged. Dave was to traverse rightwards, rising slightly to place an ice screw after 50 feet — the very most that I was able to contemplate. He was then to hold the rope while I was supposed to plummet in an enormous pendulum, and plant my axe at the end of the swing at a point, we theorised, 50 feet below and, if we were lucky and I was adept, a few feet to the right of Dave. Thus we would climb, if climb was the word. Looking back I can quickly spot several technical improvements, but these were 'Mark I' days.

Dave quickly ran out 50 feet and belayed. I hesitated. The translation of theory to practice was but a step away — a step I could not persuade myself to take. I hesitated some more.

'Pendulum,' Dave encouraged, adding, helpful as always, 'gravity will do the rest.'

But it was because I knew precisely what gravity would do that I was frozen to my spot. And I didn't want to know about the rest. I opted for the chicken run, tried to follow Dave's traverse line with a hoppity, a chipped step, a cut step. Our axes had been designed for the once-thought-to-be-noble art of cutting steps, which was why the picks stuck out straight and why they performed so badly going straight-up, front pointing; not that we knew *that* then. Or how to cut steps either. I chipped at the hard ice, a limp wristed hack, a glancing miss, a lot of energy wasted, an unusable nick of a step. Then whoosh, gravity was doing the rest. I missed my chance at the farthest end of the first swing, slithering to a stop directly below Dave. But it was progress of a sort and the first swing proved to be the worst. After that Dave was able to keep well above me so that subsequent pendulums avoided the sickening plummet of the first — despite my partner's estimation of 50 feet growing more generous with every leap-frog. All this on a sloping shelf perched atop precipitous cliffs that fell away to the Linda Glacier hundreds of feet below.

At last, where shelf and glacier met, Dave was able to lower me to flat, if badly crevassed land. I inspected myself for damage discovering that 'the rest' was the best of the arse of my pants. I had been abraded near breecherless by sharp *sastruggi'd névé*.

Nicholls front-pointed down to join me.

'Cracked it.'

We had. A bar of chocolate marked the end of hostilities, peace broke out as we sat basking in the sun and a great-to-be-alive feeling. It's a feeling I've known after a dozen mountains since but it has never been better to be alive than on that November day in 1969.

A two-hour plod through the softening late morning snow saw us to the Plateau Hut where Stu and Paul were waiting, replenished and eager for their go.

As they congratulated us I made very little attempt to hide my pleasure in our adventure and I fancied that I spotted just the fleetingest smile, smug on the stiff upper lip.

We did two more routes after that, one each on Mt. Tasman, the second highest peak in New Zealand, and on Mt. Hicks, a near neighbour. They were good, we a deal more competent, and for as long as they represented two thirds of our entire alpine experience we thought well of them. But fifteen years on, their significance has shrunk to nothing, pleasant days out at most, while Cook stands autarchic in time's test, an adventure that will never stale, never grow up, never grow old; a seminal experience.

It is hard to be sure how much we learnt on Cook. It was not then in our nature to reflect, as older men reflect, as perhaps wiser young men would have done. But tomorrow was Christchurch and the day after that Singers and there was more of life, great big bits of it, to be taken at the charge.

The lessons went home of course, subconsciously, perhaps unconsciously distilled even in the suddenness of our minds, fermenting their way into the synthesis of experience, there to lie dormant until called up by the next mountain.

Dave and I were conscious of only a few things: we had discovered mountaineering; had been intimate with it and loved it; and we had found that, as different in most important respects as two men could be, we had a partnership, were wedded, we two and the mountains, for better or for worse, in a *ménage-à-trois* that was to endure some great adventures — adventures in which there was little better and lots worse.

Flat out. Back to Christchurch. Or did we come just ever so slightly more slowly away from those southern mountains than we had gone? I think maybe we did.

'Get the wets in mate.'

At Christchurch Nicholls found the house of the party and gardened for an afternoon, weeding his conscience clear.

Gungho. Richmond. Somewhere in Australia. It was happy hour at that airbase.

'Get the wets in mate.'

Singers. Kath met us at Changi airport. She had a new mate, a fluffy powderpuff of a pup, about six inches high and more powderpuff than pup. 'Do you mind?' she asked. What could I say? She's a good woman and will not forgive me for saying it in so public a place.

New Zealand: a combination of memory, dream and desire.

2

India

MENTHOSA:
THE PRICE YOU PAY

'My candle burns at both ends;
It will not last the night;
But ah, my foes, and oh, my friends —
It gives a lovely light!'

Edna St Vincent Millay

'Well, India is a country of nonsense.'

M K Ghandi

Stu got us to Menthosa, Stu, that prodigious enthusiasm of his
and a letter he sent to the Duke of Edinburgh; not that it's a
mountain you'll have heard of. It was unknown to us too, till we
were offered a shot at it.

Christmas followed hard on the heels of our return from New
Zealand. Christmas was celebrated by Europeans in Singapore
(maybe it was only by British servicemen), with an enthusiasm,
ferocious, even by Stu's standards. It was a serious business,
occupying an average of 14 days: 7 days warm up and rehearsal,
3 days actual Christmas and 3 or 4 warming down or recovery —
which brought you perilously close to New Year and alcoholism.
A kind of crusade conducted with lionhearted fervour. A heaven-
sent excuse for a party; a better excuse for a whole battery of
parties than could be found anywhere else in the calendar — and
it was official, legitimate (most of it) — enjoying the full co-
operation of every arm of the establishment, secular and ecclesi-
astical.

So any post-New Zealand blues that we might have suffered or
any time we might have spent in quietude or reflection (both
unlikely phenomena) would have, in any case, been swept away
in this tidal wave of revelry.

The fiercest test for we Subalterns was the bi-annual visit to the Sergeants' Mess. This was an arrangement common to all Royal Marine Units whereby both the Sergeants' and Officers' Messes hosted a visit, one by the other, on alternate years. This year, Christmas 1969 was the Officers' turn to visit the Sergeants' Mess. Visits by the Senior Non-Commissioned Officers (the Sergeants, Colour Sergeants and Warrant Officers) to the Officers' Mess were usually fairly well-regulated affairs, beginning at twelve noon and finishing before five that same evening — usually because the Second-in-Command, with a nod, ordered the bar closed — and it was unwise, even at Christmas, to argue with him. But the reciprocal visit had no rules, nor recognisable end; those who were still in there at the end were incapable of recognising it — or the way home, the front door, their dog, wife or lavatory pan — whichever greeted them first. It was like one of those old-time prize fights where the opponents kept slugging away until one dropped, except that this contest went on until everyone dropped. Senior Officers, say Majors and above, were reasonably safe. No-one really expected them to make idiots of themselves and their lame excuses of desks to clear, admin. to tidy up, or Christmas shopping to do, were usually graciously accepted. But there was no escape for we Subalterns, or none that I ever heard of. We were fair game and once our seniors had departed it was lion's den stuff. And the whole paradoxical thing of it was that the better the sergeants liked you the worse you suffered. Fortunate Subalterns who were having a bad time of it with their Senior NCOs could usually escape with sufficient wit and coherence to call a taxi; those of us who were unfortunate enough to enjoy relaxed, mutually respectful, even friendly relations with our sergeants, could expect a fearful time; no quarter given, none expected. Limited damage might be two whole days lost from your life — sunk without trace — the mother and father of all hang-overs, the temporary (sometimes longer), severence of any sort of communication with the wife. (Women were allowed nowhere near the place. No rabid sexism this, rather the proper concern of a caring institution. The carnage would have upset, the daftness of it appalled them.) Other casualties would include the near certain loss of service Identity Card, wallet, car keys, car and in one case uniform — the very uniform the lad had been standing in. (The word 'standing' to be loosely interpreted.) No-one was ever sure what had happened but he staggered home uniformless, some days adrift. His wife, a woman of great humour and super-human tolerance, recounted at a later party — and in some style,

'The uniform 'e wore
Was nothin' much before,
An' rather less than 'arf o' that be'ind.'

In short, the message is that for a few weeks past Christmas there were distractions other than mountains; memories of New Zealand were drowned, thoughts of new hills were washed away.

One of my gifts that Christmas was a book *Mountain of my Fear* by an American, Dave Roberts. It is the story of the first ascent of the West Face of Mt. Huntington in Alaska. It had been a hard climb — a great one, marred by the death of Ed Bernd, one of the team of four Harvard students. He fell in descent. I read it, laid it aside, and forgot it for fifteen years. I thought it a dull book. Only about half its content was devoted to action of any sort. The rest was philosophy and psychology, the why and the wherefore; no laughs in that. Regrettably, it set the pattern for many a poor imitation. Climbing literature caught a pox of half-baked philosophising, shallow psychology, and the sort of soul-baring that only Americans seem to be able to stomach. Only injections of fun and simple sanity by the likes of Patey and McNaught-Davis in climbing magazines like *Mountain* saved the mountaineering literature of the seventies from pretentious parody. Why couldn't all these fellows just get out there, do what came naturally and climb for fun; the sheer, unadulterated hell of it? That's why Dave, Stu, Paul and I had climbed in New Zealand, for fun and because of our 'interest on the dangerous edge of things'. Good enough reasons, I thought at the time, for something so daft as climbing. I couldn't understand why climbers needed to explore their reasons in public; even less, their desire to explain. Who did they expect to care, to be inter-ested? I puzzled at it. Clearly we all loved climbing. How could our attitudes be so diametrically different? (Fifteen years later I re-read the book, partly because I was planning a trip to Alaska and I thought that it might provide some useful background information, partly because I had recently picked up a copy of a climbing publication called *Ascent* and while browsing my eye had been caught by a title 'Like wind, Like fire'. I started to read. Couldn't stop till I'd finished — and it's a longish short story. It was written by Dave Roberts. Surprised, I re-read *Mountain of my Fear* and loved it. Roberts is without peer. Perhaps it was just that I grew up. Shortly after my 'Roberts rehabilitation' he was interviewed in *Climbing,* an American climbing magazine. I read with fascination that he'd written *Mountain of Fear* as a kind of catharsis. I can understand that now. I'm not sure I would those fifteen years ago. And he'd written it in ten days at the rate of a chapter a day; a feat that ranks with the climb itself. 'I'm afraid it shows,' he added. Not to me.)

I'm not sure how long I mulled over Roberts' book that first time before laying it to rest but it wouldn't have extended beyond 1969 — and there was precious little room for thought that December. If it was more than a few hours I'd be surprised, but the result of my contemplation, whether two months or two minutes, would have been the same; not for me, nor any of the rest of us either.

Menthosa then. Still charging, still stuffing 'the unforgiving minute with sixty seconds' worth of distance run'. Stu's idea. Paul had finished his time in the East and gone back to the UK and Nicholls had gone off to learn Arabic in preparation for a stint of real soldiering in the Oman. That left Stu and me. He was the plotter; I the blunt instrument. But before he came up with Menthosa he had another plan. It was Everest.

'Fancy Everest?' was how he broke it to me.

'Know a team that's going then?'

'Yeh, you'n'me.'

'Bit thin on the ground, aren't we?'

'Soon get some more lads. Soon train someone up. And there's all those Ghurkas in the barracks down the road. They live up there somewhere and are used to yomping; piece of duff.'

Remember this was 1970. Everest was still a big deal. Stu's enthusiasms were a margin beyond my verge of the realistic. I didn't bother to pursue the issue any farther — though a seed, a tiny acorn, had fallen from the preposterous oak of Stu's ardour and for the first time I dared to think Himalayas. After all they were closer to Singapore than to Britain, and there was no war on and... Stu was aiming high, too high, but he was giving us sight of good targets lower in the gallery — it was worth watching his tracer. Though I forgot about Everest I started looking at the atlas.

39

But Stu didn't forget. He wrote to the Duke of Edinburgh. Would the Duke like to be patron to an expedition he was leading to climb Mt. Everest? Just like that. I never saw the letter and I don't suppose it was a 'Dear Duke' job, even Stu had some sense of propriety, some sense of what subalterns might or might not say. Nor do I suppose that the Duke, who might, just might, have been amused, ever saw or as much as heard tell of the letter. No. I imagine that Stu's direct assault faltered at the hands of some Palace minion whose job it is to intercept letters from cranks, madmen, scroungers, fans, and over-zealous subalterns; to divert them to some regal dustbin or, as in the case of Stu's own letter, to the appropriate authority. That would be how Stu's letter ended up at the Department of the Commandant General, Royal Marines, Whitehall, despite being clearly addressed to Buckingham Palace, just down the road — surely as unequivocal an address as was ever likely in the days before post codes confused computers. Someone dropped him in it.

A lot of senior officers were not amused. Or pretended not to be. Stu was hauled over a dozen carpets, upbraided, dressed down, until he, even he, got the message; he was a very unpopular young subaltern and he might, as long as he never wrote the like again, live to be an old subaltern; nothing more.

'Why the hell shouldn't I write to the bloke anyway?' But although Stu's enthusiasm was unbowed, it was goodbye to Everest and the dream of it. Sometimes I dare to wonder how we would have got on if we had been able to get there. Chances are that even Stu would have faltered in the rarified air just above base camp and we'd have come home to think again.

The consolation prize was Menthosa. Unbeknown to our politically naive minds, Stu had unwittingly made the first move in the classic bargaining game where you bid for something outrageous when your real target is something much smaller. This gives miles of room for manoeuvring and everyone comes away a winner. Politicians and trade union leaders do it all the time, but we were soldiers for whom talk of politics (as well as religion and, unfortunately, sex) was by long tradition a taboo subject — at least in the Mess. (Somehow the taboo stuck to only politics and religion, leaving sex to consume 100% of our conversation rather than 33.3% as otherwise might have been the percentage — though I doubt it.)

It almost became a case of 'all right Rae, you hairbrained bugger, you've got the Commandant General a rollocking for not keeping tabs on his officers and you've upset the Duke, let's limit the damage. What'll you settle for?' At least, that's the way we chuckled about it afterwards, but I suppose it wasn't really like that. More likely it was our CO again. He was a great man and recognised in Stu a great spirit, a spirit that now needed a lift to get it free again.

'Look Stewart, that letter has caused all kinds of nausea so you can forget Everest, but I imagine there are other hills in the Himalayas you can climb. Yes, thought so. I'll see what I can do, know a few chaps in Delhi, one of them's keen on Sally, you never know.' (Sally was his wife.)

And that is how we got a go at Menthosa. As things took shape it became clear that Stu and I couldn't handle the diplomatic niceties of all the back door manoeuvring that had begun. Stu had proved *that* beyond all reasonable doubt — to everyone but himself (his own faith held to the end) and I was a known diplomatic disaster, the butt of a favourite metaphor which ran 'about as much use as JB to the Diplomatic Corps'.

40 Commando was encamped on one side of Simbang airfield, the 3rd Commando Brigade Headquarters, our 'immediately superior authority' on the other. Within this labyrinthine organisation wandered the Brigade Intelligence Officer, Sam Bemrose. Sam had been a mountaineer in his time, a good one, and had enjoyed a number of successful climbs, big routes, with Tom Patey who described him in their do on the Troll Wall in winter as 'the gay Lothario'. That was Sam, old-fashioned 'gay' mind you. Sam was appointed leader to the expedition.

It was an inspired appointment. He brought to the expedition proven organisation skills, administrative experience, patience, tact and diplomacy — in fact, everything that it thus far lacked; and with Stu and me comprising two thirds of the team every one of those qualities was likely to be needed in full measure. Sam also brought with him the administrative might of the entire Commando Brigade Intelligence machine so that suddenly we, still an expedition of only three, had acquired free telex facilities, a map library whose contours spread to the four corners of the earth, an office, typists, and a team of talented lads, trained as illustrators, photographers and the like, who had nothing much else to do but to help organise our expedition, there being no war on and Sam their boss.

Sam had influence, huge influence and if he didn't know the right fellow personally, he knew someone who did. At a stroke we had food by the ton; tropical rations, arctic rations (for what contingency they were salted away in some tropical store is hard to conceive), special rations, special supplements to special rations and best of all CILOR that sweetest of military acronyms, Cash in Lieu Of Rations. And we had money, CILOR yes, but half-a-dozen other allowances besides. Allowances that Sam's imprest expert chums, armed with obscure clauses from dusty manuals, winkled free from the normally reluctant coffers of the military establishments.

And we had clothes, whole wardrobes of them. Jackets waterproof, officers navigating; balaclavas, ordinary seamen; gloves, gunners, Bofors; boots, galley, nonslip (and probably knickers, WRNS if we'd had such a fetish in the team); clothing foulweather, clothing fair-weather, clothing every conceivable kind of weather. Most of it was useless for our purpose but it was there and free if we wanted.

Indeed, we had everything an expedition could wish for except means of transport from Singapore to the mountain and, more worryingly (for Sam was not long in solving that one), climbers. We were still only three. Today that would be considered a crowd on a peak such as ours, but these were traditional times. Anyway, 'an expedition' in service parlance conjured in senior officers' minds a goodly, though unspecified, number of chaps; certainly more than three, probably not less than a dozen and ideally comprising a cross-section of ranks to make the thing look fair. Certainly it was hard to justify the concentration of a complete Commando Brigade's resources in sending three officers to some relatively insignificant peak somewhere in India — few of the Brigade knew where and, I suspect, fewer cared.

Sam then brought all this to the trip. All this and a grandiloquent expedition title, 'The 3rd Commando Brigade Himalayan Expedition'.

'Got to have a title,' Sam said, 'it impresses all the right people no end.' In this context what Sam meant by the 'right people' were those who were in a position of power or influence from which our little trip could directly benefit.

All this he brought and more besides. He brought humour, high and terrible: a high sense of what was fun, a terrible sense of what was funny. Most, anyone with half a wit of daftness in them were agreed that Sam's sense of humour was monumental. His jinks and japes were renowned although it was sometimes difficult to tell where fact and fiction separated. It was often the victim that told it best and that was the vintage of Sam's jokes; they blessed him that received and him that gave, and furnished an only temporarily discomforted individual with a story to laugh the contingent of the dullest dinner entirely under the table. For example, at one of Sam's before-dinner drinks parties (Sam and his wife Tulip were known to give the best parties on Singapore Island and the description, 'before-dinner' owed more to prandial propriety than to chronology) a guest fell, literally, early victim to Sam's awesome hospitality. As he lay slumped on the floor Sam removed his shoes, nailed them securely to the floorboards and replaced the owner's feet. The victim slumbered unawares through dinner until his bladder triggered his resurrection when, to the huge entertainment of the other guests — and no-one laughs louder than he-who-might-have-been — he rose unsteadily and uncertainly to his feet, wobbled, terribly transfixed, and crashed down again. An expression of bleary-eyed bewilderment gave way to one of wild-eyed anxiety as the implications of his apparent paralysis and loss of motor co-ordination sunk in. Luckily, he took it all in good part and now it is his favourite story.

Strenuous easy living and Sam's multi-targetted social life had filled out a frame that had once laid crash-tackling waste to opposition centre-three quarters for Royal Marines, Royal Navy, Combined Services and very nearly England. He was now very much larger than nature intended. Moreover, because the long run-up to expedition lift-off, January to September, was overpunctuated with parties celebrating the least administrative coup, there seemed no early prospect of Sam regaining his former slim glory. Meanwhile Sam loved life and all that could be squeezed from it.

But perhaps the greatest of all Sam's skills was, to use the old-fashioned term, 'man-management'. He quickly perceived that Stu was excessively energetic; I, inordinately indolent. His skill was to harness Stu's energies to more productive efforts and to leave me alone with my indolence.

43

'Got to find some more climbers, Stu. Can't justify all this to the Brigadier much longer. Looks bad, only members and all officers. All "Pigs", the lads will be saying, it's the Pigs what gets the pleasure, it's the Grunts what gets the blame.' The statement was addressed, as always, to Stu but for once I had an idea.

'How about Spot Watson, Sam? He's a marine in my troop. Rock climbs a bit. Dead keen.'

'Right he's in. Tell him will you. I'll fix getting him off duty. Anyone else?'

We thought hard; there was no-one else.

'How are we going to get there, Sam?' Stu asked.

'I've got a plan. Apparently the new BEME (pronounced Beemey — Brigade Electrical and Mechanical Engineer) is a good hand and I'll work on a couple of Navy contacts as well — it'll mean a couple of parties even if nothing comes of it.'

In the event, *everything* came of it. Land Rovers, three of them; trailers too, three of them; petrol and spares came of it; and the ship that was to take us and our three Land Rovers and trailers from Singapore to Calcutta and back. Total cost: a couple of good parties and a place on the expedition for Rory Cape, the new BEME. He had never climbed in his life but he was keen — which was only slightly less qualification than the rest of us could claim — and we needed someone to look after the motor transport on the journey across the Indian subcontinent.

The Brigadier, a good hand himself, agreed to release Captain Cape, BEME but only on condition that, under no circumstances did he venture, in mind or body, above Base Camp; Base Camp being a term that the Brigadier was vaguely aware of, suggesting to him a place of relative safety from which he could reasonably expect his brand new BEME to be safely delivered. 'Can't be losing good chaps on these hair-brained schemes.' Sam quickly agreed to the terms, promising that not so much as Cape's eyes would wander above Base Camp and that he would personally see to it that he got back to Brigade's bosom in one piece. It was a bargain — even if it left the rest of us wondering how we could be spared so readily.

Things were looking pretty damn good, the adventure was shaping up and I still hadn't done a stroke.

Rory, it turned out, was a very good hand. He was the ideal

addition, except that he suffered the inconvenience of being a Captain. That pulled the composition by rank of the team even further in the wrong direction. But there wasn't much we could do about it; he had the vehicles, we the vacancy and a deal was a deal. At least, as Sam noted, he was only a Captain in the Royal Electrical and Mechanical Engineers — that was nearly the same thing as being a corporal in the Marines.

It was Rory who rustled three Land Rovers. They were in perfect working order. He declared them BER (Beyond Economic Repair), civilized them with local number plates and the camouflage of a lick of paint: one red, one white, one blue. His REME mechanics were given reign on the things mechanical, competing to find fault, to repair three almost perfect engines, while signwriters emblazoned '3rd Commando Brigade Himalayan Expedition' on every flat surface they could find. The trailers enjoyed the same Royal treatment: new tyres, wheels, leafsprings, paintwork, signs and canvas awning. By this stage, June or thereabouts, the expedition had acquired a momentum of its own: organisational victory followed administrative triumph on logistical coup. There was simply no stopping it; it was as if there *was* a war on.

'How about some press coverage,' someone suggested, and with a nod from Sam to the Public Relations Officer, it was taken care of.

'Right ho Sam, see what I can do.'

The Himalayas! This was entirely different. The daily fare of the *Straits Times* and of Singapore Television consisted of rapes (a crime for which rubber tappers of Tamil origin seemed to take disproportionate blame), brothel keeping offences (joint product of the business acumen of ethnic Chinese and the rampant sexuality of all Singapore's peoples, brought on, it was said by apologists and braggarts alike, by the tropical heat), drunkenness, failure to pay taxi fares and brawls — specialities of her Majesty's brutal and licentious soldiery — Kipling's his country's best ambassador. The Himalayas. They could have been mountains of the moon for all the average Singaporean knew, or cared, but the press and TV loved it. In the wake of their endearingly naive reports there followed kept promises of beer from Tiger breweries and more beer from Anchor breweries, brews with ferocious properties of which not the least is the total paralysis of the sphincter.

45

There were two late additions to the team, in part further to justify Brigade's great effort, in part because Sam believed that if there was fun to be had, then the bigger the team, the more to enjoy it. Within reason. Not that 'reason' was to be a conspicuous feature of the proceedings of the next few months. So Jeff Parsons, who claimed to have climbed rock and had, and Bob Stewart, who made the same claim and hadn't, were recruited. Jeff was a Royal Marine, and like Stu and I, a yob only once removed. Bob was very proper, an officer of artillery, a gunner. Both were as strong as horses — and possessed about as much mountaineering experience as you would expect to find in a lowland variety of that species. But they were willing, fantastically keen and they could charge a bit — which counted for a lot with us. Between us, then, Sam's largely lapsed experience excepted, a total of two alpine seasons and a dusting of British rock. Hardly an impressive aggregate and one which was all but halved when Stu broke his leg with less than six weeks to go. It happened at a party. I was riding a bicycle around a table on Sam's lawn, Jeff on my shoulders. On Jeff's shoulders was Bob. It was Stu's job to leap from a precarious pyramid of chairs piled haphazardly on the table, atop Bob. Stu hesitated, estimated and leapt a mighty enough leap to be sure but an excess of Tiger had not only impaired his judgment of distance, speed and time, but the complex mathematical relationships between the three as well; in short, he missed.

Next day, Tiger's anaesthetic wearing thin, Stu reported to Sick Bay. His leg was broken the doctor said; Stu wouldn't be going the Brigadier said. There was the faintest trace, just discernible to the trained eye, of a dent in Stu's enthusiasm.

Sam pleaded. The Brigadier relented. A compromise was reached. The doc would have the final say when the plaster was removed. That event, thought to be at least a month distant, was considerably hastened when Stu insisted on waterskiing on his good leg at a beach party, while the sea washed the plaster off the other. The doctor, unimpressed by Stu's antics, and perhaps mindful of the Hippocratic oath, demurred. But he was easy prey to Sam's persuasive powers and Stu got his clearance, though no farther, the Brigadier ordered, than Base Camp. The Brigadier was becoming fond of the place. There Stu and Rory could languish together — and not a step further. Sam promised. Stu was reinstated and, still representing only slightly less than half the expedition's collective mountaineering experience, rejoined us the day before departure, body on crutches, enthusiasm on air and his hope, secret, fervent, eternal, on the summit of Menthosa. Stu's hope sprung unconditional.

The great departure day arrived; late August. The cavalcade, the resplendent red, white and blue of it, rolled to the docks with an entourage of wives and girlfriends, mates, freeloaders, Press Officers and the remains of the Tiger and Anchor supply. An LSL (a Landing Ship Logistic) waited, not entirely at our disposal, but enough for us to be late and for it still to be there when we arrived. It was the *Sir Gallahad* (later to meet a savage end in the Falklands War in 1982), then in its prime, successfully disguised as a white painted cruise ship pressed gently into the service of trooping Ghurka soldiers and their families to Calcutta on their way to a long leave in Nepal.

We drove on board through the bows of the ship which yawned open to admit us. At the time these huge bow doors were about the only concession to military intent that that good ship made. Soon after we slipped away to west and north. It didn't occur to me at the time but we might have been the last expedition to cruise to India en-route to the Himalayas, once the traditional method of approach, and one of very few of any time to sail in approach from the East. No lachrymose parting; no sweet sorrow, but a joyous, smiling, carefree farewell; another farewell, one of scores — hundreds — that a soldier and his family share in a career. After all, three months in the Himalayas was a considerable advance on twelve months in Aden or six months in Borneo — the usual away fixtures.

The cruise to Calcutta, for cruise it was, was a luxury. The Chinese cooks were superb; their repasts devoured with a relish only slightly diminished by a conscience troubled by having done nothing much to earn the feast. Days lazed away in idle ease; a snooze, a sunbathe, a short session of PT on the upper vehicle deck, drinks and dinner on the high hot sea; a tropical sunset, a tropical dawn, another day.

Stu, of course, found work. He had heard that the Calcutta customs officials were amongst the most cussed in all India. They would demand an inventory, he said, item by tiniest item, in quadruple, maybe quintuple. He wasn't sure. Day and night while the rest of us grew tired of being idle he typed away on the ship's typewriter, two whole fingers when he was going well, long lists, six copies just to be safe, of every spoon, aspirin and bootlace that we had assembled — and as we were climbing by convoy we were not travelling light. He loved it. We hated him for it. His industry touched our conscience — but not so much that any of us were prepared to help.

Our co-passengers were those happy warriors, the Gurkhas, recruited in far off Nepal and a-soldiering for her Majesty this last century and more, both in British and Indian armies, though under new management in the latter since 1947. They played volleyball on the upper deck with child-like innocence, all laughter, spontaneity and bounce. It was the way they played all their games, including war. It was difficult to imagine that some were from the same regiment that I had soldiered with in Borneo where I had watched in awe as they reacted to an ambush with savage ferocity — and that only in practice! But it *was* the same men and others have wondered too, how they tumbled into war and games alike with the same relish. But though they were great soldiers, they were terrible sailors. If they weren't playing volleyball they were being sea sick. Then never did the fierce look so fallen. Mostly though, they were at play watched by their families curiously incongruous in their saris and red tikka spots, as they sat under a lattice of welded steel or beneath boats swinging gently between davits — wherever they could find shade and fresh air.

One day, picking my way between families, volleyball players and upper deck impedimenta I recognised a soldier and he me. We had lain together in an ambush in the Borneo jungle for five days sharing biscuits, water and a view through the undergrowth of six square feet of the path that we were ambushing and the fearful thrill of what might be. Now we both grinned in recognition, shook hands and talked for an hour of what had been. His war stories were a deal more spectacular than mine (and probably more truthful) and I was outgunned completely when he reminded me that not long after my unit had quit Borneo his regiment had earned the first Victoria Cross to be awarded anywhere since the Korean War. We talked on into the dusk, his imperfect English, my non-existent Gurkhali no impediment; as soldiers young and old talk the world over. And since only a soldier could understand how that is I will not try to explain.

At last, after four days of sun and slow living, from the Straits of Malacca to the Andaman sea, from the Gulf of Martaban to the Bay of Bengal; at last the slow brown sludge of the Ganges came out into the sea to meet us. The ship slowed to take on a pilot. He steered us up the Hooghly, a finger of the broad brown hand of the Ganges delta, to dock nearly 100 miles upstream at Calcutta.

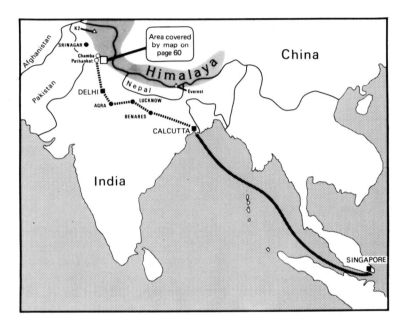

Calcutta: twenty years before it was one of the world's great ports; a tumult of shipping and commerce. Now it was dead, a ghost port. Of what the past had been there was evidence a-plenty: miles of wharfs, thickets of limp cranes hanging in disconsolate disuse, desultory lines of dull red godowns, gnawed by dereliction, housing only rats and history. And the only ship in sight was ours.

One godown was still in use, sullen testament to a busy past. Inside, its dank acres were occupied by a tangle of agricultural machinery — tractors and harvesters of the very best, implements of a wealthy West sent to purge a guilt as painlessly and as quickly as possible; a loveless gift wrapped without care, without

49

spares, without mechanics, above all without bakshish so that the stuff all fell at the first hurdle of Indian bureaucracy. It all lay dying, waiting to begin the tortuous journey through official channels, forgotten, unseen, like the beggars in the streets not far beyond. Beggars and bureaucracy; both are part of the perennial shooting pains of India, one self-inflicted, the other a western wound. It would not surprise me to learn that the stuff was still at that godown, the bright blues and yellows surrendered to the red of rust and a shroud of fine Indian filth. Or some may lie in the paddy of its destination broken by a few weeks misuse, not much more than an object of momentary consideration for the briefly redundant buffalo.

At the other end of the same godown ran a counter, a hundred feet long. On one side dozens of khaki-clad Bengali stevedors, matt black, the colour of hunger, hunched in squatting apathy. On the business side handlers of lighter loads in blue uniform. Interspersed were officers and officials in white shirts. Beyond the desks, shelves. On the shelves files; on those files more files. Files as far as the eye could see.

'Used to be one of the world's top ten busiest ports.'

I struggled to make throng these empty miles of wharfs, clumps of cranes, lines of godowns, reaches of flat foul water, and all the rusting paraphanalia of this dead dock; it was hard for the fancy to animate that sad sullage so rank was the rotted corpse. Too hard. The fancy failed; the imagination was stiff in this dismal place. It was an hour before we could find the excitement of this new world, an hour before any romance of new places could fire us. Stu was first to recover. Armed with his inventories, all six copies, he descended the gangway that had reluctantly arrived to join us to the subcontinent, weaved his way through the still squatting stevedors and bounded, all files, energy and 'it's our fault, we exploited them' up to the first white shirt. It was an act of self-sacrifice. Here was an india-rubber squash ball to be bounced about the court of Indian bureaucracy. In an hour he was punctured, confused, angry. What foreign traveller has not been all those, and more, in India. Some of the apologist in him was temporarily extinguished.

Anyway Sam had a better plan. Sam had heard that to pass through customs at Calcutta all the inventories in the sub-continent were as a camel to the eye of a needle unless accompanied, and in the proper proportion, by bakshish. The word may be Arabic, the original practice Arabian but now both word and practice extend far beyond the influence of Islam. In Calcutta the writ of bakshish runs strong. Ever prepared, pragmatical Sam had a slush fund. Stu suspected this. Sam knew it but let him play his hand first. It was an interesting debate and a depressingly effective lesson.

'Could take a while this; and some of that bakshish,' Stu at last conceded.

Some hours later an official from the British High Commission arrived, pulled, I think, by one of Sam's long strings; his job to smooth our path through customs. It took him three days.

In that time we saw something of the city. Most of it hurt, and like a bad pain, now that it is gone, I find it hard to recall.

Calcutta: the rich (the Indian system ensures that there *are* rich and that they stay rich) were fat; the very rich very fat. The poor, the many millions of them, the eternal poor, were very thin. They — rich and poor — lived in separate worlds, as if *from* separate worlds, with no common ground, with nothing in between; and never will be joined if India has its way, which, imprisoned by caste, it will. There were fine buildings, broken and decayed, bad teeth, soon to be rotten; and tens of thousands of huts of mud and wattle or cardboard or sack. Once fine wide boulevards like Chowringhee, were now rutted to narrowness and potholed with scraping craters, every one lacking repair. There were myriad alleys, no wider than a rut, ankle deep in mingled filth, in the special filth of India, in excrement, human and animal both. There were splashes of bright colour, spotless high-caste clothes, stiff starched uniforms and parades of immaculate Indian Army Ghurkas; and there were great fetid swamps of wretched rag, the drab uniform of abject poverty, the texture of the sweated soil of humans. There was dripping opulence, Indian and European; and there was the hideousness of professional beggars, children with limbs deliberately broken and deformed at birth so that they stuck at right angles, like the limbs of a cobbler's last, wheeling and scuttling on small wooden trollies or on little hands, challenging your western conscience with their pitiful whine, breaking you with the purest smile flashed from a beautiful face. You try to avert your eyes. You can't. You pay the ransom for the freedom of your stare, whether from pity or horror or compassion; or from all three. Then you pay for that too; there's always more horror, more tax on your gaze. In the end you flee to the sanctuary of a shop or hotel where the doorman kicks his countrymen to your bay. And though few of us were so guilty that our pockets ran out before our compassion, we were troubled none the less. Would you, could you, become inured, immune? India seems not to know pity of itself, to have no conscience. Indians seem not to see. I have read that they really don't see — can't see. Caste is necessarily blind to caste. Some live in luxury, waited on manicured hand and massaged foot; carrion millions live on Calcutta's streets, sleep and die on those streets, never knowing any roof but the sky. Every morning thousands lie dead, released. Every day new thousands are born to swell that hopeless multitude. I had always believed in the invincibility of the human spirit, that hope does indeed spring eternal, but to know Calcutta is to know a surrendered spirit, a place where for millions hope has never sprung at all.

We were clear to go. Now only the dockyard gate stood between us and Asia. It was locked. An impassive chowkidar lounged on a string bed nearby. He had no authority to open. I looked at him; he at me; East and West met in a glance that lasted a few seconds and spoke of a thousand years, of things I can only guess at, of things I will never comprehend. The face was expressionless — but what could be read in those deep, dark eyes? Servility or arrogance? apology or defiance? humour or anger? despair or hope? warmth or hatred? they said everything and nothing. The gulf between us would not be bridged in a few seconds — or in a few years. He was India and he had us; us and all the backshish we had to spare. We bought the gate, a loveless transaction sweetened only by Sam's grin and characteristic, 'You've seen this coming for three days, you old bugger', emptying one pocket and, 'Here's some for the missus and the kids,' emptying another.

Sam's good humour marked the end of the shock therapy of Calcutta — the end of my facile wondering why and how, the end of Stu's equally facile defence of their exploitation — and the beginning of a very long charge, 6000 miles around, that was to take us from Calcutta, via Delhi, to the top of a virgin Himalayan summit and back again, grabbing Srinigar, Agra and Kathmandu on the way for good measure.

We were acclimatized to India — no we were accustomed. We could look her straight in the eyes; its pain easier to bear. Calcutta: there can have been no-one who was ever there that was not moved to despair, to utter incomprehension at the slow sure pain of it. This was the beginning of Naipaul's 'Area of Darkness'; this would be his 'Wounded Civilization', perhaps the worst of it, the end; maybe it died here.

Sam suggested, in that firm, fair and friendly way that meant we had no choice, that we drove non-stop through the night to catch up on lost time and to put as many miles between us and Calcutta before the next dawn as possible. First, however, we had to call in at Dum Dum airport to collect Guy Sheridan, Sam's newest recruit. We plucked Guy, in real life an Olympic cross-country skier but at Dum Dum a bewildered pedestrian, from the airport melée and fed him to a truck.

Then we went at Delhi, out onto the great plain of Ganges, towards the heart of India, into the black Bengal night. We had our tempo back, sharper for the shock.

As we followed our headlights across that vast plain toward the mightiest mountains in the world, pulses quickened, humour welled back, spirit spilled in through widening smiles. The old philistine, nearly beat, was back. But Calcutta had nearly done for him. Our eager young hearts had been temporarily stilled, our quick young hands temporarily stayed as we wrestled to accommodate a world beyond our experience or knowledge, which had both been shown suddenly small.

We drove all through the night by turns, each until he could stay awake no more — some a bit longer. We were on the road. 'Get your kicks on route sixty-six,' bawled from one tinny tape cassette, the strings of Brahms screeched from another.

The road lay straight and generally narrow on a curious double camber like the roof of a house. The place to be was the middle and we tried to hang onto it, wrestling with steering wheels, bullied by potholes, trying to tame wild lurching trailers. But the middle was fiercely contested, and always successfully, by big Tata-Mercedes-Benz lorries, hell-bent on Calcutta and mindless of all else on the road. Now that I think of it there was nothing else on the road; perhaps one does not travel the roads of Big Black Bengal at night in anything other than a Tata-Mercedes-Benz.

53

We spotted the first one, a tiny white dot in a wider loom of light, miles away down the straight road ahead. Closing, closing, closer. We dipped; no reply. We flashed; no response. Closer! Closer, close! We lurched off the apex of the camber and down the side to the edge and whatever that held. The lorry roared past, full throttle, not an instant's hesitation, unheeding, uncaring, perhaps unseeing. King of the Bengal road. We got the message — jungle rules — and dodged them all night, 500 miles to Benares.

Somewhere on the road we stopped for a bleary-eyed brew. One minute there was nothing, just the seven of us, a ubiquitous thin cow, or two; a couple of hefty buffalo, miles upon miles of rice paddy and not a village in sight. Next minute a crowd, a multitude; wordlessly peering, staring at our every possession.

It was to be like that throughout India and it remained an irritation to be always the object of so much mute curiosity by always so many — and whilst the curiosity was by no means hostile, indeed it was utterly passive, it could be unnerving. Most of us were accustomed to the curiosity of youngsters the world over, but here the crowds were of all ages, granny and grand-dad too. It seemed. . . odd.

At every stop Rory would scold us. 'You're driving like bloody madmen, the vehicles'll never last.' Then he'd drive at least as hard when his turn came.

Mid-morning, Bengal plain, a hot place. Midday, hellish hot, 'redders'. Off came the canopies, top and side: the doors and windows came off. A fifty mile an hour dust storm was to be preferred to a windless cab. We stripped to shorts. Guy introduced the *shemagh*, an Arabian version of the turban. Most adopted it. A lurch to avoid a raging Tata-Mercedes-Benz found a Land-Rover sized pothole that claimed a leaf-spring. The raging lorry stopped, backed up. Out jumped a huge Sikh, black beard framing white grin. He turned and towed our bent truck to a tiny village, its focal point a smithy shop. Then, having delivered us, our destroyer roared off with a wave, with *élan*, the bright painted butt of his lorry proclaiming 'Horn Please'. For what purpose I wondered.

At the smithy, another Sikh took over, he as big, black-bearded and white-grinned as the last, a craftsman, a graduate at the schools of improvisation and necessity. From nothing but bits

54

and scraps, and with nothing but a hammer, tongs, a ringing anvil and some bellowed heat, he fashioned a leaf spring, good as new. An hour; fashioned and fitted.

We sped on, Rory full of praise and promises of promotion for the smith and 'I told you so's' for us.

Benares: early afternoon, a very hot, very holy city.

'Some geezer called Buddha was born here.' Spot was reading a tourist handout — none too accurately.

'That's not quite the case, you'll have to read Sidartha and stuff like that.' Stu, our Indianologist, had been hard at his homework, inventories forgotten.

'Well Buddha can keep it, it chucks-up something rotten. Look at those buggers boojee-ing (washing) out! What a place for a dhobi!'

Stu tried to explain, 'Benares is one of the holiest cities in all India; and one of the oldest. That's the smell of burning flesh — they're cremating their dead — and those others are washing in the holy water of the Ganges.'

'Well it might be good for Benares, just so long as they don't try it in Bradford.' Spot was a Yorkshireman and not altogether in sympathy with the sixties' love affair with all things Indian.

From a long bridge over the Ganges we could look down on Benares; a splendour of stately waterfront steps, *ghats* and funeral pyres — 'the industry of death' — aswarm with earnest pilgrims. It was all that was Calcutta and had the look of that place, but not the feel. Here was faith and hope and humour, three things that made it altogether easier. The difference was evident, almost palpable — even to us.

But we were exhausted by the driving, by dust and heat, in no mood for a heavy dose of Eastern mystique. The escape from Calcutta and the happy headlong huzza down the Ganges plain had us philistines again. We fled the shriek of the city centre and the pervasive, pungent whiff of charring human flesh for the tranquility of a rest house on the western outskirts.

Rest Houses or Guest Houses are a happy legacy of the Raj, clean and run well whether by the Public Works Department or Forestry (also legacies of the Raj), or new agencies such as the Department of Tourism. Indians love agencies and have heaped new on old. This rest house had been the Royal Mint. An ancient employee told us so with curious pride. His English was perfect.

The Queen had slept in this very room. I was sceptical about that even though the room was fit for a queen. He said the old days were good and that the British could come back if they wanted. (I didn't think we did.) I was to discover that this attitude, whilst far from common, was by no means unique. As I lay resting on a very comfortable bed looking up at a sky-high ceiling I reflected on the this of Calcutta and that of the Royal Mint, its Raj-loyal retainer, the other paradoxes that India had revealed, and wondered if there might not be more in those days of Empire than it was fashionable to admit.

That night, the cook, pleased to see British tourists, as distinct from other Europeans or Americans, showed the same curious cheerful pride — when a lesser welcome could have been expected — serving Lancashire hotpot — and serving it with some flourish and obvious pleasure. We all know how he came about the recipe but goodness knows where he got the ingredients. It would have gone down big in Bolton.

Next morning after a better 'great British breakfast' than British Rail has so far managed we headed for Lucknow and Delhi.

We stopped for petrol in the cantonments of Lucknow my schoolboy memories dancing to 'Dinna ye hear it? — Dinna ye hear it? Thepipes o' Havelock sound' — and equal nonsense. There, under a broken, once fluorescent Shell sign, stood an Indian soldier. That in itself was unremarkable: there are literally a million Indian soldiers. What was remarkable was that this soldier, a captain, as proclaimed by his shoulder badges, was dressed neck to foot in the casual elegance of an English cavalry officer. That is to say a fawn viyella shirt of superior quality, tight cavalry twill trousers, stable belt and desert boots. To the neck the likeness was uncanny. Above the neck — a big black beard and a mighty turban. Foot to neck, Britain, army and Raj: neck on, India. He was splendid. Splendid! Other shoulder badges discretely advertised '6th L'.

'I say, that 6th L wouldn't be 6th Lancers by any chance?'

'Absolutely old chap. You cavalry?' The drawl! Professor Higgins would have had it somewhere between High Street Ken' and Sloane Square. Geography insisted it was Utter Praedesh. The parody! The pipes, the pipes! Bob turned down an invitation to the Mess for a 'G and T', shook hands and rejoined us as we pulled out.

'Super chap, Indian you know.'

'You'd never have known it.'

I asked. 'Why do you upper-class chaps drawl so, it must take you twice as long to say anything.'

'Ya-aah,' Bob began, but too slowly as Spot cut in 'When tha's got bugger all to say, it don't make much difference.'

We laughed a good few of the dusty miles to Delhi on that. Bob too.

Delhi, very late August, a blur of heat even after our year's stewing in Singapore. We drove headlong, bandits now in our dusty stripped-down wagons, with bare chests, *shemaghs* and stubble beards. The city's propulation seemed at that moment to have taken to their bicycles, but then there were also the tri-shaws, thin men peddling fat men, and the motorized trishaws, and the taxis and the pedestrians, the stall keepers, shop keepers, busy crowds, jangling crowds. And the noise! If they weren't shouting or ringing their bells or tooting horns, they were gesticulating or feverishly transacting. Fantastic, frenetic, a blur.

Sam had contacts. The British Embassy, when at last we found it, was a haven of peace and order. Rooms had been booked on our behalf in the YMCA about half a mile away but that night we were to dine at the Embassy at the house of the Naval Attaché. He was a good hand, had recently completed the London to Sydney car rally. We regaled each other with yarns and ate bangers, beans and mash. Sam spent the next few days tying up various loose administrative ends — there's never a shortage of those in India — and beating at the door of that bastion of bureaucracy the Indian Mountaineering Foundation. The rest of us relaxed at the Embassy pool and played at being tourists — there was a promise of life in cacophonous Delhi that allowed frivolities like tourism to be undertaken with a clear conscience, without the sense of despair and guilt that accompanied every exploration in Calcutta. We enjoyed Delhi; to the hilt.

All expeditions to Indian mountains must needs be escorted by a liaison officer. Our first-appointed was a very pukka Major, a Brahmin, as he told us soon enough, who, on introduction regarded our motley group with obvious distaste. Fortunately, just as I suspect he was contemplating his resignation, Bob appeared in twills and cravat, sartorially spot-on and rescued us all from humiliation. That night in a disco down at Connaught Circus we worried that we would never measure up to Major's high standards of efficiency, dress, behaviour — or anything else that his caste held to be important. Moreover, rumour had it that he was a mountaineer of some note — bad news indeed! In the end we were spared each other. His father had been shot by Naxalites and he went home to attend to family business. In his place we were awarded Shayam Singh, an easy going, fat, happily inefficient Major, healthily averse to hardship, and with not the slightest interest in, or knowledge of, mountaineering. He was perfect — whatever his caste.

There was one piece of bad news that, had we had a plan, would have affected us badly. Sam cited this as evidence of the superiority of our, as he liked to call it, 'flexible approach'. And flexibility, he would remind us, was the first principle of war. Or at any rate it's one of them. The bad news was that the Rhotang Pass was closed to non-Indian traffic. The Rhotang Pass at 13,000 feet led over the first ridge of the Himalayas to the inner ranges of Ladakh and Zaskar. It would have given very easy access to our mountain, allowing a drive to within twenty miles of its base. A flurry of maps, much excited jibberish from us and a calm plan from Sam produced the following: we would drive via Dalhousie and Chamba to the village of Brahmaur, park the trucks and hire porters (Shayan Singh assured us that porters would not be problem and he was wrong about that as about many other things) who would carry the necessary over the Chobia Pass (about 17,000 feet) and down into Udaipur on the Chandra river — the point to which we might reasonably have expected to drive had the Rhotang been open to us. Then we would climb Menthosa.

All went well at first as we enjoyed fabulous Dalhousie, hill station of the Raj, cool and clear, almost a slice of Switzerland; wonderful high Chamba town, fresh grilled trout and 'the rough male kiss of blanket' at night; a dizzy drive up a Public Works Department track to a PWD bridge that was no bridge at all: wooden slats, suspended on wires, frail railings in which jeep-sized gaps drew the eye to jeeps, wrecked in the torrent 200 feet below. And the whole tenuous thing only inches wider than our vehicles. Bob and Rory conferred. Rory knew a bit about vehicle-weights. Bob, being a gunner, and artillery being concerned with trajectories and things, knew a bit about angles. They pooled their knowledge, none of which had any direct bearing on the problem at hand which was a bridge that was patently not designed for truck and trailer. But they pronounced anyway. Someone should drive an unloaded, trailerless truck across to see what would happen. Sam drew straws. I lost. Armful by armful we carried the contents of the first truck to the far bank, oblivious to the obvious flaw in our planning. I tried not to notice that the construction swayed to our tread. Nor could any rest be taken on the railings. Those that we left were ornamentation only, merest gestures. Rory stood on the far side his arms aloft in indecipherable standard-NATO signal while I aligned, with much good advice, the first truck for a tremulous tilt at the gap between. As a late refinement Stu had me belayed on a rope through an open window (we had refitted the doors in the cool of the hills). It had apparently occurred to no-one that, if the truck toppled, I had first to be pulled through the window before the rope, an idea of doubtful efficacy in the first place, could bring any advantage to my safety. And so I crept to that far bank, amid a splinter of slats, on a swaying bridge, twitching in timorous response to Rory's confident, but to me meaningless, gesticulations. A glance back along the droop of a 100 feet of rope to Stu's waist-belay made it manifest: the belay ploy, window or no window had no great merit. By the time I was safely across our collective patience was exhausted. The remaining two vehicles were brought over fully loaded without benefit of belay or Rory's hand signals. A few miles of track cut into the precipitous right bank of a gorge led to Brahmaur. At the bottom of the gorge, never less than several hundreds of feet below, the rusting remains of a dozen hapless predecessors, exercised a life-preserving restraint on our progress.

Brahmaur. We all fell in love with the place; a village of eighty temples, or so it was said, and about as many inhabitants. All this holiness was altogether too much for Stu, who, already rigged in Indian cotton pyjamas and *chuplis*, went completely native within hours of our arrival. He spent his days suffused in local culture, his early evenings with one or two of a dozen local gurus and his nights at the headman's house. That the headman's daughter was a vision of great loveliness was first spotted by Sam who could scarcely contain himself until he had opportunity to confront Stu with his discovery. Stu affected great, if unconvincing, offence. How could we possibly so misinterpret his intellectual curiosity;

how mistake his pursuit of a higher state of mind with low pleasures of the flesh. But we did, we did, and Stu whether for reasons cerebral or carnal became increasingly at one with his inner-self with the passing of each day — and night. Stu protested, methinks too much.

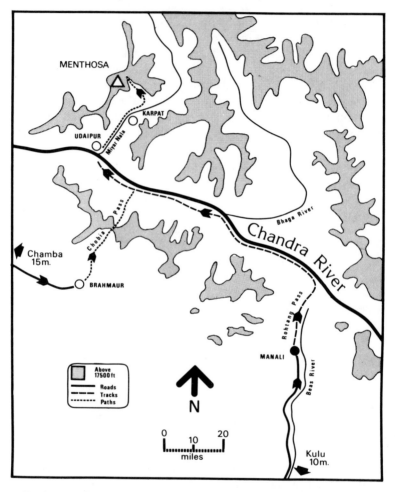

Brahmaur had everything, it seemed. Everything that is except porters. It was harvest time and Shayam Singh could interest no-one. No amount of his bombast, bullying or bribery could tug any of the likelier looking local lads away from their work. We were well off the beaten expedition path — we may well have been the first Europeans that way in years — so that the expedition game was unknown, and cut no ice. Nor, to their great credit, did our money. In the end Shayam was able to assemble only a handful of very unlikely lads, so unlikely as to be useless to the harvest, and nowhere near sufficient to hump our paraphernalia across the Chobia Pass to Udaipur — where Shayam assured us, they'd be queuing up to carry for us; he would see to it personally.

Sam amended the plan. Stu, because of his leg, Rory because he knew engines and because they were only base-camp wallahs at highest, and Shayam Singh because the police post guarding the Rhotang Pass would require his presence and because he was horrified by the thought of a week's trek over the Chobia, would, between them, take two of the trucks and trailers around to Manali to see if they couldn't get permission to cross the Rhotang after all. The rest of us and our half dozen failed farmers would take what we could, and what we couldn't (tents, stores, food etc.) went to a grateful village.

Chobia; three days later. It had been an idyllic walk even under sixty pounds of rucksack. Now we halted and camped at 15,000 feet while Sam, the great persuader, tried to coax our six porters to agree to cross the Chobia, 2000 feet higher. Village unlikelies they might have been but on the walk up to the Chobia they had shown themselves, like hill people the world over, inured to hardship by hardship. With heavy loads, not the fabulously heavy ones often reported, but heavy enough, bare feet, a single threadbare blanket to our lofted goose down, chappatis and nothing much else to our range of gastronomic goodies — they soldiered well enough. Their village first eleven must have been a fair team!

But fine as our unlikelies were they wouldn't be persuaded over the Chobia. Again like hill folk the world over, they were suspicious and superstitious of things and places they didn't know. The Chobia was high, snow covered and glaciated. It was therefore, untrodden, therefore unknown, therefore feared, each interdependent factor compounding the others; and earning the Chobia Pass a holiness. Furthermore, it led to the valley of the Chandra Bahaga River; a different world. The Chobia like the lower Rhotang further east were low points in the spine of the

61

Himalayas, the whole a watershed, literal, linguistic, racial, cultural and religious, between the lush aryan Hindu valleys of Manali, Kulu and Chamba and the dry mongoloid Buddhist valleys of Ladakh and Zanskar to the north. The boys simply wouldn't go.

I welcomed the delay. 15,000 feet was too high for me and Guy. We lay for two days wracked by terrible headaches, knowing nothing then of the gradual process of acclimatisation or its random selection. Here was Guy, fittest of us all by far, an olympic athlete, laid very low while Sam, who hadn't raised steam above a trot in years and two stones heavier than when last he had, settled as easily into 15,000 feet with its rarified air as he would an armchair with a gin and tonic. We had much to learn about altitude of whose painful lessons this was only the first.

It took Guy and me three days to recover. The porters were still unpersuaded so Sam amended the plan again. Dividing what we could of the porters' six loads amongst us, we set off for the Chobia, they for Brahmaur. It was heartening to discover that now we all went well up to the crossing point at 17,000 feet despite loads upwards of seventy pounds. Our first few steps on the glacier that led to the top of the pass, however, gave cause for concern, though, like everything else on this great adventure, it was soon converted to humour. Reaching the snow-line and the beginnings of the small glacier, I suggested to Bob that we roped up and donned crampons. This was a New Zealand lesson that had been well learned. I managed my crampons fairly quickly and was for a while too preoccupied with the magnificence of the scenery to notice that Bob was struggling. But he was, and with the wrong feet. It happens to the most experienced now and then. I pointed out his error and thought no more of it. We roped and he, at my suggestion, set off first up the hill. Within half-a-dozen steps he'd encountered a crevasse into which he fell headlong. He being uphill from me, it was easy enough to hold the fall. He emerged shaken; but of fear, not an emotion that featured on the very short list of those permitted to one of his class and background, he showed none. Two wobbles later he was in again. This time he emerged badly bruised and bleeding; but of pain, he betrayed not a wince. It was simply not a recognised sensation.

'Sorry about that old boy,' he said through a goodish trickle of blood from nose and lip.

'No sweat Carruthers!' I had taken to calling him Carruthers some weeks before in mickey-take of his upper-crust Englishness — that being the best name I could come up with on the spur of that particular beer.

'You'll forgive me for mentioning it mate, but you didn't look all that steady on your crampons.'

'Absolutely right old boy. To be perfectly candid, until five minutes ago I couldn't have told a crampon from a tampon. This morning is the first time I've seen the bloody things.' His invective and humour were surprising and welcome discoveries. We laughed and Bob acquired a new double-barrelled nickname, Carruthers-Crampon.

Two days later, without further incident, though with much slog, we reached the road which joined Udaipur to Manali via the Rhotang Pass. It had been a hard yomp with heavy loads. We were stuffed. 'Fatiguing little jaunt that,' Crampon made his point.

'I'm buggered,' Spot made his.

It was ten miles to Udaipur. No-one much fancied the walk and we were contemplating a bivouac there and then, when along came a dilapidated PWD jeep. Without any signal from us it stopped, a hugely smiling driver offered us a lift and we bundled in — or rather on. Soon we were rattling happily along the dusty road, all smiles and badinage, the trials of the last few days forgotten, thoughts occupied with the morrow — or the night's dram at earliest.

Udaipur was a meagre scrap of a place (it may be more now), a road-head hamlet of a few adobe houses, a bridge (the proud responsibility of our driver) over the Miyar Nullah and a substantial Forestry Rest House — though scant afforestation to justify its eminence. The Chobia had been a water-shed indeed. Here the ground lay parched, the houses were flat roofed, mud the building material, buddhism, or varieties of it, creeping down through Zanskar from Tibet, the prevailing faith.

Stu, Shayam and Rory were waiting, their smugness ill-concealed. Shayam had smooth-talked his way through the formalities — it could have never happened in Calcutta but here in the sanity of the mountains humanity could sometimes triumph over

63

bureaucracy. They had sped up and over its 13,000 feet in no time, Rory nursing the unacclimatised engines, rescuing them more than once from oedema, pulmonary or carburatory, with a timely tinker. This, after all, was what he'd come for and like all mechanics he loved to be needed.

'Two trucks and trailers at Udaipur, a dump of food at the Chobia, a truck and trailer, a ton of gear and a broken heart at Brahmaur and we're only sitting at the end of the road, the walk-in still to go and the mountain Christ knows where.' Sam was gleeful. 'Break out the brown wine.' The whisky flowed.

The next day Shayam recruited a dozen porters. They were a tough looking bunch, light-skinned and Italian handsome, a great contrast to the black beauty of Bengalis. They were greatly amused by Stu's attempts at Urdu though they soon developed an instant deafness to his cries of *'jeldi, jeldi'* (hurry, quick, faster). They smoked a great deal of *bhang* which did them no apparent harm, except to make them deafer still, care less and laugh more. Two were father and son, a particularly striking pair. Davi Chand, the son, had youthful good looks and the build of a 400-metre man — the performance too as it turned out — while the father a handsomer Marcello Mastroianni, had the rugged looks of a man who could have named his fee in any spaghetti western. He certainly did with us. It was Shayam's job to fix the price for the job. He put on, largely for our benefit, a great display of strut and bombast but the boys stuck fast; they knew that we needed them much more than they needed us. I suspect it was Shayam who had told them that in the first place. Whatever their source, market forces prevailed and they got their asking.

At last the walk-in began; that necessary preamble to the proper Himalayan expeditions that we had all read about. With most of our ordinance and a good part of our victuals spread thinly between Udaipur and Delhi, with a small, scruffy team of porters, a scruffier team of climbers and a modest, unsung objective at the end of it all, it wasn't perhaps as grand a departure as we had imagined in halcyon Singapore. But it was a start; more, it was *the* start.

We made Karpat, twelve miles along the spectacular Miyar Nullah gorge, in a day. The night in the village schoolhouse was bliss. Next day a similar distance led to a point where the moraine of the Urgus Glacier ran off the eastern flank of Menthosa, the way of our approach, down to the Miyar Nullah path. That was a memorable day. A day when our heavy loads were borne on feet made light by sweet enchantment. That beautiful valley! Views of new mountains, new places, smiling faces, sunny villages, prayer flags, *chortans,* streams, meadows; soft carpets of flowers, the excitement of new things and of old things newly seen. Here we nearly saw our first yaks — but not quite. In this valley, perhaps in others, they had been crossed with cows, or maybe buffalo. Whatever the breeding the farm animals hereabouts were not pure yak. We wondered if they had indeed been crossed with cows and if so whether they were then 'caks' or 'yows'. (I know now that in Nepal this hybrid is called *zhom.)*

We gambolled under Sam's paternal eye. The porters ambled a cheerful stroll from hamlet to hamlet, *bhang* to *bhang,* happily oblivious to Shayam's unnecessary haranguing. I found it heartening that these tough mountain folk showed scant respect for Shayam, that neither his caste nor rank impressed them. Here, perhaps, was evidence that the human spirit could endure centuries of the charted degradation of the Indian system of caste, and survive it. I certainly hoped so and rather unhelpfully gave them every encouragement. Shayam seemed genuinely puzzled that Stu's clowning and smattering of Urdu could have good effect while his own hectoring, rank and status earned only grumbling insolence and reluctant effort. It was a lesson in man-management — a science (or is it an art?) — not recognised in that sub-continent.

On the third day we turned west and climbed steadily for several thousands of feet to the snout of the Urgus glacier. Jeff Parsons and I, both fancying ourselves as 400-metre runners, competed fiercely on this steady climb, but whatever our best speed, Davi Chand, bearing a similar load, would cruise past on easy legs, breathing softly. We could not match him.

'There's-a-sub-50-second-man, -if-I-ever-saw-one,' Jeff squeezed out.

At 15,000 feet, to one side of the glacier snout we found the perfect site for a base camp; a flat grassy patch, meadow almost, with a brook, a boulder the size of a house as a bad weather marker — and, best of all, a superb view of Menthosa, our first of any kind.

It had two peaks. The East-most was dauntingly precipitous; that to the West, welcomingly rounded. We feared that the first was the taller and were relieved when the map showed otherwise. From the summit at 21,140 feet two ridges, in horseshoe formation, came north toward us. They led down for about 1,500 feet to a vast plateau from which a steeper slope, perhaps 50-50° dropped some 2000 feet to the Urgus col at the head of the Urgus glacier. Of the horseshoe summit ridges the easterly, or left-hand one as we viewed it from the north, looked to be the easier (in those days climbers were able to take the easy one and feel good about it) but it bared a row of serac teeth about half way up its length. This we knew was where a previous attempt had been stopped. The right-hand ridge though steeper, and therefore shorter, appeared to lack obvious obstacles. But there was plenty of time before we had to choose. For the moment the scene and situation were grand beyond words.

In an hour we had a base camp of two heavy canvas Command-Post tents; tents from which Commando Colonels conducted war. They were big and square, ideal, if unusual in this deployment. The porters arrived in good spirits thanks to Stu's good-natured chivvying and an hour later came Shayam in a most uncastely lather. It was, he boasted, the first sweat of his whole life. He flopped down and was scarcely to rise again for the duration of the ascent — some ten days.

That night, all crowded into one tent for the communal meal, and of course a dram or two, Sam tried, not very hard, to calm our blather with a simple plan or two but he soon gave up and gave us our head. Gave it to us the next day too when after a hurried porridge breakfast we charged off to recce a route up the Urgus glacier to the Urgus col on the north flank of Menthosa from where our proposed route really started. We were eager young pups, Sam the master. And like pups we scurried and sniffed, and covered about three times Sam's distance — his was the master's route, the sensible and the shortest between two points. By the end of the day we had reached a point half way between base camp and col, a height gain of only about 1500 feet. The snow had been soft, the going hard, the glacier complex, our route through it necessarily tortuous. And while our nose-down snufflings unearthed only false trails and dead-ends Sam's head-up, steady tread found sure alleys through the glacier's chaos.

It was a tired pack of pups that followed their wise and gentle master home that evening. None, Sam excepted, knew or cared much about conservation of energy; it was a lesson that New Zealand had not been quite high enough to teach. It was one I was to learn the hardest way.

The babble at base that night was subdued at first until a gigantic meal stoked it. Thereafter, bedlam and brews ruled. Somehow Sam got the shape of a plan through to us all. It went like this. Establish and mark a route through the Urgus glacier up to the col at about 16,000 feet. This looked a good place for Camp 1 (all books we had ever read about Himalayan climbs had a Camp 1, 2, 3 and so on, so we wanted them too, the more camps the more respectable the effort we thought). Hump kit and stores from Base to Camp 1 — no mean task since our tents weighed twenty pounds each and the stores included an HF radio which weighed at least fifteen. From Camp 1 at the col up the 3000 feet 50-60° slope on the north shoulder of Menthosa to the plateau. This looked a good Camp 2 (we registered disappointment that there weren't going to be more — why some of the trips we had read of managed 7 or 8). Another hump of gear and stores from 1 to 2 then the summit by whichever ridge looked the better bet.

All was well with us. Stu had the runs, it was true, but that was a minor problem. We settled in for the night, cosy in that contentment that comes from having a pleasantly tired body, an untaxed brain, and a mind free of any greater burden than what to have for breakfast. There were five in the other tent, Bob, Jeff, Davi Chand, Rory and Spot, and four in ours Sam, Stu, Guy, Shayam and myself. I was by the door, Stu farthest from it. I read by candlelight and while Sam and Shayam snoozed, Stu wrestled with his digestive track. Suddenly there was a flurry at the far end of the tent. Stu was fighting to wriggle from his sleeping bag. Curious, I rolled over in time to see Stu stepping quickly over the others towards me. Slowly now and less sure he hoisted an uncertain leg over my torso. Then he hesitated, standing athwart my chest, assailed by a terrible doubt. His mind fought a battle with his bowels for control of his sphincter, a desperate and losing battle.

There was a loud report followed by a sound not unlike that made by a flock of starlings taking flight, or in a tight turn (the simile occurred later). Bestridden by Stu I looked anxiously upward, supine now in more ways than one. His longjohns, whether worn for warmth or containment, were tight-stretched at the crutch. A foot above me and frail protection, they sagged suddenly and alarmingly low. There was a quivering pause while gravity and the finest British wool contested these new contents; a pause just long enough for me to rip the tent door assunder and roll to cover. Stu returned bare legged and washed ten minutes later to find Sam still hysterical, Shayam still affecting horror — though from a nation that defecate more publicly, more randomly than any other, I am uncertain why. Stu and I were relieved — in our different ways.

The next morning we left Stu and his longjohns to their ablutions — a chore Shayam thought unthinkable and found untouchable — and sallied back up the glacier to the end of the previous day's efforts. From here, with only a little more disciplined expenditure of energy we gained the col and satisfied ourselves that it would serve as the site for Camp 1. In two more days of heavy load carrying Camp 1 was firmly established. Jeff and I, who were going better than the rest, decided to stay there the night. The others went down — Stu and Rory, already trespassing above base camp against both doctor's and Brigadier's orders were well pleased.

'Not bad for a BEME,' said Rory.

'Or a convalescent,' added Stu.

Jeff and I rounded off a satisfying day by tuning the di-pole aerial of our HF radio set and making contact, at the first attempt, with our Indian Army control station 200 miles away — yet another product of Sam's wide influence.

I kept no diary, and my memory, fickle at best, refuses to dredge up all those fifteen-year-old details. It hardly matters. The details of who did exactly what, exactly when, precisely how, are unimportant now. The big events are still clear.

Jeff and I recced the way to Camp 2. It lay up that 50-60° slope above the col, 3000 feet to the plateau. Technically it was straightforward, but it was hard work in soft deep snow and for a few hundred of those 3000 feet our line was threatened by ice cliffs high above — not that we noticed them then.

Sam, Spot, Bob and Davi Chand (who, as the only porter who had agreed to carry above the snowline had been issued with suitable kit and clothing) had all moved up to Camp 1. Together we set off to establish Camp 2. It was overkill but we were all keen and 'why not', Sam said. Jeff and I were to stay up. We were probably the strongest pair and that day, and as if to prove it, foolishly charged up the deep, steep snow of the way we had recced a few days before. Most of our old steps had been filled in by wind-blown snow. It was tiring work. Idiotically we competed, soon leaving the others far behind and when Jeff sensibly slowed, I forged ahead, breaking a new trail from 18 to 19,000 feet with the same profligacy as I had shed on Mt. Cook nearly a year earlier. But 19,000 feet does not forgive as easily as alpine altitudes. I arrived at the plateau twenty minutes ahead of Jeff and a good hour ahead of the others, suddenly aware of a sagging tiredness. I gave it little thought beyond registering the fact, and lay down to rest in the sun until the others arrived. After a breather, a horizontal plod, through very deep snow (Jeff and I now well to the rear) led, in a couple of hundred yards to Sam's declared Camp 2. Kit and food were dumped, the tent erected. Then Sam and team retreated to Camp 1 leaving the plateau to an only slightly chastened Jeff and me. We sat for a while resting and studying the two limbs of the horseshoe. The left-hand limb looked easy, except for the serac barrier, and it looked as if a way might be found round that, but it was farther from our tent; and distance in that soft snow was now a prime factor. We were both shaken by our recently discovered vulnerability. We thought to go for the right-hand ridge, nearer if steeper.

A glorious sunset raised our spirits and largely banished our tiredness. Then the cold drove us into tent and bag.

'I'll flash up the stove, you get the pots.'

'Can't find them. Must be outside somewhere.'

A minute later.

'There's no pots, John.'

Somehow, in that big lift, in all that overkill, we'd forgotten the cooking pots. We should have gone down, there and then, or certainly the next morning for we were badly dehydrated and liquid is important, crucial, at those dry energy sapping altitudes. We had been throwing away energy all day and now we had no pots with which to pour some back.

'Maybe Sam will bring some up tomorrow when he realises — if he realises.'

We improvised, like good soldiers, we thought then (like foolish virgins we know now), ate the contents of a 7-oz tin of baked beans and used that to produce ludicrously small brews of tea — about one fifth of a pint at a time. Then, when we should have been drinking pints we got bored with the ritual and went to sleep.

Next morning, by now severely dehydrated, but unaware of it, we set out for the right-hand ridge. The plateau was exhausting: thigh deep snow, yard after yard. It took hours to reach the ridge, then another hour to wade and climb onto its crest where we had convinced ourselves the snow would be blown hard and firm by the wind. From just below a little cornice on the lip of the crest I reached over to plant my axe in what I prayed would be névé. Arm followed axe up to the shoulder in softest powder. We furrowed onto the ridge and sat for a few minutes in tired disappointment before beating back to the tent. It had been a long hard day and we had only 500 feet of height to show for it. The lesson was in the learning.

While we had been struggling up to the ridge Sam and team had appeared at Camp 2 with new loads. They had watched for an hour or so before retracing their steps and though we had tried we had been unable to shout any communication.

There were all sorts of luxuries in these new loads — but there were no pots. Sam had no way of knowing that we had none — short of a stock-take and one of Stu's inventories — and he had not unreasonably assumed that we had taken our own.

Now we really should have gone down. We didn't. Instead more improvisation. That night when the first Bluet gaz cylinder ran out, we cut the top away, washed it, none too carefully, and continued to brew with this new, slightly bigger pot, say one-third of a pint.

When Sam arrived the next day, this time to stay up, Jeff and I were lying, laid very low in our tents, the summit, by either ridge, a forgotten dream. Dehydrated, exhausted, poisoned, possibly suffering high-altitude sickness, we neither knew nor cared.

I suppose that now I ought to be able to diagnose the sickness. But I have never looked back. 'Ain't no percentage in it.' It's only now, fifteen years later, in the writing, that I've been able to muster the courage to consider it. The facts are simple, even if their recollection is painful. The reasons — well what the hell.

The sun got up. We couldn't. Tried, tried, tried. Couldn't.

The young pups were tuckered out, punctured, beaten, finished. The body wouldn't go: the mind couldn't make it. All my life everything had fallen to the charge, to the mindless frontal assault and no prisoners, nothing had ever happened to cause me pause, to doubt my strength or spirit. And how that arrogance, that vanity, mocked now on this modest Himalayan hill; mocks yet. Suddenly, in fact not so suddenly, my charge had run out and there was a mountain still to climb. If I had been older I would have cried but I wasn't man enough for that yet.

'You'll have to go down mateys,' gentle Sam, gently commanding.

Neither of us could muster the smallest protest. Someone packed our essential gear, someone helped us out, someone carried our rucksacks, someone broke trail. Now that there was no fight to be fought, now that all the opposition had been removed for me, whatever fight I had left in me fled. Pride was all I had left.

'Give me my 'sack, please.'

'No. Don't be daft.'

'No-one has ever had to carry my gear before.' A soldier's legitimate pride? Perhaps, but more likely hubris. It's a long way from stupid strong to weak wise but I had slid the full length in two or three days. Never was the economy of effort lesson, the one we escaped learning in New Zealand, so painfully learned; never were recalcitrant pupils so brutally educated.

Slipping, sliding, stumbling, falling, dead drunk on defeat, we reached the plateau's edge.

Stu, trespassing, enthusiasm undiminished, longjohns refurbished, had fixed a rope on the steeper bits of the slope between Camp 1 and Camp 2. Sam had forbidden him the summit, the Brigadier's dire warnings still ringing in his ears, so Stu had made busy doing whatever he could. Fixed ropes, he'd read in the books, were *de rigueur* in these big mountains and that was what he had spent a happy day doing — fixing rope. I held on to it rolling and tumbling down to Camp 1. Jeff too.

Guy had escorted us down, though I hardly knew it. He was still suffering as badly from the altitude as he had on the Chobia Pass. He appeared to have a ceiling of 16,000 feet or thereabouts. (He has since been much higher without ill effect.) Nevertheless, he was still in far better shape than Jeff or I and looked after us well, cooking a meal and brewing endless tea — which was what we needed most. By morning we were stronger and able to walk, unassisted, down to Base Camp where Stu and Rory were kicking their heels, by now somewhat bored. Guy had a message for them from Sam; he had no-one left with any climbing experience who was fit — did Stu and Rory fancy a go at the top? That was all Stu needed. He was off, Rory in his wake. I hope it will not be thought churlish if I mention that in their random ascending and descending, climbing relatively high, sleeping fairly low they had, inadvertently hit upon the perfect acclimatization programme. And so it was that they climbed from Base to summit, by the left-hand ridge, in three days. A trip that had begun in jest, had been borne on jest, that thrived on jest, ended in jest; the summit team comprised a convalescent and the Brigade Electrical and Mechanical Engineer, both permitted to travel only on the express understanding that they didn't venture on the mountain 'proper', as the Brigadier himself had quaintly put it.

While all this was happening Guy, Jeff and I were making our way down to Karpat. Shayam bored by his lonely vigil at base camp came with us. It was our intention to rustle up some porters and to begin the withdrawal. The police at the Rhotang had impressed upon Shayam that we had to recross by October 15th. That, they insisted, was an absolute deadline for on that day, they would have us believe — and had Shayam believing (he was positively desperate to believe; the comforts of civilization beckoned and he was a sybarite to his soul) — on that day, year in year out, the heavens opened and a mighty blizzard blocked the Rhotang until the following spring.

The thought of a winter in that wild area held a certain fascination for us. It filled Shayam with horror. He was galvanised as never before, found half a dozen porters and actually escorted them back up to Base Camp. He was going to get across the Rhotang even if it meant carrying a load himself.

The three of us reached Karpat with a hefty downhill load and decided to rest for a day at this beautiful village. Jeff and I read and convalesced, even though we were strong again now, and felt sorry for ourselves. Guy busied himself with logistical and administrative details (the few that he could find), despatching spare kit, tents and the like with a couple of locally recruited lads, to Udaipur. The radio, which Guy had carried down from Camp

1 where it had been not much more than a toy, went too.

'Can't see us needing that now.'

We breakfasted on *parhattas,* wild honey, fresh eggs and local tea, all provided by the hospitable village folk.

Lunch would be more of the same and dinner an enormous 'up homers' repast with one of the locals, all sorts of great Indian food and half the village in attendance.

This tranquil existence was shattered the next day. A porter arrived, breathing hard, with a note from Sam. Bob Steward had been hit on the head by falling ice whilst descending the slope above Camp I. He had a broken skull and was unconscious. It was serious. Stu and Rory had got to the top. Now everyone was carrying Bob from Camp I to Base. He presumed we had the radio. Call for a helicopter.

Sam, the gay Lothario, was telling us it was serious. We needed no more encouragement. But the radio was at Udaipur.

'Damn!' Guy regretted his administrative tinkering — he had just been trying to make himself useful as we all do when we feel partly redundant and, blaming himself for the error, quickly took the initiative.

'John you run to Udaipur and get on the radio for a chopper. Jeff, you and I'll go back up to Base in case we have to carry Bob right down to the road. Depending on how you get on with the chopper, John, you can decide what best to do next.' Not orders these, but ideas, plainly spoken. Discussion was pointless. It would waste valuable time and a better plan than the one we had was unlikely to emerge quickly.

I shot off, pumps, shorts, stripped for action, a man with a mission. A man delighted to have a mission and though no distance runner, determined to run as never before. Guy would have run it faster but I think he felt that would have been running away from Sam's expected wrath about the radio and that the better thing for him to do was to go up and admit to the error, if error it was with anything other than hindsight. He was probably right. In any case the minutes that would have separated us were hardly likely to be crucial. I shed guilt with every sweated stride, misery with every bounded step. It was Aix to Ghent, Marathon to Athens; it was sweet therapy, it was catharsis. It was twelve miles at 10,000 feet and it would kill me now and many who live at sea level. But I was thin from my exertions

73

at altitude, two stones thin, fit as any fiddle now that I was rested and rehydrated; and I was needed. To be needed, that is the great panacea. I was Wilson of the Wizard, Walter Mitty, Jim Ryun, anyone who could run and run. On what wonderfully childish dreams can grown men drive themselves to greater things. I didn't say *great* things but I would have done them too if they had been needed.

I have no idea how long it took, but it was half the time of any state of fitness before or since. I arrived at the Udaipur Rest House close to genuine exhaustion, panting, 'The radio, the radio', to an uncomprehending chowkidar. I found it under a jumble of kit, matched the di-pole to frequency, laid it out in the best direction I could think, switched on, and still heaving wildly, grabbed the headset.

'Hello Zero this is Menthosa Base (which it wasn't quite). Radio check, radio check, over.'

And straight away, crystal clear, 'Zero, OK over.' A soft female voice.

'Menthosa, read-back message, over.'

'Zero send, over.' She was sharp and pencil and paper handy, that operator.

I gabbled half a message of no great conciseness then...

'Roger so far, over.'

'Zero, Roger, over.' I was in love with this operator.

I gabbled the rest, the gist of which was that one of our number was seriously injured at 15,000 or 16,000 feet and could they send a chopper to Udaipur where I would direct them onward. (I had no map so that I couldn't give them a grid reference to which they could have flown direct.) I emphasised the altitude because I knew that among their range of helicopters the Indian army had some Alouette Mark III's, and it would need to be one of these to cope at that height. (No current British helicopter could have performed the task.) I finished.

'Message ends. Read back, over.'

She read the message back word perfect, if anything word improved, and ended,

'Helicopter leaving this location figures five, your location fifteen hundred hours. Good luck, out.'

She, whoever she was, must have learned her radio procedure at the Royal School of Signals at Blandford (there's a good chance that she did), and I loved her.

The helicopter arrived five minutes early, catching me washing my feet. It spotted my hastily prepared landing site and landed neatly on the fluorescent 'T' I had arranged. I greeted the two pilots in bare feet. Yes, I was sure it was no higher than 16,000 feet; yes, I could take them there. They were worried about the time and daylight. Have to hurry they said. I jumped in as the pilot took off. He arrowed with élan to the entrance of the Miyar Nullah gorge. What a flight, what a view, what excitement! There was Karpat, far below, and the school-house. There were the dots of other hamlets and, there, just discernible upturned faces. There was steep Phabrang to the East and other mountains all around. It was spellbinding. The co-pilot offered me an oxygen mask, indicating the altimeter which showed 5000 metres. I felt no need, having lived at that altitude for some weeks, but joined them on oxygen anyway not wishing to appear ungrateful.

We swung west beyond Karpat and I began to worry whether they had managed to get Bob down to Base. There was Base. They had heard our approach. A 'T' was clear to see. The pilot flew straight in and landed without the usual circling reconnaissance. He flew with élan this fellow.

Bob was propped, conscious now, against a boulder. Spot had unwrapped a bandage from his head and was about to replace it with a clean one.

'Thou's got to 'ave clean nicks and a clean bandage for 'ospital.'

Sam examined Bob's head. There was hole, about the circumference of a penny, drilled clean through his skull. Whatever it was that occupied Bob's head was plain to see. Sam decided that he must have a photograph, focused and began adjusting the meter.

'Two copies,' Bob said with a weak laugh.

'Hey mate, keep your mouth closed,' Sam said, 'all that daylight is fooling my meter.'

It looked as if Bob would live after all. We loaded him inside and I jumped in after, keen to be away, my bare feet were freezing. Shayam jumped in too pulling rank on pilot and co-pilot, both, like me, lieutenants. The engine roared, the rotor gathered speed, the chopper shuddered — and remained where it was.

75

'I haven't got enough power,' the pilot shouted at me above the noise, 'you'll have to get out.'

'But I'm barefooted,' I protested, 'I can't walk twenty miles like this. Shayam you get out.'

'But I'm a major. You're only a lieutenant.'

Stalemate — Indian rank and caste in confrontation with soft western feet. The pilot, a wise man, saw that the key to unlocking this impasse lay in the technology at his hands and pulled power well above the regulation limit, pulled it with gusto and pulled us away in a standing start at 16,000 feet with five aboard. No mean feat of flying; no mean helicopter.

Shayam and I got out at Udaipur. Bob was flown on to hospital where he made speedy progress and a full enough recovery never to want to climb again.

Two days later Sam declared a party. Shayam sent invitations hot foot everywhere. We wondered about the response; we weren't even sure that such a thing as a party existed in the social order of things in this part of the world. They do, we discovered, they most certainly do. They came from Karpat and from the four valleys that converge at Udaipur and far beyond. They came early, stayed late. Days late. We had alcohol, the chowkidar and some of his mates did the food, the guests brought more food and *bhang* and *chang*. With the women came music and soft song, with the men the dance. The women sang and sang, their men danced and got stoned. We danced with them and got drunk. Sam chatted amiably to the local headmen and other dignitaries, they chatted amiably back, the mutual ignorance of the other language no bar to comprehension. Stu was a fever of photography and tape-recording — anxious, as ever, about culture — and his memoires.

'Oh the culture of it all!' Stu was unable to make up his mind whether to dance, sing, drink, take photographs or make tapes. He tried all at once, succeeded in none.

'Bloody culture,' said Spot. 'You'd get all this at any Glaswegian wedding,' adding after a short pause, 'plus a good punch up.'

He spoke too soon. Shayam had been approached by the headman of a village above Karpat that we had passed on our travels. The man wanted to know if Shayam could pull strings to help him secure permission to fell a few, it might have been more, of the Forestry Department's trees.

76

Shayam thought it might be difficult until he saw that the man had an especially nubile daughter. Then he was absolutely sure he could manage something, no doubt about it, no problem. Shayam named his price obliquely, but not obliquely enough. The father was justifiably angry and an altercation followed during which, in an act that crossed several centuries of social engineering, Shayam was pushed to the ground amid a sprawl of happy male dancers. Pushed mind you. By the high standards of Glaswegian weddings it was no punch-up, no brouhaha; bloodless and toothless it wouldn't have raised an eyebrow in Sauchiehall Street where it could have easily passed for an 'excuse me'. But here it was an act of violence, an act of defiance in the face of rank and caste, an act that appealed to our simple values — simple country father defends daughter's honour against bullying city slicker, and never mind the complications of religion, caste, culture, country or history. This was a good fight, a right fight. We hustled Shayam away before another push was thrown and did him the favour of getting him drunk. Drunk even by high Glaswegian standards. Next morning the party was still in full swing and no-one seemed to remember the incident — or to care.

We drove over the Rhotang on October 15th. There wasn't a snow flake in sight, nor any for a month after. Then back around to Brahmaur to collect the third vehicle and on to Delhi where we discovered that the ship we were scheduled to take from Calcutta back to Singapore had been diverted. It had sailed for Bangladesh to help with the flood relief in the first of a series of calamities that overtook that unfortunate nation in the 70s.

It would be at least a month before we could leave Calcutta — and we were in no hurry to go back there.

'May as well split into three and see a bit of India,' Sam suggested.

I decided to phone Kathy and make the most of it. But phoning Singapore from Delhi's General Post Office isn't the simple operation that Alexander Bell may have had in mind.

By the time the combined efforts of a good proportion of a not inconsiderable staff had managed to set the phone ringing in our home in Daffodil Drive, Singapore, I was a lather of ridiculous rage, of fatuous frustration. Seizing the handpiece from an oversolicitous telephonist, I strained to hear a faint crackling voice. It sounded all of a sub-continent and an ocean away. I judged the voice to be speaking Chinese and took it as belonging to our part-time *amah*, Lucy.

'Lucy, Lucy is that you?' The unnecessary question was answered with stacatto smatterings of disembodied Urdu, Gujerati, Hindi and I know not what else — there are 270 languages to choose from — as equally anxious callers from all round India, and maybe beyond, contested my line. To this confusion add a battery of telephonists' hands flashing every which way across their switchboards, making and breaking connections, crossing and uncrossing lines with mercurial random. Two dozen would-be telephone users all took their interrupted attempts at conversations, business deals, international transactions, proposals of marriage, illicit assignations in far better part than I wrestling with a holiday with the equanimity of those surrendered to chaos.

'Lucy, get Missy please.'

This time there was no audible reply — in any language.

'Lucy, get Missy *please*, this is Master speaking.'

I was shouting now, at the top of my voice, hot with heat and range. My efforts had attracted a sizeable audience. The switchboard operators were looking my way, reduced to a pianissimo as they wondered at my distraction. Fellow telephone users, puzzled, amused, shocked, by my invective were gazing too and the hundreds of by-standers, few of whom seemed to be there for any purpose, some of whom were possibly permanent inhabitants, watched intent and impassive, quietly grateful perhaps that this spectacle should brighten their day. The situation was rich in irony — though I think India on her own is incapable of irony — my idiocy the catalyst. Or was it farce?

Here was Master, the hapless victim of an imperial invention, phoning a colony from an ex-colony, shouting outmoded colonial appelations that embarrassed him despite their harmlessness and worried him that they offended the crowd, late subjects of the 'Master' nation. But if that crowd understood they would not have found the appelations curious or offensive in the least. It was all rather acceptable by the standards of their own society.

The strongest and commonest comment conveyed by those impassive stares seemed to be how silly to get so cross with a telephone, especially when it's working so well. Fair enough comment.

But Master threw a wobbler, partly from embarrassment at his own anger, and partly from anger at not being able to control his anger. A great big neo-colonial wobbler.

The line crackled in reply.

'Missy speaking you silly bugger.'

'Come to Delhi.'

It was, it remains, one of my best lines. Kathy came and she, Stu, a Land Rover and I had a ball. Agra and the Taj Mahal of course, and by moonlight. They did not disappoint. Maini Tal and the Corbett National Game Park. They did not disappoint. Kashmir, Srinigar, the Dal Lake; a house-boat, the *Lady of Shailot*, late October, autumn, coolness and colour. They did not disappoint.

Returning from Srinigar late one night, Calcutta bound, our dynamo blew, just before the Banihal tunnel which is miles long and not a light in sight. As it was dark outside anyway we reasoned that it was as easy to continue as to return. Stu and I sat on the bonnet directing the feeble light of our head torches at anything we thought should be avoided, especially at rampaging lorries coming hard in the opposite direction, while Kathy got her first taste of high adventure at the wheel.

After the tunnel, which debouched in the middle of nowhere, we floundered on for ten precariously dim, torch-lit miles. There was much to hit and too little road to miss much. A village brought relief and, amazingly, repair. A tiny shack of a garage had a reconditioned Land Rover dynamo in stock — though little else. It was fitted that night.

The next day brought the gauntlet of a perilous road that ran for miles along the side of a steep and deep gorge. The bottom bore the brutal proof of an appalling standard of driving. Jeeps, lorries, buses lay dead and dying in the river below, mute, but terrible testimony to the consequence of a spill. This was the road to Jammu.

Some way down it, Stu at the wheel, we came up behind the rear truck of the daily convoy from Jammu to Srinigar returning to base. We knew from an encounter on the upward journey that it could be up to seventy vehicles long. Kathy and I exchanged a glance that wondered if Stu was going to be content to sit behind the convoy for the fifty-odd miles to Jammu. It was travelling very slowly.

79

The answer was no. Seventy times, no. Now I don't doubt that if you measured that road you would find that it was several inches wider than the combined widths of an Indian army lorry and a Land Rover. But there is more to the equation than that simple addition. There was the erratic course of the army lorries — seventy erratic courses. There was the wobble of the wheels and there was the crumbling edge of a rutted road, a 500-foot drop to the river and all that evidence. I remember it all clearly, Kathy remembers it vividly. To overtake — this was done on the right as in Britain — the same side as the gorge, Stu would come up almost to beneath the tailboard of a lorry, lurch suddenly to the right and scrape and bounce down its right-hand side, one eye on the road edge just beneath his foot, the other steadfastly ahead, lookout for oncoming traffic. Kathy and I reckoned, independently, that if Stu got it wrong we might have a chance of abandoning to the left while there was road left to go for, leaving Stu for however long it takes to tumble 500 feet at 32 feet per second, per second to rue his miscalculation. Once was exciting, twice enough, but seventy?

That was Kathy's second taste of high adventure at the wheel. She got her third in Patankot, hardly recovered from the first two. Patankot, in the heart of the Punjab, is a city of Sikhs, millions of them. We were intent on Delhi, nosing our way through the seething mass of city India made solid by the evening rush hour crowd, as fast as its bustling density would allow — about 3mph — no more than walking speed at most. It was very hot and we had the Land Rover as naked as a beach buggy, no doors, roof, canopy or sides, nothing. An engine, chassis, self at the wheel, Kathy in the middle, Stu beside her. Chubby vespas, sleeker lambrettas, each bearing a turbanned, bearded Sikh, flowed slowly toward us, parting in a bow wave at our bonnet.

One scooter bore down faster than the rest in the manifestly unsteady hands of a giant Sikh soldier. Another giant Sikh soldier rode pillion: some advertisement for the structural properties of Vespa scooters. This Vespa did not join the bow wave to left or right but forged inexorably ahead, slap bang into our Land Rover, by now stationary.

'Damn.' It was the very least Stu could have said.

The two Sikhs rose to their full six feet plus, full thirty stones between them, and moved, no steadier on their feet than they had

80

been on the scooter, to where I sat unhappily at the wheel. The tide of scooters, of humanity had stopped to watch. There is nothing so quick in India as a crowd. I was apprehensive.

'I demand an apology,' — this from the erstwhile scooter driver and the bigger of the two. His breath betrayed the reason for his unsteadiness, and, as far as I was concerned, the collision. He was drunk; dangerously, pompously, gloriously drunk. The demand was declaimed, more to the crowd than to me — he had his stage and the biggest audience of his life. He was the star. It seemed unlikely that there would be any prizes for supporting roles.

I was exquisitely aware of all this so that I cannot begin to explain the stroppiness, the perverse pride of principles that seized me now.

'Apology? What for?'

The crowd, bigger by the second and uncommonly quiet, strained to see and hear. All India, it seemed, was watching.

'You have just knocked me and my good friend Captain Amrik Singh of the 7th Punjab Cavalry, from my scooter. I demand an apology.'

I looked at my tormentor, his eyes blazed weakly with false anger, the forced anger of bombast — I hoped. All around his home crowd; thousands of pairs of dark eyes, impassive, so that it was difficult to tell whose side they were on. I was in no hurry to find out — for me this was an away fixture; and not as much as a pane of glass between the two sides.

'No, I did not. You ran into me. It was your fault.'

The crowd thickened, pressed in for a closer look, the better to hear, peering from behind, before, to either flank. India had us surrounded.

'I, a captain in the Indian Army, an Officer of Artillery, demand an apology.' Slightly slurred, but there was no mistaking it; he knew what he was entitled to and he wanted it. He wanted that apology. Worse, having played all his cards so quickly and so publicly he now *needed* that apology. He'd had me cornered, but now he'd cornered himself too. I wished he hadn't; I would have settled for a draw but he had gone for broke. I gambled, desperately, badly, and said, as fraternally as I could manage in those dire circumstances,

'A Captain, oh really. I'm a captain too,' I lied, 'in the Royal

Marines, you know the Commandos, you must have heard of us.'

He hadn't. And if I had hoped to strike a common chord of military solidarity or impress him with the affix 'Commando', I had my psychology and my history all wrong.

'But you don't rule us anymore.' What was surprising was not the childishness of the statement, the drunkenness would explain that, but that in all our thousands of miles in India this was the first time anyone had said it, or anything like it.

'No we don't and I'm sure you're better off without us.' Now I was childish, not entirely sincere and, more to the point, a long way wide of the psychological mark again.

'If you don't apologise, I will have this woman raped by all this crowd.' The bluff had taken a turn for the worse. Kathy who up to this point, had been trying to lose herself in a road map took a sudden interest in the developments.

'Apologise,' she advised. It was uncharacteristic of her to be so unreasonable — though I concede that now she had a vested interest.

His threat struck me as such obvious bombast as to be empty. 'No,' I said, still reasonableness personified, 'it was your own fault.' Kathy was looking unhappy.

'Then I will have you and your friend buggered by the crowd,' adding unnecessarily, 'all of them.' Now Stu was looking unhappy. Now I had a vested interest. I was effusive in apology, abject in it; I was remorse itself. And we were gone — nosing off into the crowd as fast as it would part. The result was entirely to their satisfaction, and they were in motion again.

'What about the damage to my scooter?'

The captain saw mileage in me yet. I shouted back that we were going to the Government Guest House and he could come there to settle this new problem.

We drove to the outskirts of town, to a Rest House that we knew from the outward journey. It was dusk as we arrived and the night, earlier and quicker than at temperate latitudes, approached. We rushed to register and get a room, a motel-like affair looking out over a verandah onto a central lawn. We waited, all three in the same room, Kathy calm but tense, Stu worried, while I affected cheerful insouciance.

'Doubt whether they'll bother, eh.'

We waited, five minutes, ten. Then just as we were daring to hope — the phutt, phutt of a heavily laden scooter. A shout from the lawn summoned someone. Stu followed, first locking the door with Kathy inside, then positioning himself on the high ground of the verandah in a dark shadow, a heavy chair to hand. He held the ground of tactical importance. I High Nooned along the verandah — all East is East and West is West — to where my would-be adversary stood four square at 'God's great judgement seat' — the lawn. His mate stood one pace, right flank, rear. A single bare electric light weakly lit the drama.

He drew first. 'As a Sikh, in order to satisfy my honour, I must fight.' He was too drunk to see that he was overplaying his hand, that farce was taking over, that he was no longer occupying the ground of tactical importance, nor even the ground of his own choosing, nor that he no longer had a home crowd and that I could afford to gamble a little longer. He was a foot taller than I and a good three stones heavier, but he swayed and there was Stu lying in ambush, and there was the chair. The odds weren't bad.

'Fine,' I lied, but only a little, 'we'll fight.'

The game was as obvious as it was ridiculous. He was momentarily unbalanced, but quickly recovered.

'We must fight with knives.' Puffed up bombast, it's the same the world over.

'OK,' I replied. He was bluffing, wasn't he? I found room for doubt.

He recovered again, 'Sikhs must fight to the death.' He puffing and spluttering, a dog barking from behind a fence. This had to be bluff, didn't it?

'OK,' I was no longer sure who was bluffing who. There was a pause as we both realised that there was nowhere else to go. The denouement was due. It was time to collect.

His mate saw this too. He allowed the pause to nag a tick or two then, choosing precisely the right psychological moment like the good second he was, he made a great play of reading his watch and announced, 'I say, the bar's open. Why don't we all have a drink.' The timing was consummate. It may be that he'd had some practice but no matter, here was honourable escape from this daft farce for us all. We all agreed eagerly and moved quickly to the bar before embarrassment could raise another hurdle.

'And bring your charming wife,' added he of lately-threatened mass rapes and buggeries. It was well that India does not know irony.

'Where are we going now,' asked Kathy as I sprang her from her cell.

'For a piss-up.'

'When will you men grow up.' It was a general condemnation — I hadn't been excluded.

We, the men that is, fell to drinking with some enthusiasm. Kathy watched, a tolerant observer to the curious ways of men the world over.

In a few rounds we were all the best of mates, a band of brothers; soldiers, slapping backs and swapping stories that we had swapped a dozen times before, would swap a hundred times again, some our own, others borrowed, some made up specially for this occasion. Before long a Kipling quoting competition ensued. Amazingly, it was their idea and they won, hands down. We were handicapped, for callow though we were even our rough tuned sensibilities baulked at the bits we thought sure to offend. At these gaps, beside themselves with glee, whether at our embarrassment or their triumph I know not, they would supply the missing lines. It was they who said, 'So here's to you Fuzzy Wuzzy' and 'pore benighted heathen'. They who, howling with laughter, tears streaming into their beards, laughing fit to burst their bristles, said, 'An' for all 'is dirty 'ide, 'E was white, clear white, inside'. Kipling may have understood. We were puzzled. Some time later one of them rose and made to toast. Swaying, he began in that sincere, solemn way of drunks,

'But there is neither East nor West, Border, nor Breed, nor Birth, when two strong men. . . ' and he slumped asleep in a chair before he could finish, before he spoilt it or killed it with parody. We parted swearing eternal friendship.

Calcutta, second time around. It was just as bad as the first but I had done with my observations. 'India is the poorest country in the world. Therefore, to see its poverty is to make an observation of no value; a thousand newcomers to the country before you have seen and said as you.' I kept my eyes closed, easy enough in the cloistered seclusion of a small, very English, hotel we had found. It had a high wall around that kept England in and India out. It was culture-tight, forever England. It may be still, I wonder sometimes.

There was no ship, would be no ship. We would have to fly. We left the trucks; I wonder about them too. At Dum Dum Airport, Kathy all double boots and duvet against the 40lb baggage limit for the second time in our short marriage, we stepped from the hot soil of India into an airconditioned airborne fragment of the West. Easily, across that hopeless gulf, wider than anyone should be able to step; getting wider.

I reported to my C.O.

'Does that chap still fancy Sally?' he wanted to know. I assured him he did.

'Good-oh! I am hoping to take some time off in Kashmir myself.'

I reported to the Stores, empty handed. What little I had managed to keep tabs on had been abandoned in Calcutta at the end. I tried to explain.

'Sorry, can't accept that, not nearly good enough. We'll have to have an inquiry or couldn't you invent a storm or one of them bloody great avalanches.'

I invented both.

It had been a great trip, we had taken something of a hammer to crack something of a nut it was true, and we had made hard work of it even then. But we had started good friends and had ended better friends, the best of friends; we had laughed the 90 per cent of it and most of the thousands of miles we had driven; we had climbed a virgin peak, be it ever so little or simple; and hardly a cross word uttered. I have been on dozens of mountains since but this trip is still, by far, the one that was the most fun. Every expedition should have a Sam and his genius of humour. Sure-Touch Steady-Hand Sam. Sadly no-one can ever have Stu or Rory. Stu, 'boisterous as March, yet fresh as May,' was shot and killed while soldiering in the Oman the following year. Rory, the Brigade Electrical and Mechanical Engineer, the Expedition Motor Transport Officer, who could turn his hand to most things including Himalayan summits, died soon after of leukemia.

The lessons? They were postponed for another day. It wasn't that we hadn't 'the courage to submit to impressions; to be delighted, touched and exalted,' we never seemed to have the time, there was always a party or something else to do.

We knew a bit more about mountains, a bit more about mountaineering and a bit about India — though Vishnu was still no more than a name.

3

The European Alps

BIG BITS AND LITTLE BITS

Oh yesterday the cutting edge
  drank thirstily and deep...
But tomorrow
By the living God, we'll try the game again!
John Masefield

I returned to the UK from the Far East in 1972, mad keen on mountains and even keener to get back to them. Three years in Singapore was a long sentence for any mountaineer, although we really hadn't done too badly out of it: a terrific adventure in New Zealand and a greater one still in India — even if, for me, that second trip had been tainted with the bitterness, the disappointment of personal defeat. Not a bad start. A sound foundation to work on and a dozen lessons well learnt.

We, 40 Commando that is, were originally destined to sail from Singapore to England on the aircraft carrier *Albion* via the Persian Gulf (as it then was) and Capetown where we were due to spend Christmas. It was a cruise that I countenanced with ill humour; three months of stultifying boredom relieved only by a few days of highlight and, we hoped, highlife in South Africa. But the plan was changed and, steaming to the whim of the politicians of the day, pieces in a game that was grandly referred to as 'the British Withdrawal East of Aden', we cruised instead on a magical mystery tour all around the Indian Ocean.

One day we found ourselves in Mombassa. We were to be there for five days. Mt. Kenya I thought. It might just be possible. Hurried homework with an atlas, a six-inch ruler and the local bus timetable told me that it wasn't. But I ignored the sums, dug up Spot Watson, who alone of the Menthosa team was still with the unit, and prepared to make a dash for it. But we sailed early. To Gan, an atoll in the middle of the Indian Ocean and uninhabited except for an RAF staging post and surely the least mountainous place on earth. From here we flew to Britain. By the time I arrived at Brize Norton, I was desperate for a mountain.

The Alps, the European Alps, seemed to be the thing. I had read bits of Rebuffat, marvelled at his pretty pictures, scoffed at his poetry, read bits of Terray's *Conquistadors of the Useless* and quite liked it. I'd flipped through *The Hard Years* and I put a brief nose in Blackshaw's *Mountaineering*.

Hardly painstaking research, I agree, but sufficient to convince me that the European Alps was a dangerous place to be and best suited to supermen. So I went cautiously — unnecessarily so I think now — to those Alps.

What had happened to the charge of New Zealand and Menthosa I am not sure. The Menthosa wound had healed well; it wasn't that. It certainly wasn't that I was beginning to take my responsibilities as a husband more seriously. No, that was to be postponed indefinitely. What was it then? I'm still not sure, even now. Certainly, to some degree, my superficial reading of mountain literature had the effect of deterring me when it would be reasonable to suppose that it should have encouraged me. I can't explain that either. I'm sure the books were written with every intention of encouraging for that surely was their very purpose, their *raison d'être?* Nor do I imagine for a minute that Brown or Terray had any mind to deter; entertain perhaps; make a bob or two even — but deter? I doubt it. But that was their effect on me; I was deterred and went with far greater caution than was the case in New Zealand or India. It may have saved my life, but imagine what the effect on our young hearts and minds would have been if, before charging to New Zealand we had read the following which I have extracted from a glossy entitled, *The Alpine World of Mount Cook National Park* which I saw recently.

'By any standards, many of the classic routes around Mt. Cook are very long climbs. When this is linked to the fickle nature of the weather and the length and severity of storms, it may help to explain why mountaineers who learned their craft in this region have acquired not only high technical skills, but also strength, endurance and stoic patience, qualities which have repeatedly stood them in good stead in expeditions to the

88

world's great mountain ranges. Thus Edmund Hillary toughened and trained on Mt. Cook on the way to the 'conquest of Everest' in 1953.

Digging deep now, I could guess at other reasons. Being servicemen we climbed, mostly, with other servicemen, and though we climbed as keenly as any other group, we tended to remain within our own fold. We knew little of the mores, practices and developments of the civilian climbing world, which was a rumbustious thriving little world even then. It wasn't that we were cloistered — there was nothing to stop or hinder us busting out; it was simply that we never looked out — we had no gaze to follow.

That might have been some of it. Then too, there was *Mountain Magazine*, at that time the foremost mountaineering periodical. It was the source of a lot of very useful information (the first of its kind available to every mountaineer) and full of good stuff on when and how and what. I was an avid fan. That was probably a mistake. The alpine information, unimpeachable as it was, meant little to a lad whose entire mountaineering experience had been gathered some way east of the Alps and half of that some way south of the equator. The information itself, details and times taken on routes and mountains I had scarcely heard of, was of little significance — my mind hadn't started a file on Europe. The details fell on barren ground and blew away before seeding. But climbers' names from the reports, from the stories, from the profiles — they stuck; a kind of hierarchy grew into the sub-conscious. And if there are stars there must be ordinary mortals and ordinary mortals do not follow where only stars dare to tread. Maybe it was some of that that slowed the charge — not that any of it was ever the conscious intention of *Mountain* or its then editor, Ken Wilson. But I think the 'stars and commoners' syndrome, this hagiography, was rooted firmly in Wilson's sub-conscious too. He was passionate about climbing and a fund of accurate information on every aspect of it; but he didn't climb. It must have been very frustrating; like a doctor knowing *Gray's Anatomy* inside-out but not being able to find the pulse. Because he didn't climb he allowed himself heroes, small cliques of them, and their activities he faithfully reported.

None of which should be taken as blame for my caution. *Mountain* was meant as information. It should have been taken as information. It was my own weakness, my fault that I flunked my early European alpine challenges. I should have imported a chunk of that New Zealand charge but I was weak enough to allow myself to be educated out of it.

That first season I travelled by train to join some Marine mates at a part-time barracks in Val Veni, Courmayeur, that the Italian military authorities had allowed us to use. They had all been there for some while and were fit — frighteningly fit. No sooner had I arrived than I was whisked by Land Rover to the little village of Gressoney-la-Trinité on the south side of the Matterhorn from where, I was told, the Lyskamm would be traversed.

That night Doug Keelan and I lay in a field arguing about Ulster. Our Marine mates lay round about. I am an Ulsterman. Doug is very English and he hated Ulster and all things Northern Irish with a fierce and, I thought, blind hate. At least in one sense he was fair; he hated all Northern Irishmen equally whether Protestant or Roman Catholic. He did not discriminate, and this so far as I was concerned, merely compounded his wrongness. (He might also have hated all things Southern Irish but if he said so I can't remember.) Doug was very stubborn. And, being an Ulsterman, and because I was right, so was I. We argued long and loud — both determined to have the final word — so long that we argued our way to dawn, out of sleep and into breakfast. The walk to the Quintino Sella Hut is a long one. We argued that away too, though in the end I had to give Doug best; I simply couldn't walk, breathe and argue as the altitude increased.

The hut is high by Alpine standards. Doug slept with the sound content of a man who has won a big point. I spent a restless night, unable to sleep because of the altitude — it's a problem I always encounter in the first few days of every season — unable to forgive or forget, and unable to argue because Doug was soundly asleep — and though I could have woken him we were already unpopular with the rest of the team for having kept them all awake the previous night.

'Why don't you two sirs shut your gobs' had been the Sergeant Major's suggestion. I didn't dare ignore him twice.

When we left the hut at two the next morning my body-battery was run low; two nights and not a wink of sleep between them. Our plan, or rather Doug's plan, was to traverse the Lyskamm from the Italian side to Zermatt on the Swiss side. The route, though technically not much more than a plod, was a high one (14,692 feet) for the first of the season and Zermatt was a long way off. Doug and the others (Guy Sheridan was in there) already acclimatized in the Mt. Blanc range, went at it like greyhounds. I fell to the back, unable to keep up. Doug noticed and rubbed salt into my Ulster wound by pausing every now and again to ask, as though to everyone in general

'Everyone OK? Not going too fast am I?'

For the others, the question was superfluous, they were lean and hardy, could have gone for days. For me the question was taunting torment. I had recently escaped a desk across which I'd been pushing a pen for months. I was not so fit as the others but I was determined to die before I called for quarter from Doug. There were times that morning when the pride of all Ulster, orange and green, hung in the balance and I was sorely tempted to ask the minute that would have been unforgiven, unforgotten. The summit came in time, just in time; the plod seemed interminable. By the time I arrived Doug had been resting fully five minutes. I was almost pleased to see him.

From the summit a fine dawn could be seen awakening all the Alps. I was reminded of that seminal New Zealand dawn on Mt. Cook, as a hundred dawns have reminded me since. There can be few things as pleasing as an alpine dawn. It melts away the reluctance of a body slow from cold, stiff from a cramped bivouac. It brushes away cobwebs from sleepy hut-eyes. It hushes the belly's breakfast whine and it reminds you, and some of us need to be reminded after the necessary purgatory of those pre-dawn alpine starts, why we climb and how we love these mountains.

There followed a pleasant scramble along the summit ridge and a long descent on the Swiss (north) side down the Grenz glacier, an interesting outing in itself, to the Monte Rosa hut. From there a rather dull walk led to Zermatt. For the first route of my first European alpine season things hadn't gone too badly. A wink or two more sleep would have been handy and something a couple of thousand of feet lower would have been kinder on the lungs but, all in all, I couldn't complain. Compared to our first flounderings in New Zealand, this had been a masterpiece of planning and execution. Not all my alpine seasons were to begin as smoothly — come to think of it, this was the only one that did.

In Zermatt, where we spent the night, I met a lad bursting with enthusiasm, who was looking for a partner for the North Face of the Matterhorn. This was a route still shrouded in the gloom of a fierce and dangerous reputation (which like most reputations was largely undeserved) but so effusive in his keenness was the lad (and I have genuinely forgotten his name) that I allowed myself to be cajoled into it. We went up to the Hornli Hut that night and set out for the foot of the North Face at 2 am the next morning. My third alpine start — I was really getting the hang of them — though I was never to get to like them. The route begins on a hanging glacier shelf which is reached by a snow slope of about 50°. It was here that I realised that I had something left to learn. My partner scampered up this slope planting his axes with confident swings and pulling hugely on them. When I tried this with mine they came straight back out again. It was not until the following winter that I learnt about curved axe picks. At that stage mine still stuck, nearly useless, at right angles from the shaft. Nor were my crampons much better. They were an old grivel model and although they sported frontpoints these were fashioned in such a way as to allow one front-point to move independently of the other on the same crampon. They inspired little confidence and I doubt that they would have worked much wonder on the best ice-climbing feet in the business.

Fortunately a tragedy overtook us; saved me from the face that day and from exposing my inexperience and poor equipment — if both hadn't already been spotted. Two climbers, Spaniards, slipped roped together, from a point not far above us, and fell a fair way past us, one alternately plucking the other. By the time we got to them they were conscious but in poor shape. We made them as comfortable as we could before returning to the Hornli Hut to alert the Rescue Services. My partner returned to Zermatt. I suspect that he had decided that I wasn't fit company, a fair estimate, and I have never heard from or of him since. I walked over to Cervinia, where I was to join my mates, following along the foot of the East Face, marvelling at the mountains all about and relishing being alone amongst them. I forgot about the North Face of the Matterhorn for that year but the seed was sown.

We moved back to our barracks in Val Veni and in the week of leave that I had left I had a great time with Guy Sheridan, Doug Keelan and an old mate, Bob Hudson on the North Face of the

Tour Ronde which must be the friendliest and shortest North Face in all the Alps — my first taste of alpine ice and pleasant tasting stuff I thought it was. There followed, the next day, a romp up the Brenva Spur of Mt. Blanc. From the summit we descended back into Italy via the Dôme glacier and thence to Val Veni. Strolling happily through the pine forest towards the barracks — an unlikely base for an alpine season I admit — I reflected on the last ten days. They had been pleasant, without being spectacular — the accident on the Matterhorn I somehow discounted. There had not been the elemental fire of New Zealand, or half the energy either, but it had been a very useful introduction to some of the best mountains of France, Italy and Switzerland — a topping-up of the well of experience, a period of consolidation. I was content rather than happy. There were alpine fires within me that had been fanned by that view from the summit of the Lyskamm and by the majestic mountain scenery of the Vallée Blanche and the Brenva. I would be back next year.

But there was to be a piece of history between me and my next alpine season. We walked into camp feeling pleasantly tired and rather pleased to have been to the top of Mt. Blanc by any route, to find Jim Goldsworthy and two formidable looking Italian policemen bent in earnest conversation, awaiting our return — at least Guy's return since he was technically in charge. I say technically because Guy, a Captain, was not the most senior person in our number; that was Jim, a Major. Jim, crippled by new boots on the Lyskamm, had decided that his blisters were too painful to take him up Mt. Blanc and had remained in the valley while we climbed. And for reasons I have never quite understood but accept, reasons that the Italian authorities could neither understand nor accept, Jim was not in charge of our party: Guy was.

The two police, who spoke no English, and who had sensibly assumed that we could speak no Italian, had brought with them an interpreter. She was a girl of stunning beauty such that it was difficult to voice three coherent words for her to translate — a grunt meaning much the same in any language. She had a fair command of English and, I would guess, a total command of men of any language. A silly story unfolded. Apparently a couple of the lads who had stayed in barracks had gone out on the town and run amok. One of them had relieved a discotheque (the result of a bet we discovered later) of an ornamental engine about the size of a sewing machine (it was the artefact's bulk and evident weight that formed the substance of the bet for when it was not serving as decoration the thing was useless and valueless). Not unnaturally, the owner wished for its return. All this was revealed with much gesticulation and a spell-binding translation or two. A disappointing feature of the Italian language was that a twenty-minute monologue from one of the policemen could be refined in translation to one very short, albeit delicious, sentence from the interpreter. This was a pity, we could have listened to her dulcet translations all night long.

Guy was anxious to avoid a diplomatic hiccup — obtaining permission to climb as a military group had taken a deal of negotiation — and he was keen to smooth over the problem. He would sort it all out personally, he assured the police. There followed one more delicious translation, and with a *'Si, si, arrivederci'*, they were gone in a squeal of tortured tyres and a cloud of dust.

Guy quickly traced the culprits, who were in any case already feeling very foolish about the prank (the sort that lose their funniness when viewed with hungover hindsight), and told them to find it, take it back and apologise. This they did with some graciousness. Indeed the apology seemed to have gone down so well that Jim, Guy, the two culprits and Sticks Booth, the driver, decided to have a beer at the place on the strength of it. (Sticks? Booth had joined the Marines as a drummer, transferring later to general soldiering duties: all drummers are nicknamed 'sticks' for life.)

What happened next, happened quickly and the details, like the action are blurred. Booth excused himself, didn't return. The time came to go. Jim sent me to find him. I found him in the courtyard outside being badly beaten by half-a-dozen large, dark-suited fellows. I rushed back to tell Jim who rushed out to help Booth. He was quickly subdued by more large dark-suited fellows and badly beaten too. We all piled in; and were badly beaten by yet more large dark-suited fellows, who it turned out were carabinieri — the police. You will have to form your own conclusion as to why they were there, why they were not in uniform and why there was an armoured van at hand to cart us off to the police station. All I know is that we lost — badly.

I have one happy memory that I will cherish long after all Europe is united. Sticks, in his youth (which was sometime before this incident), had been a boxer of note, famed throughout the

Marines for his fleet feet and fast hands. He had been fast even for a welter-weight and not all had been lost in his easy years as a driver. True he was heavier, a bit slower, but the residual speed he had retained as well as the footwork and the timing. And when the rest of us piled in to the affray the balance of power had been upset long enough for Sticks to free himself and rise to those fleet feet. Then he got the rhythm, gave them a lesson in footwork and feint, danced them a merry and defiant dance; Sugar Ray round chairs and parasoled tables, Astaire up steps and Flynn down again; flicking out stinging lefts that had them in a civil war of evading collision. It lasted perhaps only thirty seconds before his legs and luck ran out, but it was a magnificent act of noble futility and I will not easily forget it; it was his best fight 'E'en the ranks of Tuscany could scarce forbear to cheer'.

The night in cells was uncomfortable. The next morning a helicopter landed outside. The British Military Attaché had flown up from Rome. We were brought before him. He was caparisoned in a uniform the like of which I had never seen before — the sort of thing one associated with Generalissimos of Central American Republics; it struck me that he might have designed it himself.

> 'Came there a certain lord, neat trimly dress'd.
> Fresh as a bridegroom; and his chin new reap'd
> Show'd like a stubble land at harvest home:-
> He was perfumed like a milliner;
> And twixt his finger and his thumb he held
> A pouncet-box, which ever and anon
> He gave his nose, and took't away again:-'

Clearly he was an important chap; and more clearly, we were in deep disgrace, big trouble.

A Court of Inquiry followed our return to Britain. We were sworn-in and Booth, still on crutches as the result of his, as he put it, 'narrow points defeat', was first to give evidence.

'Now Booth,' said the presiding Colonel, 'the Italian police claim that no fewer than four of their number received hospital treatment as a result of this most unfortunate incident. Did you see any that were hurt?' All this had to be written down which took time, giving Booth time to compose his reply. Nod from the President and he began,

'Well Sir, there was this one bloke on his knees. Mind you,

they're a religious lot and knowing the Italians, he could have been praying.'

The reply was adjusted on the President's instructions.

Round 2: 'Now Booth, did you at any time strike or use any form of physical violence against the police?'

Booth was quick from his corner and head down into the reply, 'Bloody right, sir, I knockéd ten bells out of as many as I could lay a punch on, London rules, know what I mean?'

The President adjusted that too, 'Put down, Booth used minimum force to defend himself.' He was doing his bit that Colonel.

The result was a very senior dressing down for us all and a lifetime's supply, for the episode is infinitely variable, of after-dinner stories.

The Italian authorities had the last word, however. Years later I received an official-looking letter in Italian which I took to the local chippie for translation. It was a summons to trial for the incident — six years late. I didn't attend the trial and some months later the following letter arrived.

Department of the
Commandant General,
Royal Marines,
Ministry of Defence,
Old Admiralty Building,
Whitehall, London, S.W.1.

Captain J Barry RM (Ret)
National Centre For
Mountain Activities
Plas y Brenin
Snowdonia.   7th September 1978

Dear John,
Incident at Aosta — 17 August 1972
Your trial in relation to the above incident was held on 8 February 1978 at Aosta. At the trial you were awarded a conditional suspended sentence of seven (7) months imprisonment with a non-registration of the sentence.

Costs relating to the trial have been borne by the Ministry of Defence.

The incident is now closed.

Yours sincerely,
Malcolm

The chip shop proprietor, in common with most of his race, despised the Carabinieri; they, along with football referees who awarded penalties to the opposition, occupied a lowly position in Italy's social structure — Italy's untouchables. His chips were free for years to come.

The next alpine season saw Nicholls and I reunited. The lean intent young man was, if anything, brighter eyed and bushier tailed than ever, looked as if he hadn't suffered a decent hangover since we'd last climbed together four years before. Four years! Dave had spent most of the time between soldiering in the Oman where the Sultan, with British help, was fighting a counter-insurgency war against Chinese/Russian trained and supplied infiltrators from the Yemen. He had gone at the Jebel and the enemy, as he'd gone at Mt. Cook and though these new games and rules are very different Nicholls treated them the same, earning a deserved reputation as a fearless fighter. A grateful Sultan showered him with gallantry medals so that the last time I saw him, all got up in his military finery at his wedding, there was scarcely room on his slim frame for all those ribbons — especially since the Falklands had crammed on another one or two. (He was to write to me from the Task Force, on its way South to say 'There's six thousand of them and two thousand of us. Could be a ding-dong scrap'. See what I mean about Nicholls!)

He was all that he had been in New Zealand, if a little more serious, but still the walking, talking epitome of the British upper-middle warrior class: selfless, courteous, brave, true, ruthless when the odd occasion demanded — and badly read.

'Two things greater than all things are,
The first is love, and the second War.'

He'd had his war but his love, those days, was mountains and he was raring to go after a four-year abstinence. Together we returned to our joint apprenticeship. It was a strange thing, though we were very different we made a good team, sparking well on the mountains and rarely seriously disagreeing about them. Whatever weakness we had as individuals, and I had more than my fair share, the other was able to make up in good measure. We played New Zealand rules, tempered by some experience, but still keen to get amongst it. There were years to catch up, hills to climb, adventures to savage; the sky was no limit.

We stretched our apprenticeship over two seasons' climbing where fancy or the chance road took us. Mt. Blanc de Cheilon, North Face, 'a doddle', says Nicholls. Was too. Grand Capucin, East Face, a terrible electrified escape off the summit and a good fight back to the valley in a storm. 'Impressive,' says Nicholls. Was too. The North-East Face of the Piz Badile with Bob Hudson; three mates romping in the sun, spaghetti in Viscosoprano that same night and where shall we go tomorrow? 'Fun,' Nicholls says. Was too. Lost on the Dent du Crocodile, sick on the Dru's Bonatti Pillar, sweetest success so far on the North Face of the Dent Blanche. 'Wazzer' that, Nicholls says — was too.

So it went. Adventure here, misadventure there, triumph, disaster, good do, cock-up; they all tumbled one on the other in heady profusion and we treated them all the same. We enjoyed the whole alpine game so much that a summit gained was only a few laughs better than one lost — neither one the subject of retrospective consideration for more than a beer — by the second drink our guns were trained forward again.

Somewhere, in a rare moment of introspection, I got to wondering why it was that I had treated the European Alps with such caution after so cavalier a campaign in the New Zealand Alps which are, I now know, far more serious; where there was little hope of rescue, no *téléphériques,* worse weather, where the distances were longer, climbers fewer, where guide books didn't exist. That was it! Guide books; their absence. Literature; none of that either. Not much anyway. That was the difference. I suspected it earlier. Now I was sure of it. There was no guide book to the Southern Alps and very little literature about those mountains or very little that we had been able to find. We went there openminded, *nothing* preconceived, fearless, literally fearless, we knew nothing to base fear on — the fearlessness of glorious ignorance. A friend of mine used to claim in a half serious way that if you knew your mountain and where the route lay it was better not to read about it in the guide book or anywhere else. He's right. The knowledge conferred by reading about mountains is second-hand experience. Unbalanced and unconditioned by actual experience it lies, unrefined but fermenting in the mind's 'labyrinthine ways', with no weight of personal experience to hinder it. Fear begets fear with compound interest and so reputations of mountains and men are built. This is the effect of careless guide books, careless literature. This is what *Mountain* did in its early days when the people responsible didn't understand that the game of mountaineering was more than an index, however accurate, however useful in correct application, however painstakingly collected, however professionally presented.

Fear from personal experience is very different. The thing happens, the fear strikes, sudden, sharp; quicker than a paragraph; than the shortest sentence. The senses register their response, the mind records, sometimes the body too. You are frightened — it keeps you alive but straightaway the reason starts its damage limitation and, not long after, its healthy purge. This keeps you sane. In time the reason filters, refines that fear, argues with it, reasons much of it away leaving a fine clear residue called experience; something invaluable from something valueless. Information gotten from books and magazines seldom benefits from the mind's automatic response to live fear. No reason assails the opinion or the response received from those pages. Damage is done. Sometimes it is irreversible. In my case it was only temporary but I should have trusted the philistine when he had served so well. The cure came when I stopped reading and started climbing. That is why I was incautious in New Zealand, cautious in Europe. Fear is insidious and mountaineering is first a psychological game, poor second a physical one. Man is an animal version of the same thing. It took two years for my own experience to tip the scales back in favour of the charge — but it was fun and no waste.

Nicholls was luckier; a happy warrior, happy philistine, he had never read anything and so still possessed a raw mountain mind, a free spirit and unnotioned hope.

Two summers later we were ready for anything, according to Nicholls. He fancied the North Face of the Matterhorn. I wasn't so sure, this was one reputation personal experience had done little to dent and since the season's first routes, or rather half-routes, had all been a shambles, they had done nothing to instill confidence.

On the way back to the camp from our latest shambles we

stopped to quench a not especially well-deserved thirst, drown a mighty sorrow, reappraise the whole alpine scene and generally hang one on. Two beers and a muddled mull of an inquest later, someone produced a glossy tome entitled *The 100 Finest Routes in the Mont Blanc Massif,* slippery with lyrical prose proclaiming the virtues of the author's 100 finest; each more beautiful, more compelling, steeper, harder and demanding more *mousquetons* than the last. On every page cloudless azure skies competed with crisp névé while elegant alpinists posed seemingly just above the surface, immaculately attired, neatly accoutred, bronzed and smiling and oh so obviously unfatigued.

Certainly it was pretty. But somehow it didn't correspond to my latest, most painful alpine experiences — which comprised a snowplod, three failed routes and about fourteen forays into the 'Bar Nash'; every foray getting us higher than anything we'd managed on the hill — though they were scarcely less arduous. Nor did the author's smug description of the interminably boring snowplod we had just failed to plod as a 'serene and beautiful route' seem entirely accurate. Still less could I explain by what feat of mountaineering incompetence had we turned one of his smiling, sunlit four-hour sprints into an eighteen-hour bivouaced marathon of misery, ineptitude and exhaustion. To me, alpinism was something very different. (Though if I was being honest with myself, which I wasn't quite, I knew the feeling was only temporary.) My immediate memories, painfully etched in cruel chronological detail, were of a blistering and well-over-the-guide-book time hut walk; of luke warm brews, forgotten food, burnt fingers, handleless pots and anglophobe hut wardens; of pre-dawn stampedes, wet snow, breakable crust, loomless lamps and Zambesi *bergshrunds;* of supercharged long-life sardine-fuelled belches, bust crampon straps, fumbled gear and slings all too big or too small; of woolly breeches too cold at dawn, too hot in the sun and too ticklishly heavy in the wet; of cold feet, sweat, chapped lips, chaffed crutch and charred lips; of queues and queue jumpers, aching calves, bursting lungs, summits fleetingly glimpsed, painfully gained and soon departed; of viewless victory and plod, plod, plodding — and all at rip-off prices.

This to me was Alpinism — I'm sure you'll recognise it. But here was this French smoothie all got up in clinging reds and blues proclaiming it otherwise — and with hundreds of handsome pictures to prove it.

But by the fourth beer on a stomach no fuller of anything else the disappointment had evaporated, the pain all but gone. By the fifth I was anybody's and beer-bold I was ready for any route Nicholls cared to mention. Stewed in those not uncommon ingredients, sun, alcohol, hardwork, and failure I surrendered to a wonderful state of soporific euphoria. In one more beer I would achieve indestructability. I always did.

And that's how Nicholls got me back on the Matterhorn. The booze and the unblinking gaze of those honest blue eyes, earnest exhortation, sweet reason, flattering sincerity and beers. I was seduced — my better judgment less than equal to the alcohol, my reluctance no match for a vaulting ambition that had yet to trip the crampon straps of reality.

So it was that we found ourselves the very next day, propelled by, for me at any rate, a fast evaporating wave of enthusiasm, in Zermatt — Nicholls still intent on the North Face in defiance of my swiftly recovering judgment and two ferocious hangovers. The weather was superb but my morale began to rain.

The campsite sported every nationality this side of Nagasaki — with more than a few from Nagasaki itself — and every colour and creed too, from zen buddhists through holy rollers and seventh-day adventists to this still-green heathen. Nicholls who had long affected multilinguistic pretentions, approached the proprietor with a purposeful air and engaged her in monosyllabic, sub 'O' level French. Unabashed when his opening burst fell on stony ground, he reverted to the time honoured English habit and of bolstering linguistic inadequacy by adding decibels. Lots of them. The result was three very damp square feet on which to pitch our tent. A poor start.

Rescuing the remains of a dehydrated food pack, I sat disconsolately gnawing my way through a partially reconstituted 'chicken supreme'. 'What a bloody shambles,' I thought aloud, contemplating the cosmopolitan community about me. Too loud. For I was quickly reproached by an American who bore a striking resemblance to Mahatma Ghandi. He harangued me with evangelical eloquence on the virtues of internationalism, ending the lesson with 'Peace brother'. 'Balls brother,' I thought, though not aloud this time.

101

The rasp of file on metal announced that Nicholls, oblivious to this microcosm of humanity about us and all else but the Nordwand, was honing his front-points to a fine tune. He threw me the file. My crampons were blunt beyond rescue from the years of misuse; and worse still only one was mine, there being two right feet. Now with the same undivided attention Nicholls addressed his ice-axes. Models of pristine perfection, they gleamingly proclaimed any attention to be superfluous. I removed some rust from my own axes, mainly for form's sake.

The next day dawned blue and cloudless.

Nicholls fully booted and rucksack neatly packed, was pawing the ground like a thoroughbred, impatient for the off. A solitary cloud drifted high confirming the settled state of the weather and deepening my gloom. I half-heartedly suggested that, to experienced hillmen, that particular cloud formation pressaged a storm — if not Armageddon itself. Ignoring my learned forecast he hoisted a gargantuan sack on to his slim shoulders and set off in purposeful three-league gait, through a tourist throng towards the cable car that was to whisk us half way to the Hornli Hut.

Apparently irrevocably committed, I belatedly packed an untidy rucksack, bounced it on to a much broader back and plodded in pursuit. Moving through the narrow streets I took refuge in Walter Mitty fantasies and even pondered whether, if asked by some inquisitive tourist to which route I aspire, a reply of 'Nordwand', 'Face Nord' or simply 'North Face', would extract the greatest awe. But no one asked.

The guide book advises that two or three hours should be allowed for the climb from the cable-car station to the hut but Nicholls, as if intent on an Olympic qualifying time, set off at a suicidal pace. I struggled for half a mile before the face saving 'ventiliation'. 'I'll catch you up,' I said without conviction and collapsed breathing heavily.

As I lay there a gaggle of nubile teenagers replete in pert lederhosen, passed in the wake of a guide and mentor. Spotting a sensible mountain pace — even from the horizontal — I fell in. Fortunately, just as my lungs were about to mutiny again, the *bergführer* announced a five-minute breather alongside one of those touristy sign-posts that point the miles to everywhere. The girls, needing no rest swarmed excitedly over this edifice identifying a number of smaller peaks. I wished myself on any one of them. The five minutes passed in seconds and on and upwards continued this happy band exuding health and vigour. I stumbled behind exuding something more odiferous, until at last, we reached the hut.

Nicholls was nowhere to be seen. Entering, my eyes adjusted more rapidly to the evening gloom than my lungs to the altitude or muscles to the exertion, and I spied him cosily ensconced in a far corner, flanked by two well-proportioned blondes. They regarded him with obvious admiration. He thoughtfully omitted to say that he'd been there half an hour, while the blondes eyed me with interest — no, disbelief. 'Is this the one?' asked Brunhilde. Nicholls looked just a wee bit pleased with himself. Machismo undermined, I grinned a feeble grin that would have unearthed the maternal instinct in Rosa Clebb and was nursed for the remainder of the evening on spoonfed stew and elbow-tested tea.

We were to be off at one — am that is; I prayed for a storm. It was too high for me to sleep. I dozed fitfully while Nicholls snored contentedly through the appointed hour. I let it slip by and dared to hope of redemption as two o'clock crept up. Only another hour and we'd be too late. He woke up and in one smooth movement was into his breeches, boots and gaiters. 'Hell we're too late,' I said with conviction. He answered with a brew of his speciality — cold, burnt porridge. No easy thing that — but he managed it every time. Then he was out into the night and toward the hill in that same purposeful three-league gait that I had plodded after 5000 feet below.

Crossing the scree behind the hut it was obvious that the weather was perfect, very cold, clear and starlit. Reaching the glacier we stopped to fit crampons. A barrage of expletives and the evidence illuminated by my partner's headtorch offered this drowning man a serpent. 'I've broken a strap,' he wailed. I commiserated gleefully, 'nothing to do but retreat, fully justified in the circumstances — a brave attempt after all.' However, he read it — it was better than an obituary. But I had seriously underestimated my man who, cast as he was in the heroic mould, quickly tied a couple of grannies on the broken strap and set off at redoubled speed. I made myself the promise of a new partner, as had Nicholls, I later discovered.

I was resigned. We roped up and moved across the glacier,

negotiated the odd darkly yawning crevasse by fast fading torch-light and after an easy preliminary slope (where the Spaniards had fallen three years before) arrived, in an hour, at the foot of the North Face. Final preparations complete and gear carefully slung about our bodies we set off up the first ice slope, a thousand feet long and the dominant feature of the first third of the face.

Climbing by torchlight was tolerable. A dim pool of light illuminated the only bit of the world that mattered, while darkness camouflaged the exposure. One hundred and forty feet on front points, calves fit to burst, a cry of '10 feet' from below, chop a step big enough for one and a half feet and a smaller one for Nicholls when he arrives, in with an ice screw and tie on. Up comes partner, change belays and off again. Four rope lengths each and swap the lead.

It was exciting. I was almost beginning to enjoy myself when a couple of stones whistled past. I was reminded of one reason for my earlier lack of enthusiasm; stonefall, cripplers from penny size up, as Nicholls said, stiff upperlipped, 'bad news'. 'You OK?' — 'Yup.' On we go.

By first light we were at the top of the ice slope and lost. The route which had looked straightforward from below was now lost to us in the acreage of the face. We consulted the guide book and agreed to wait until it was fully light to see if we could espy the way.

Daylight came but not the route. The guide book said blandly 'from the top of the ice-slope follow a shallow but obvious couloir trending right'. I could see a couloir way to the right and volunteered, a sure sign of desperation, to lead across. The rock was loose and such holds as existed were covered in snow. I took my gloves off to get a better grip and got cold hands. I put them back on and nearly fell off. After a hundred feet my nerve ran out before the traverse and I announced that I was returning. For some reason this proved even harder — it was difficult to ignore the thousand feet of space between my feet and the glacier.

Regaining Nicholls and temporary relief it dawned on us that the crisis was only just unfolding — we were still lost and were wasting precious time — incredibly that traverse had cost us an hour. Two thousand feet to go.

Nicholls, as yet unmoved, cast his blue eyes about and decided that a thin ribbon of near vertical ice directly above was the elusive couloir. My protest that it should have been to the right and that anyway couloirs weren't vertical were of no avail. 'You found it — you can lead it.' He did too and what a lead. For an hour he battled upward encountering rotten ice, snow and rock while I could but admire and offer a few limp words of encouragement. And while he battled away I worried; that alpine nag was at me; what about the belay, how was the time, the weather, the toes... At length, a small but victorious voice yelled, 'come on up' and making best use of the rope, stomach, knees and arse, I joined Nicholls on a tiny ledge. It was as hard an ice pitch as I ever want to be dragged up. Clearly this was not the right way. Where now?

Above, steep rock led to the Hornli Ridge, the *voie normale*, and safety — some 600 feet away. His eyes said, your lead, and after his magnificent effort I could hardly demur. 'Besides,' he said, ever the gent, 'it's your turn.' What a time for protocol!

I led, picking the easiest line, to the bottom of a steep 50-foot crack which invited my inspection; repelled my first assault. It was the only way — try again. After 30 feet I was exhausted and tried to rest on fist-jamms but this, at 13,000 feet, made monstrous demands on fast diminishing reserves. I looked below. Not a pretty sight. 'Watch the rope,' I whimpered (the accepted euphemism for, 'this looks hard and I might fall'), but fighting, grunting, snarling and swearing I made it. (Obviously.) Nicholls arrived but made no comment. He must have been impressed.

Several hundred easier feet later I half pulled onto the Hornli Ridge — half because I hadn't the strength to do it in one, and half because who should be picnicing not a few feet before me but Nicholls' two blonde admirers. There being no retreat, I completed an undignified stomach roll and lay in a dishevelled bundle, all sense of relief drowned by this new humiliation. He vaulted easily from the vertical onto the horizontal and stood, sartorially immaculate before my two sirens. 'Hi girls,' he said without a trace of strain, 'made a slight route-finding error.'

I have little recollection of the descent, though I do remember missing the last cable car and the blisters of an extra 3000 feet of toe-stubbing trudge.

With every cobble assuming Himalayan proportions, and tired as we were, we took cover in a bar rather than face the camp site.

Nicholls bought the first round — a rare event — and the second, third and fourth — a unique event. Well, you know how it is — we'd been on the go eighteen hours or so with nothing but spoonfuls of cold porridge in the belly and — would you believe it — I was seduced again!

We went back up to the Hornli Hut the very next day and fairly romped up the route — all the way to the top this time — the day after in about six hours, which in those days was a respectable time. Mind you, so it should have been; for me that was third time round. (And if you said that that description's a bit super-sixth-form sesquipedalian, I'd agree. I wrote it soon after the climb; it betrays the fact that I was beginning to take myself and mountaineering too seriously.)

The following summer saw us out in the Alps again, this time based at Lauterbrunnen, a little tourist village of hotels and campsites in the Bernese Oberland. My partner had raised his sights one notch. I'd taken to calling him Young Lochinvar such a gallant was he,
   'So faithful in love, and so dauntless in war,
   There never was knight like young Lochinvar.'
Beside him I felt,
'A laggard in love, and a dastard in war.'
Anyway it amused me to pull his leg and we both enjoyed playing the roles. Nicholls, when his blandishments brought him success with fair ladies, especially so. But that wasn't nearly so often as he felt a young Lochinvar deserved — or needed.

He had acquired a smart pair of binoculars which he toted like a new toy. I had mocked them rather unkindly saying that I couldn't see the least use of them in the Alps. One morning I awoke to find him at the tent door — he was always first up — training them on the Lauterbrunnen Wall — a sweep of north faces, Gletscherhorn, Ebnefluh, Grosshorn, Breithorn — that overlook the village.

'Hey, I've spotted a new line on the Gletscherhorn — to the left of the Welzenbach and the Direct — bloody useful these binos.' He made his point and we did the route, a fairly respectable effort of 2000 feet of steepish snow and ice which I reckoned had earned me a rest.

So there I was planning a touch of personal administration, a few pints or two when up bounces Nicholls bursting with all his usual vigour which past painful experience would normally have led me to regard with deep suspicion. But here we were, a rest day and a new route under our belts. Surely even he would be happy with that!

It was eleven o'clock and I was contemplating breakfast:

'Just got the weather forecast from the heliport,' he chirped.

'One or two eggs?' I replied.

'Reckon we should crack straight up today,' he enthused, 'Plan B.' Plan B! The full horror of its implications scrambled my two eggs and any vestige of coherent thought:

'Plan B,' I whimpered in anguish, 'that's the bloody Eiger.'

''S right,' cut in Nicholls and with the convoluted logic of a man who doesn't recognise a rest day when he sees one, he proceeded to turn night into day, black into white and a dream into reality. He proved beyond doubt, at least to his own satisfaction, that the time to spring Plan B was upon us.

I knew better than to argue and started to pack. Carefully we laid our gear out over an acre of ground. We'd talked of this day for years and our kit was carefully prepared. I had cut the route description from a book to save weight and covered it in polythene to keep it dry. A large photograph we had taken from Heinrich Harrer's *White Spider* to show the route more clearly, was similarly protected. He was to take the stove and the fuel, I, a cooking pot and a bivouac bag. The rest we shared equally — or so he still thinks. Packing the sacks very carefully we tested for weight and, deciding they were too heavy, unpacked and thought again. Out went half a day's grub and a spoon, a few ounces saved, and the process repeated until we were convinced we could go no lighter. The sacks still weighed too much by far, but they included the ropes, which would seem lighter when worn, and clothes that would eventually end up about us — still weighing the same but feeling less.

The train ride to Kleine Scheidegg was a curious affair. Hundreds of passengers crowded onto this little toyland train, and none of them Swiss. About fifty per cent American, fifty per cent Japanese, each armed with a camera more expensive than anything you ever imagined. An immaculate conductor waved us imperiously, and with badly concealed disgust, to a far corner which we were to share with a dog who had apparently disgraced himself. There we crouched on our sacks, the object of a great deal of almond-eyed curiosity, assailed by a dozen daft transatlantic questions and captured on a thousand centimetres of celluloid.

Nicholls was disrespectful enough to suggest that it was my legs that excited this curiosity; I countered that it was probably the way he had to cross his rucksack straps so that the load just teetered on non-existent shoulders. For sure, it was ironic that in this land of mountains we were rendered oddities by virtue of our mountaineering attire.

The short ride to the Eigergletscher station was quieter, most of the tourists regarding the Scheidegg as the edge of the known world and anything beyond, even though it was rail-roaded, café'd and pastured, as Columbus-only terrain. Our repartee slunk into silence and, for me at any rate, contemplation. Nothing I had read about this face had lessened my respect for the seriousness of the undertaking, nor my admiration for those who had climbed it well. Toni Kurz intruded, and hard as I tried to dismiss him with rationalisations about the superiority of our equipment and clothing, and the fact that the route was now well-known, it was difficult to dispel belly trepidation with cold logic. From any perspective it remained 6000 steep feet from bottom.

You'll remember Toni Kurz and his three mates and how, in an early attempt on the face back in 1936, they had died of exhaustion in their retreat from the Second Ice Field. And how, after his three mates had perished, Toni Kurz fought for his life days and nights until, literally within a hand's grasp of his rescuers, he too had no more to give and died. I think I was nervous. I *was* nervous. But as the train stopped, so did the reveries and though the fears yet lurked, action lent them boldness.

A short level walk around the buttress below the West Face brought us in half an hour below the North Face — this the longest best-documented, worst-represented, wrongly-feared face in the Alps — perhaps in the whole mountaineering world.

It's an extraordinary setting. No long hut walk the day before, no glacier approach, indeed no glacier; the Kleine Scheidegg, 'Tokyo' and 'New York' visible the while, and there rising straight out of cowbell-clanging pastures, this huge ugly face; a piece of gigantic stage scenery. Not a pretty sight; no classic sweep of sculptured rock or pleasing rock architecture, while even the ice was pockmarked by stonefall and looked second-hand.

ove: Mt Cook from the east. The route taken follows the couloir above the skier's right shoulder
then the ridge to the summit. *(Photo: Nigel Shepherd.)*

w: Menthosa taken from Base Camp. The route follows the right-hand shoulder from the saddle
Urgus pass). The summit is the right-hand peak.

Above: Aiguille de Leschaux. Dave Nicholls on steep ice near the top of our new route.
Below: The North Face of the Eiger. Dave Nicholls above the 'Difficult Crack' at the foot of the 'Rote Fluh'.

Above: Aiguille de Leschaux. Nicholls on steep ground.

Below: The Eiger. Nicholls approaching the 'Hinterstoisser Traverse'.

Above: The North Face of the Matterhorn seen here in shadow on the right-hand side of the picture.

Below: The Eiger. Swallows Nest where Nicholls organises the bivouac.

Below: The Eiger. Nicholls approaching the 'Spider' at the end of 'The Traverse of The Gods'.

Above left: Red Wall at Gogarth, North Wales — note the lighthouse in the background. *(Photo: Nigel Shepherd.)*

Above right: The author and others on 'Dream of White Horses' a popular climb (HVS) at Gogarth. *(Photo: Nigel Shepherd.)*

Right: The author on sunny rock.

Below left and right: Father and son 'Forty Years Late' in Normandy.

ove: The author on steep ice at Cwm Dulyn, orth Wales. *(Photo: Malcolm Campbell.)*

Above: Devil's Appendix, Cwm Idwal, North Wales. Davey Jones climbing just above the crux on the first pitch.

low: The author on vertical ice on Central Gully, at Meall Garbh.

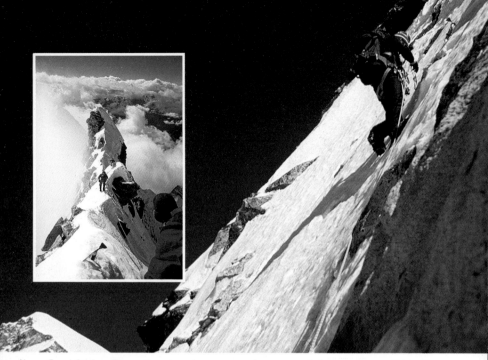

Above: Gauri Sankar. The author at work on steep and unprotected slopes leading to Camp II (Neuschwanstein). South Summit visible to climber's left — still more than a mile away! *(Photo: Guy Neithardt.) Inset:* Gauri Sankar. The author returning to Camp III (Fawlty Towers) after the accident — belayed by Guy Neithardt and watched by Pemba Lama. *(Photo: Pete Boardman.)*

Below: Gauri Sankar. Camp I (Nid d'Aigle). *Inset:* Gauri Sankar: The author one week after regaining Base Camp but still showing the strain. *(Photo: Pete Boardman.)*

Opposite page: Gauri Sankar: Returning to Camp II after a day's work.

Above: Deborah. The third bivouac. The sun 'like a Bishop's bottom' morning. The ridge beneath the tent — 3000 ft below — is where we spent six days in a snowhole. *Inset:* Deborah. Roger Mear on the crucial traverse on Day 2.

Below: Deborah. Rob Collister begins the descent of the South-West Ridge (the Beckey/Harrer route). *Inset:* Deborah: The aircraft at Base Camp. We skied to beneath the col at the head of the glacier, approached the col on the right before descending to 'Col Camp'.

Looking up into the Stygian gloom I shuddered, for the top half of the face was shrouded in cloud, descending cloud at that. 'What happened to your perfect weather, mate?' 'Oh it'll clear up, just a drop of afternoon cloud.' It started to rain.

We found what seemed to be the start, decided the rope was unnecessary at this stage, and began. The first pitch up some steepish cracks was a struggle, with the sacks. Half-way up I regretted the decision not to rope up, but a couple of grunts and a snarl or two led to easier ground. The easy ground led uncertainly upwards though the cloud, which happily cleared from time to time just long enough for us to recognise the odd landmark.

The guide book description mentioned two pitches where difficulties might be encountered, but we were unable to find them and soloed on up until we recognised a steep traverse that led rightwards to the 'wet cave' and the 'difficult crack'. Here melted water Niagara'd down the face, so after roping up we donned our waterproofs in the vain hope that we might escape a soaking. We both waited for the other to take the lead.

Rather unchivalrously, I thought, Nicholls reminded me of recent routes I claimed to have done. 'Much like this I imagine,' he said with mock innocence. What could I say? I led off rather quicker than was entirely safe to try to escape the deluge, but not so quick as that water, which poured into my carelessly open neck and sleeve. In no time I was soaked. Belaying in the comparative shelter of the 'wet cave', I took in the rope as Nicholls sprinted across — faster with the security of the rope, and drier with his sleeves and neck secured — a wise virgin.

Immediately above rose the 'difficult crack'. Having seen photographs of it and read so much about it, I almost felt that I'd already climbed it a dozen times. Technically it's about 'Severe', I suppose, but with heavy sack and in a waterfall it made me puff a bit. I ran out 150 feet of rope and belayed just below the Hinterstoisser traverse. Somewhere left of here Toni Kurz had fought that great fight.

Out came the stove and both tea and soul were warmed. A couple of pegs in the roof of the cave and a stock-take and a sort out. I was drenched right down to my socks and was already missing some of the spare gear I had ditched to save weight. And worse. The weather was not good, even Nicholls was admitting it

— rain, avalanches and stonefall were difficult to ignore. Still, the big decision could be left until the morrow.

We addressed ourselves to the preparation of a meal with the undivided attention of men with absolutely nothing else to do. We wolfed the lot, soup and all, and washed it down with a gallon of tea, the sweetest smiling tea you ever saw.

It was not until about 11 pm that we began to make preparations for the night. As bivvy sites go the cave wasn't too bad. There was just enough room for both of us to either half-lie dry, or full-lie wet — and if it was damp it was at least sheltered from stonefall, which made it as good a home as any on the Eiger.

In his near-dry gear Nicholls snored as an innocent man should, like three pigs. I shivered the night away and gazed longingly at the twinkling lights of Grindelwald thousands of feet below. It was a long night — they always are — and the water trickled all through it, which meant no freeze higher up, and stonefall all the next day, which counselled retreat.

A wet, storm-laden day dawned. There was really no decision to be made, and yet we held a council of war. I was in poor shape after a miserable night — I would have been prepared to finish the climb in that condition, but to start it? And what with the weather and all, down we went; it would still be there next year.

Ten abseils and two hours later we were at the foot of the face, and looking up in a mixture of anger and relief. Anger that we had been thwarted, relief that we had been able to retreat in good order and were safely back at the bottom.

For the umpteenth time we justified the decision to retreat to ourselves. I reflected that there was something in the old military tenet 'time spent in reconnaissance is seldom wasted'. We now knew the line to the Swallows Nest; that would save time next go. We knew too to take care to keep dry and to wear waterproof leggings as well as jackets for the first few thousand feet — and on the last abseil we had found an easier first few feet. But more important than any of these we had stepped on the face and had dispelled the mystique and much of the fear; it no longer held us in its thrall.

'If you take the first step you will take the last.'

The very next year, we saw it on a sunny day and climbed it in another two — and I'll remember them forever.

We had been drawn to the Eiger again. Its attraction was not easy to explain. No-one had told us what a fabulous route it was; it didn't look particularly pleasing — we knew that, it was undeniably dangerous — or could be — we knew that too. What was it then? I don't think either of us was ever honest enough to face that question. We never examined it beyond this simple notion that we both shared; we wanted to climb the Eiger. Everyone does. Most get no further than dreaming about it. Some get as far as talking about it, a few get on it. And when they get up they nearly all say the same thing; great route. But we didn't know it was a great route, we only knew that we wanted to climb it. We never examined the reasons. I fear they were the worst ones — the name, the reputation, kudos — silly things like that.

I had a sillier reason still. I was lying in the sun at Sennen beach; beside me a German girl that I was trying desperately hard to impress — so far without success. It was 1966 and we were listening to the World Cup final; England was doing far better with Germany than I. She had a German boyfriend who was a fine mountaineer — a *bergführer* in fact, who, she said admiringly, had narrowly failed to climb the Eiger Nordwand that very summer. Next year he would try again.

I said, 'I'm going to do it next year.' I couldn't help it. It just slipped out: a vain-glorious lie, I hadn't so much as worn a pair of crampons or set foot on snow or ice at that stage. The lie didn't deserve success and it didn't reap any. You may remember that England won four to two. That didn't help either. But I felt obliged to climb it after that and, come to think of it, of all the reasons I have heard for climbing this particular mountain that is no dafter excuse than any other — a debt of honour, even if it had to wait ten years to be settled.

Anyway, we were back at Lauterbrunnen. At least I was. Nicholls who was at Staff College, learning to read and write at last, could only fix ten days leave and arrived by train a few days after myself. I met him at Interlaken station with 'O young Lochinvar is come out of the west'. He grinned, but the blue eyes showed not a flutter of recognition — Walter Scott was not on the Staff College's reading list. All that rehearsal wasted. He was ready for the Eiger.

'Don't you want to warm-up on something else first?'

'Haven't got the time mate. If the forecast is good I think we should go.'

The forecast was good, for days the man at the heliport assured us. That was good enough for Lochinvar, good enough for me too. We packed that evening, this time lighter, more sensible 'sacks, and set off the next day. The plan was still the same; amble up to the Swallows Nest for a cosy bivouac and go like the clappers for the top the next day. This was before Mesner made nonsense of the bivouacked approach (though not for ordinary mortals) by climbing the entire thing in ten hours. At the time ours was a fairly ambitious plan. Not my own — Tom Patey had put it in my head years before when he and I were strolling up Buchaille Etive, he a seasoned veteran, a sixties hero — mine too; I an awed tyro, agog at his every word. We were talking about the Eiger. He was looking back, having recently retreated from it with Whillans, I looking forward, daring to dream — but only just.

'How's the Hinterstoisser?' I knew all the names. (Not long before I had watched a terrifying TV film about the Eiger — a melodramatic film that must have ruined the chances of a hundred Eiger hopefuls long before storm or stonefall sent them home to think again. At the finish of the film I was trying to fix my own reactions when a friend said, 'Well that puts us in the peanut league.')

I knew I didn't want to stay in the peanut league but now I wasn't sure if I wanted to climb the Eiger either.

Patey said, 'Piece of duff. And all that business about having to leave a rope across it in case of retreat is nonsense — you can abseil straight down off it.' Then he let me into his plan, the bivouac at the Swallows Nest and going for the top the next day. In a couple of sentences, sensible and truthful, he had repaired most of the damage of the TV film, given a young dreamer more than a shred of hope, a young hopeful some good advice.

The previous year, remember, our failure had at least succeeded in dispelling the mystique. Now we were ready for another shot and this time the weather was good — the forecast better. It all went well, but not so well as to be unremarkable — that would be no fun at all. The day, the way my memory holds it, the way I like to think of it, went like this — at a fast beat.

Scrambled easily, unroped, to the foot of the Difficult Crack.

This was where we had paid our Eiger dues the previous year. This year an obviously brand new rope dangled from above — we couldn't see where. Lochinvar gave it a hefty pull. No-one came down, nor rope either.

'Must be fixed.'

Made a useful handhold. Made three or four useful handholds. At the top crampons. To stay on all the way to the top, every foot, all 6000 of them. The face was heavily snowed. It was September, the snow stayed — slower but safer climbing; all the stones were glued in place.

The Hinterstoisser. A web of old ropes, none good enough to use. Patey was right, a piece of duff; about 'Severe' in crampons; no big duff anyway.

Swallows Nest. Cruise of an afternoon; bivvy berth, luxury class. A night star-gathering. First Ice Field. Between dawn and the day. Fine day. Fine snow. No stones, good news.

Ice Hose. Nice Hose this year; good to axe, kind to crampon; steep enough to befriend both.

Second Ice Field. Who has seen it and not wondered the angle of it; big white cheek, cracking, scrunching today with smiling, singing neve. Up, across. Diagonal. A thousand feet. Moving together, 'tread we a measure'. Lochinvar and I. The rope, forgotten, dangled between. In no time. In time. No stones! To Rolling Stones. 2120 South Michigan Avenue. Never heard it? Shame. Made for toe-tapping good neve. Not a Lochinvar tune. I hummed it. Two by two we drummed it. Jagger takes two minutes and eight seconds dead. We spun it for twenty minutes more. Twenty two minutes to the top side. Can't think of the 2nd Icefield now without getting that tune. Good music for good snow. Steep to the Flat Iron. Some hard mixed pitches. Lots of snow. Lots of ice. Death Bivouac. Damn silly name. Nice place except for a boot. Just a boot! Dark thoughts. Don't think about the rest of him. Third Ice Field. Down. Pity to have to lose height. Hard ice here, steeper. Pitched it on ice-screws. The Ramp. More ice. Should have been the rocks' turn. But not enough ice to be useful; enough to make the rock useless. Too little for crampons; too slippery without. Crampons. Slow work. Careful work. Hard work. To a bulge after 800 feet. Heck this is hard. Didn't Heckmair think so too? Lochinvar thought so — and though 'he staid not for brake and he stopp'd not for stone',

113

he fell off. Slightly. Swore his way up. Grunts and sweat. Then, on a rope 12 stones tight,

'Good that, I wish I'd led it.'

A second's line; he meant it though.

Stonefall. Shelter at the Brittle Ledges. Fear for the Spider which we imagine will be swept by stones. Bad time to cross. Wait and do it early in the morning. Second bivouac. Steerage class. Sorry Tom. Nicholls sits and wakes. I sleep and lie. Anyone would have complained. Not Lochinvar.

'He kipped on the Eiger where ledge there was none
And in his good polybag he shook ere the sun.
He shivered and shuddered, but voiced not a care,
There never was knight like the young Lochinvar!'

But it was a good night. Starbright. Cold. Dreaming I chased the maiden of the moon. No breakfast — a hard pitch instead. Weather good, climbing perfect; last year's dues were worth the price. Traverse of the Gods for brunch. Some burger! The name no more dramatic than the place. The Spider. White Spider, crisp spider; 'tread we the measure' again. Exit cracks. The Sting. Not made for crampons. Summit slopes. Lochinvar, dead keen to balance the shifts, plods the lot. Knee deep, and him from the class-room. 'A' for effort. The top. Big grin, two bigger grins — the stiff upper so forgets itself. A silly pose, a 'happy snappy'. The Eiger, more than a mile of three-star route that we had wanted to climb for all the wrong reasons. But climbing it, found all the right ones. It's the best route in Europe and you can sit on your bum and slide home. Don't forget — 'If you take the first step you will take the last'.

We felt only pleasure — and a profound admiration for Heckmair who climbed it first, in bad weather, more than thirty years before. Now that was a climb — and a climber. I think we felt that we had graduated too — even if it had been our own syllabus and we examiner and examined. Easy way to pass.

'Where to next year, Dave?'

'How about Courmayeur? You'll have to behave yourself though.'

I hadn't been there since the incident those years before; the idea had its attractions — some of the best mountains of the Alps and beautiful interpreters.

114

This time Nicholls was there first and full of plans; good weather plans, wet weather plans; plans for new routes, plans for fun, plans for adventure but nowhere in his wildest contingency was there a plan for what followed. He persuaded me that there was a route on the North Face of the Aiguille de Leschaux that was worth a go. It had only been done once, by a lad called Gogna and his mate Rava; looked to be a 'wazzer'. He told me what to take and what the weather would be — this plan had been well laid. He'd done some homework too — all that Staff College training was beginning to tell. He was drinking dangerously large at the Peirian Spring. He knew where the route lay, how long it was, the way off, the gear we were likely to need — everything. It was as good as in the bag; all over bar the shouting. We piled into my car prattling the excited nonsense of those with an adventure round the corner and no care between, and took the road to Val Ferret and the Leschaux.

Half of Italy, it seemed, was parked in the Val Ferret that same day. And not your orderly British parking either, but real hot blooded Latin stuff with modest family saloons serving in the office of Grand Prix thoroughbreds, four-wheel-drifting into the happy spaghetti chaos. Panache, perhaps, was the word for it. We parked: *sans* panache, nicely off the road and decently square to at least one of the surrounding Regazzonis. Smug was the word for it.

Then it was off up the path toward the Triolet hut and the second ascent of the Gogna/Rava route on the North Face of the Aiguille de Leschaux — at least that was the plan.

For a hut walk this one was a pleasant plod — 'doddle' was the word for it — and since it was a Sunday the way lay dotted with shapely and occasionally entwined diversions. Nicholls, Sebastian Coe'd it as usual while I made my token attempt to keep up until heart, lungs and legs mutinied — successfully — whereafter I fell, wonderfully diverted, to the rear.

Arriving at the hut some hours later, I found Young Lochinvar engaging a Lorenesque Italian in a one-sided conversation based on home brewed esperanto. She was a cracker with shorts of Whillans brevity, legs 3 pitches long and 5C all the way and a Dad suspicious of Young Lochinvar's intentions — and rightly so. Unfortunately for my partner, she'd never heard of Gogna or Rava. He scored no points at all with his North Face name dropping and soon tiring of Nicholls' chorus, she flounced gorgeously away leaving him to Signors Gogna, Rava and me.

'Must'a lost something in the translation,' said Lochinvar lamely.

Next day the weather was shaky — very warm and cloudy — but we decided to have a look all the same. Half way up the initial ice slope, adjudged 50° in the guide, but happily little over 40° we called it a day. Water was running everywhere and we backed off at the thought of what the conditions would be like on the much more serious top two-thirds of the route. 'What do you think mate?' that time honoured euphemism for 'let's push off, this is ridiculous'. It takes the braver or saner man to deploy either version, for it force-feeds the other's ego and affords him a distinct tactical advantage. Before I could agree my ego said 'could give it a couple more pitches'... and my heart sank as he agreed. Then a couple of bouncing bricks said don't be daft and down we went.

From the glacier as dawn broke we looked back at the face to get a close-up of the line for future forays. Our gaze was drawn leftwards to a couloir which ran out of the top left corner of the initial ice field. It led uninterrupted to the summit ridge, steepening in the last third to a near-vertical seam of ice. Well they're all near-vertical, aren't they? It was an open invitation to anyone who has traded punches with Scottish ice, or wildly flailed a shorty axe in a wet Welsh winter and dulled a dozen crampon points in between. A new route? There was no mention of it in our guide or in the Vallot, 'Give it a try next time up?' 'OK.' And so, faint failure soothed by half-hearted hope, and fuelled on procrastinating dreams we retreated to the hut and a brew. A gallon or so of tea later we decided that two axes apiece and perhaps some ice screws would be handy — not to mention some liquid courage — so it was back to the valley.

Half way down a patch of snow that interrupted the hut path we overtook 'Legs Loren' tripping delicately and deliciously downward. This was the signal for Nicholls, who'll stoop to anything for a friendly smile or more, and who in winter masquerades as a ski instructor of sorts, to burst into a tight-legged, short-swinging glissade that would not have disgraced Stenmark. 'Legs' was much impressed as our hero jet-turned neatly round a rock and paralleled casually to a stop at the bottom. In a vain attempt to follow, I fell heavily at the first gate and gashed my forearm on the pick of an axe that was too carelessly attached to my 'sack.

Salvaging what dignity I could, I limped down clutching the wound with the other hand in an attempt to conceal the damage. But blood dripped onto the snow and with it my morale and machismo. Nicholls, with ever an eye for the main chance, gained more points by bandaging my arm and rather too literally adding insult to injury. With a triumphant wave to 'Legs' he bounded off towards the road with a whole new enthusiasm.

'Troubles always come in threes,' said Lochinvar as we neared the road. 'Probably find your car has been nicked. Should round your day off nicely,' he added cheerfully. Rounding a corner, we came upon the car, now parked in splendid isolation, just in time to see it being towed onto the back of a breakdown truck — Italian style. Now you might imagine that the nation that created Ferrari, Maserati, Lamborghini *et al* would be car lovers and you'd be wrong — unless it was just that this particular BL vintage was beneath their contempt.

For whatever reason, a winch cable had been attached to a distinctly sub-standard belay and before a panic-stricken sprint brought me within distance, my wheels were hauled unceremoniously onto the back of the truck. Off came bumper and silencer and down went four tyres.

I know my Italians (but sadly no Italian). They are an unreasonable and wildly excitable race and a bit of British calm would soon sort this out.

'What the bloody hell d'you think you are doing with my car,' I howled, gesticulating in a most Italian way in the not entirely mistaken belief that this would translate English into passable Italian. From somewhere beneath a hugely sad groucho moustache the *Carabiniere* who was supervising the growing shambles replied, *'Calmo, calmo',* very calmly, very reasonably and in a thoroughly Northern European sort of way. Something seemed to have gone wrong. The only word of Italian I knew was *grazie* which wasn't quite the word I wanted just then.

'Parlez-vous Français?' I asked without being too clear how I would proceed if his answer was *'oui'*. My French is fine for pens, aunts, charabancs and postilions but not so hot on more useful phrases such as 'get my bloody car off the back of that

117

bloody lorry, etc. etc.' *Il* simply *no comprende* and despite my reversion to English reinforced by animated semaphore, we remained *incommunicado.*

The breakdown truck took-off all but literally, with my car perched precariously atop, siren wailing and all lights flashing — somewhat unnecessarily, I thought, for apart from the *persona dramatis,* the place was deserted for miles. It two wheeled into the first hairpin and Regazzonied into the blue.

We set off in hot, steaming hot, pursuit, doubting whether we'd ever see our car again, but hours later, having tracked smouldering rubber and sundry BL accessories to a third rate garage in down-town Courmayeur, we traced my offending wheels. The necessary repairs had been carefully botched and release was eventually secured at a mere umpteen thousand lire.

'Just one of those days,' said Nicholls helpfully. That night, beer-cheered, I consoled myself that at least he might have forgotten about his new line.

So you'll forgive my lack of enthusiasm when the very next day my partner announced that we were going to have another go. Confident that sanity would ultimately prevail, I allowed him to indulge himself in a bit of gear sorting. I pointed out that between us we had six pegs and had not Gogna used 70 on a route not a couple of rope's length away? This deterred him not at all. Knowing my man I gave up and buckled to. We decided against bivvy gear — more than a stove that is. Dave's theory was that since the route was mainly ice we wouldn't be slowed by technical intricacies and what wouldn't fall to stealth could be reduced by frontal assault.

And so it was that we found ourselves crossing the same glacier the day after at two in the morning. By three we were at the top of the ice slope and preparing to sally onto new ground. The way ahead was uncertain and fairly steep so we decided to await the comforting and hopefully revealing light of dawn. A brew helped to while away the time and top up morale. At last the day came and, spotting a line, we climbed on.

It was great. Exciting as new ground always is; but more than that the climbing was superb, the protection passable and the belays not half bad. It was warm too. A bit too warm really, but at least the ice was soft and sensuously rubbery — if you like that sort of thing. On we went searching, seeking, sensing the way if

118

you were leading and with one eye on the pitch after if you were holding the rope.

For the most part the ice gave the line so we followed our noses and they rarely lied and though the ground steepened it was still all very reasonable. We were happy in our work and chatted cheerfully whenever we met. I led a pitch; drove in a peg and belayed. Dave came up, at the gallop, took some gear and led on. 'OK mate,' he yelled, meaning that he was belayed. I untied from my peg and began to knock it out when a steady roar caught my mind's ear. Leaving the peg I glanced around the cirque in the hope of a glimpse of something spectacular. Nothing doing. Returning to the peg I became aware of a darkening above. A quick look up. Damn! Dave had already seen it and was road-runner flat against the hill. The vision was quick, the impression quicker and the memory hazy but I recall huge blocks of ice and seemingly endless cascades of slow snow streaming off the summit slopes and out, out, out into the sky above us. Escape looked unlikely and too frightened to panic we cravenly cowered — and survived. Ice broke on rocks all about, but none on us while snow buffeted but left us attached until at last the sky cleared and the discovery that I was unscathed encouraged me to enquire after Nicholls. 'Dave, Dave, you OK?' No answer. Panic. How to get down... rescue... insurance... me?

'I'm OK, what will we do?' — a small voice miles off at 150 feet away. 'It's this bloody couloir.'

'Same up or down — and we're nearer the top,' I answered with half-hearted, half-convinced reason.

There being nothing more to say the rope went tight, I removed the peg and went on up to Dave. Together we were braver — though still very shaken. But it would be safer ahead, steeper and therefore safer, and in any case there was probably no more to come — we argued with a logic short on alternatives.

In other circumstances the remaining 800 feet would have been exhilarating but the joy had been swept away and we had even stopped pretending. At the time survival seemed a serious-ness business only regaining its sense of humour in the retelling. Our banter evaporated altogether as the pitches grew wild, the belays precarious and the protection pretence. The joke was done.

The penultimate pitch was a crippler. Six feet of the couloir had fallen away at its narrowest point leaving smooth crampon-resistant rock beneath. A long reach failed by miles and a full tip-toeing stretch by inches. A peg for help, some wild piolet a panic, a couple of what your modern crag rat describes as 'armlocks' and enough height gained to get the front point, alarmingly close to the bottom of the ice, onto the continuation of the couloir. A few feet later I belayed with all four remaining pegs. 'Short pitch that,' Dave noted.

The last pitch was a beauty — virgin white ice leading at 80° up to the sun and what appeared to be easy ground. I led on. Oh boy, beautiful ice. Steep but compliantly axe-worthy, though a touch too soft for screws and a long way to anywhere. The expos-ure was sobering. 'Relax, man relax,' I coaxed myself aloud. But if the ice stays you can't fail with modern tools, can you? It stayed and so did I — all the way up 150 feet to a belay boulder that couldn't have been improved on. I let a wild hoot of un-abashed joy. No need for coy smugness here; we whooped our pleasure at being out of it. Chuffed was the word.

Climbing was fun again and private promises of future pru-dence made lower down were well on their way to being forgotten, as was the avalanche, though that was sure to be resurrected, elaborated and adorned in a dozen versions and a hundred beers from now.

We sat in the sun and admired a fantastic view of the north side of the Jorasses. 'At least ED Sup' Nicholls judged. 'No doubt about it,' I replied without having the slightest idea what 'ED Sup' actually meant. A wet of tea later we had moderated 'ED Inf', and later still, recovering our sense of proportion and fearing ridicule, TD Sup seemed to be popular. I have no idea what grade it really was — and what does it matter, for doubtless in but a short while some callow youth will have reduced it to a 2-hour *Difficile* — and perhaps Legs Loren will show it to be an easy day for 'oh! what a lady'. And good luck to them; the only advice I'd presume to offer is, 'mind where you park your car!'

But not all attempts on new routes have happy endings. Com-ing down off the Leschaux we had been rewarded with a front row view of the mighty East Face of the Grandes Jorasses — a neglected facet of that much climbed mountain — and curious neglect because the East Face is one of the biggest faces in the

Alps and the rock is generally of good quality. Admittedly, the one route that does lie up the face, somewhat to the left side of it is a masterpiece by Gervasutti. To the right of his route, between it and the Hirondelles Ridge lies a vast exposure of rock with an obvious line, more or less up the middle. It is clearly visible from the Gervasutti Hut. Too good to be true. A year later I was at the hut with Nick Banks, a New Zealander who'd have a go at anything as long as he didn't have to take it too seriously. Trouble was neither of us took this seriously enough. Gervasutti was a genius — as understood by the sense of the word before nearly everyone became a genius; it never struck us for a second that there might be good reason why he hadn't taken our intended line, obvious as it was. Indeed, he had walked right underneath it to get to his own. By 1980, Gervasutti's route, nearly 40 years old, had seen only about half a dozen ascents. That should have given us pause for thought. But it didn't. We were going to go where Gervasutti should have gone, we said, with a grand arrogance but no great seriousness. We toyed briefly with the idea of taking EB's for the hard bits but, in the end, with that same grand arrogance, and still only half serious, we decided that anything that had pushed Gervasutti leftwards we could climb in big boots. Our reasoning was not so much arrogant as uninformed. Our research, a long look from the Val Feret road, hadn't included reading *Gervasutti's Climbs* or we might have thought differently. He'd used rope-soled espadrilles — the EB of the time. And that long look was about the sum total of our planning. Not much for a major new alpine route on a remote face, already *Extrêmement Difficile* by the only existing route and well over 2000 feet high. Not enough either — it's waiting still — but Banks never did like having to take things seriously and I am easily led.

Banks, because he is a New Zealander, loves long approaches and likes to take them early. I, having been to New Zealand, hate long approaches and like to take them as late as possible — better still, not at all.

This, according to the guide, was to be a long approach, four hours and several thousands of feet to the start of our route — a start common with Gervasutti's line. I reasoned that since we could not hope to begin hard rock climbing before dawn and preferably not until the rock had been touched by the sun, there

121

was little point in arriving at the Col des Hirondelles, close to the foot of the face, much before 7 am. This suggested a 3 am start. Now Nick can do one of two things; start at 1 am — or not start at all. Whether this affliction is common to all antipodeans I have often wondered, but there was no moving Banks. At least this early start would allow for a more leisurely approach than the guide book author had in mind. That was not, however, what Banks had in mind. His other problem was that he only had two speeds. Full tilt and dead stop. This morning it was full tilt, beginning 1 am. As he sped uphill he had breath to spare to pro-pound the perplexing theory that it was less tiring to walk quickly than slowly. Had I the breath I would have pointed out that the evidence of a million races run from mile to marathon did not support his argument. Not that it would have made much difference; Nick was as impervious to impirical evidence as he was to puff — or my complaints about the pace.

We arrived at the Col at three and shivered to seven. That Banks shivered the more violently was scant consolation.

Seven. We followed Gervasutti to a snowy ledge that crosses the East Face. This is where we were to go straight up and where Gervasutti, bigger on skills and realism had headed hard left.

The first pitches, up to the snowy ledge were 'mixed' — snow, ice, rock and everything in between. Banks declared them, 'my sort of country'. He led with gusto, crampons and axe agressively aflail.

At the snowy ledge the 'country' changed to vertical rock. This, Banks declared was not his sort of country — and you can't argue with Kiwis. We made a few pitches fairly quickly to where the face reared steeper and clearly harder. 'Rip it to bits', Nick advised. I climbed fifty feet. It was getting harder. Another twenty, harder still. I wanted to remove my rucksack to lighten the load but I couldn't spare the hand — I needed them both to stay on. Try out left. I traversed left, maybe twenty feet. A crack offered hope above. Another foot. I was tiring badly and to the weight of the 'sack, the rope, mismanaged and twisted through a dozen runners and round the two corners of the traverse, added its own disc brake drag. I wished I had left my 'sack with Nick, I missed my rock boots that we had originally packed but later contemptuously discarded, I regretted not taking the whole enterprise more seriously and I wondered what I was going to do

122

next. Another foot. I'd run out of slings, used prusik loops, then a wire in a thread, the spine of which was fatter than the wire's length. I hooked a carabiner into the loop at one end, hoped the chock on the other would act as a stopper. It did; when I fell about five feet later, strength puffed to 'the twelve clean winds of heaven', control vanished close behind, the mind a battlefield of wildness and concentration and wildness an easy victor. I fell forty feet, clean into space. Fifteen hundred feet above nothing in particular, and below and some way to Nick's left. I shot him a glance. A glance which said nothing and everything. His answer was a camera. A camera! Banks had always claimed that taking photographs was a waste of time. He had climbed Everest the year before and managed to take only two on the way. That in itself must establish some sort of a record. Neither came out. That must establish another. Now, uncharacteristically he was all lenses, filters and exposure meters, intent on a photograph of me hanging somewhere above Italy. 'After all,' he explained his sudden interest in portraiture, 'there's no more hurry. Might as well enjoy ourselves.'

An hour later I regained the rock. It had been overhanging slightly — the rope was plumb-line proof of that. Two hours after that, I regained Banks, whose enthusiasm for our 'enjoyment' was beginning to wane. It waned out of sight when I suggested that he might try a lead, and in its place a whole new enthusiasm welled — an enthusiasm for 'about fifty pints of piss', as New Zealanders rather inelegantly refer to beer. We went home.

His enthusiasms nearly always carried the day. As far as I know the East Face of the Grandes Jorasses, Gervasutti's great effort excepted, remains inviolate — unless you consider that our efforts amounted to penetration.

That episode went a long way in developing my sense of the ridiculous — an important alpine attitude.

'It wad frae mony a blunder free us,
An' foolish notion.'

This next excursion perfected my sense of the ridiculous.

It was my first winter season. Nicholls had become serious about being a Marine; I had become serious about not being one. Our paths crossed less often and we seemed no longer to be able to fix time in the mountains together. He had also become married to Dierdre, a Scot, and lass fit for a young Lochinvar. Dierdre was claiming most of his attention and all of his energies — and he was catching up on what he reckoned had always been Lochinvar's dues.

I had arrived in Chamonix at Christmas alone and too late. The weather was good and everyone was out on the hill. I cast about for a partner — and finding none decided that conditions were too good to waste; it would have to be a solo, something not too serious, not too hard. The Swiss Route on the North Face of the Courtes fitted the bill perfectly; a down-hill ski approach after using the *téléphérique,* across a straightforward glacier, a cosy hut, easy to the route, a route I knew from a summer ascent, a way off I thought I could handle on my own and without the need of a rope. Then the perfect end of this perfect day — a downhill ski home.

And that's how it went until near the end.

I regained the glacier, after a satisfying day, at about 4 pm. A storm was brewing (I had seen the tell-tale clouds from the top), the weather worsening by the minute. By the time I found the Argentière Hut a blizzard was blowing full hooligan and it was dark. The simple thing to do was to spend the night in the perfect safety of the hut, then ski down the next day — or whenever the weather allowed. There was ample grub around the shelves to survive on. But life isn't simple. I knew that just down the glacier and around the corner the lights of Chamonix were twinkling, while at the Bar Nash all sorts of delights awaited. The temptation was too much. Besides the hut was a spooky place. I mounted skis and set off by head torch. The terrain was flattish, the skiing would have been easy in normal conditions but a rucksack filled with bits for winter, a howling blizzard and a weakish lamplight ensured that it was pretty grim. An early fall put paid to the lamp's problem. In the struggle to my feet I lost it altogether. It wouldn't be found. I considered turning back, would have turned back if I had thought that I could re-find the hut. I didn't think I could and continued by map and compass.

My big worry was an ice fall over which the glacier tumbled a mile or so further down. It lay right across my path; I would have to turn left some way before it. Here I would meet a marked piste run, with poles, ski-tracks, moguls and soon a *téléphérique* station and a café; warmth and safety not much more than a mile away. I fell now more often than I skied. What in daylight would have been a ten-minute schuss was fast becoming a monument to incompetence. I was unhappy. The icefall loomed large in my imagination; I mustn't go down the glacier too far; I must pick up the poles and piste; I couldn't miss them. Surely not?

I'd missed them, I'd blown it. This was it. I was falling. Floating through space and darkness. These were the wages of bright-lights foolishness. But a quick, and not very painful crash, told me that this was not the icefall; or maybe only the beginning of it. I was in a crevasse. Blind gropings told me that. I pondered. It was as good a place to spend a night as any, comparatively sheltered and snowily soft. The hut would have been better, Chamonix better still, but since neither was available, this would do. The sleeping bag, which I entered in company of a blast of spindrift, brought warmth and soon, sleep.

The sky! I could see the sky. It was ten-thirty. What a place to oversleep. I packed and addressed myself to the problem of escape. This would be a big fight, the good fight. I steeled myself, braced myself. Tried to think what Messner would have done; set my jaw accordingly, screwed courage to the sticking place, strapped crampons the extra hole, wound both axes tight, Yes Sir! I stood square, Marciano square, to the crevasse wall, hunched in determination, and raised an axe with sacrificial deliberateness. Then it occurred, in the accidental way these things do, that it might be worth a look farther along to see what might lie around the corner. I advanced, axes held low and wide, OK Corral style, a few steps to where a tight squeeze allowed me round a corner. Another step and I stood blinking, bathed in warm winter sunshine, the wide open ski piste before me and a hundred holiday skiers swooping all around, Attila before Rome, Tamerlane before Samarkand, Ghengis Khan before all China. I felt a fool and overdressed. And must have looked it, all girded in crampons, double boots, overgaiters, goretex suit, axes, balaclava and helmet while casually elegant punters swept by all silk, sunglasses and Ambre Solaire. I fled to the sanctuary of the crevasse before I was seen by one of the skiers standing about gossiping, enjoying a spot of sun. Back at my bivouac I stripped off every shred of mountain apparel, packed every incriminating item into the 'sack, adopted as recreational an appearance as my wardrobe would allow and skied, as casually as I could, onto the piste and into the sun. Fifteen unsteady minutes later I was sipping coffee at the *téléphérique* station — with a heightened sense of the ridiculous.

'O wad some Pow'r the giftie gie us
To see oursels as others see us!
It wad frae mony a blunder free us
An' foolish notion.'

4

Britain

BITS OF BRITISH ROCK

I was luckier than most. At least most would consider me to have been luckier; I was taught to climb by my father. He, a country lad from rural Ulster, had learnt to climb during the war with the Commandos, mostly in Glencoe. Glencoe; he still refers to that place as his spiritual home, a phrase which, in old age, he regards as a bit silly; the product of a soldier's sentimentality and Irish romanticism. And make no mistake, all soldiers, especially old ones, are sentimental, incurably so, even if all Irishmen are not romantic, though I suspect that they are.

There I was at six years of age scrambling up and down boulders and bits of cliff with a naturalness that was not strained by instruction, in the safety of a father's fond gaze; fear as yet unlearnt and not a thought for name or grade or why. It was fun; a game, nothing more, nothing less. And as boys play without self-consciousness, then so I scrambled and gambolled and climbed. It's a shame, in climbing as in most things, perhaps especially in climbing because it is a game that is played into old age, that a self-consciousness creeps up on us and brings with it all sorts of pretensions and affectations. The pity is that there is no going back; we start out fresh, end up faded. That, for all but the free-est spirits is the way of it.

Now my father had a theory that the fear of heights was not innate to the human species, but rather that we learned it from a mother's fearful cry when her children wandered into dangerous places. So I tripped along perilous walls and ledges at the age of two or three with a terrified mother suppressing her rebukes, though not, of course, able to conceal her anxiety — which by one means or another is always transmitted — and received. That, I think, is why the theory remains theory and I am as afraid of heights as the next.

But what is the rock climbing game all about? Well it's about turning up at the bottom of a rock face and bearing away until you arrive at the top. Nonsense, you say, there must be more to it than that. Yes, there is, a bit; not much though. There are easy climbs and hard climbs and, therefore, grades of climbs. Or to look at it another way, there are climbs you can do and climbs you can't. There's rope, carabiners and other bits and pieces, and nowadays there's bags of chalk and sticky boots. There are guide books which tell you where the cliffs are and the climbs to be found there and their every coded difficulty (sometimes to the last ten feet of it). Then there are the names themselves. They are awarded or inflicted, according to taste, by the first up that way who can then give it any name they want. It is said that the names given reflect the author. What then, do we make of he who names his climb 'Wombbits' (a really clever pun on a nearby route called Woubits), or, by the same chap 'Systitis by Proxy'? Or what of someone who in the summer of 1982 calls a route 'Bye-bye Belgrano'. Perhaps it's better not to answer and ponder instead the lad who can call a very hard route 'Ordinary Route' or the fellow who can call one 'Jenny Wren' after the little bird of that name that had walked whistling by as the climber struggled desperately to stay on the rock.

Then there's the doing of it. You reach up, grab a hold, another hand another hold, a foot here, the other there; pull up, stand up, reach up again, and again, and again, until — the top. That's all there is to it, really. I defy anyone to find anymore in it. True, on some climbs the holds are further apart than you'd call ideal and often they are longer away than you'd have in a perfect world. Sometimes they are smaller too than they should be — though they have been big enough for someone. Occasionally, everything is perfect; the holds perfectly positioned, ample in size and number. Unfortunately, this seems only to be the case on easy climbs. On harder climbs the holds are harder to find and fewer; sometimes so scarce or so small that they can't be found at all. These are the climbs that you read about and recommend to others.

That it? Certainly is. Not much, you'll say. Not much indeed. Of course, there is a heck of a sight more to it than that if you actually do it, but, in truth, not a lot more than meets the eye. There's the essence of it *(reductio ad absurdum,* I admit). It's not a spectator (or reader) sport. Ten feet of upward movement can consume hours of viewing time. Definitely for the *cognoscente* only. It is hard to see how the description of a successful ascent of a rock climb could be made interesting which is why I intend to take that risk only once. Rock climbing only means anything when your entire world is that few square feet in front of your face. Then it means everything. Then you can run your hands over continents, seek out rivers and valleys with febrile fingers, stamp feet on islands of hope and fight the whole of life's great fight for six inches of height gained. It's done; and no photograph, no page, no tale will every bring back a tenth of it. But I can tell you of the fun, the laughs and the cock-ups and that is what I will try to do — risking just that one straight-to-the-top tale.

I gave up climbing at the age of fifteen, first to play rugby, then to chase girls. Then, at twenty three the Marines sent me off to learn again. Eight years. Eight years I wasted. I'll want them back one day. The Marines had a climbing wing which had been founded during the Second World War and which soldiered on afterwards under various names, accumulating a talented band of climbers and impressive range of expertise. My father, an Army Commando, had climbed Genges Groove at Sennen in 'pumps' in 1947 — it's still graded 5B. Mike Banks had climbed Rakaposhi (25,550 feet), Dick Grant, Annapurna II (26,041 feet), Viv Stevenson and Zeke Deacon were putting up routes as hard as any around, Guy Sheridan was in the British Olympic Cross Country Ski-Team. I was joining a talented team with a solid mountaineering history: an élite — before that became a dirty word — and like most élites a happy band of brothers.

When I joined them they were called the Reconnaissance Leaders Wing. It was commanded by Guy Sheridan and though most of the stars had departed the tradition and spirit remained.

I embarked on a Reconnaissance Leader's Course. We began in Cornwall, climbing at Bosigran, Sennen, Chair Ladder, Lamorna — places rich in Royal Marine climbing history. Great days of PT, pranks and wonderful Cornish granite. Later we moved to North Wales. Then we parachuted into Scotland and afterwards went to Norway for six weeks of arctic warfare — learning to ski and move and live in arctic mountains in winter. It was one of the happiest periods of my life: no responsibilities but what the day brought, and hard work which seemed, minded as we were, nothing more than one long game. The 'we' were instructors and students of all ranks and seniority — rank was seldom mentioned, hardly ever mattered and certainly brought no favours. The instructor I remember best was Scrim, Corporal James Archibald Scrimgeour; Jim the Scrim as he was known universally and with some affection. He'd been a sergeant once, for about twenty minutes — just long enough to thump a fellow sergeant and even an old score. The price — demotion — he considered a bargain. Now he was a superannuated corporal looking forward to his imminent retirement and a new career as a publican — and he'd been hard at his homework these last few years.

Scrim was a character. Everybody was agreed about that and everybody had their favourite Scrim story. My favourite happened in the third or fourth week of our stay at Cornwall. The course students lived in a Royal Marine cottage in St.Just, the instructors were billeted in digs throughout the village. Every day would begin with half an hour's PT and perhaps a wrestling competition, catch-as-catch-can, shoulders on the ground for a count of three or a submission. It was usually a submission, a pained, choked submission. Then a day on that Cornish rock — the best anywhere — with Scrim or one of his mates — the best anywhere. I had been climbing at Sennen with Scrim for about four days. On the first of these we broke for lunch in the sun at the top of the cliffs. Scrim dived into his sack and unearthed a carefully wrapped pack of sandwiches. These he lay in one of his huge hands and with the banana-fingers of the other unwrapped the contents.

'Ah sarnies. Wonder what's in them the day.' Scrim all relish and expectancy, peeled back a corner of the first sandwich.

'Och bloody spam, I canna stand spam,' and he threw them all to the seagulls, a thousand grateful seagulls.

The next day exactly the same thing happened. And the next. And the next. It was becoming a ritual; the seagulls would have agreed.

On the fourth day of 'och bloody spam', I suggested,

'Scrim, if you hate spam so much why don't you get your landlady to put something else in them?'

Scrim looked at me, a quizzical Sauchiehall look and said, utterly solemnly,

'Ma landlady be buggery; I make 'em mysel.' No smile, no hint;

130

he was serious. Or was he? I never knew and I never did find out. That was Scrim.

It was also Scrim who lit a fire under me as I struggled in the Logan Rock Chimney. This was a chimney twenty feet high, about a millimetre wider than I was at the bottom and tapering at half height to exactly my thickness. Scrim pointed me at it, sort of ordered really, for though a corporal, he was the instructor after all and I, though a lieutenant, was the pupil. I was keen, which Scrim knew and counting on when he said,

'Intae that chimney. I bet ye canna climb it faster than 30 seconds; that's the record.' I was also arrogant. Scrim knew that too and was counting on it. In a trice I was into the chimney and up to the point where it exactly fitted. Here my enthusiasm and arrogance combined to thrust me that further fatal inch. I was stuck, stuck fast; couldn't move, down or up. Glancing down (the head was already to one side), I saw Scrim lighting a great green fire. He must have had the ingredients stockpiled just round the corner. The chimney was a chimney right enough. In no time thick grass smoke had funnelled up and engulfed me, and as I struggled and fought, spluttered and swore, Scrim and his mates (clearly they were in on the act too) fell about in good natured hysterics, one occasionally getting sufficient grip of himself to stoke the fire with another bundle of green grass. I got up somehow, or at least out, and now I reckon I'm one of the best chimney-men around. How much credit Scrim's unconventional instruction can take for this is not certain.

That then was Scrim, and, getting my own back, so was this. It was a Friday morning and Scrim was in a terrible state. Hung over with a 'heid-bangin' hangover, and drained by a combination of half-a-dozen consecutive 4 am 'lock-ins' at the local, the energetic attentions of the local virago, and long neglect of what had once been fine physical equipment, he was, that morning, a wreck; self confessedly 'knackered', even by his own high Glaswegian standards. No matter — he was used to it and he'd get over it — in time to repreat the whole crippling catalogue the very next weekend, which, it being Friday, was looming large in his plans.

But I was still keen, even after weeks of Scrim, on a climb at Bosigran called Raven Wall. Scrim wasn't used to that — to keenness. He looked as if he might not get over it, not in time to get us up Raven Wall that morning anyways. 'Friday's a V.Diff day,' Scrim said. 'You have to think about the weekend and tomorrow's the St. Just Feast — the pubs'll be open all day.' You had to save a bit for that. And we were to march in the parade, between the Boys Brigade and the Rotary Club; we'd have to prepare for that. And anyway, Friday or not, it made no difference, he was a V.Diff man, everyday — couldn't see the need to climb any harder at the best of times. Certainly couldn't see the need to terrify himself on this, this Extreme, just a month or so before he was due 'outside'. Couldn't see the need for it. This, Scrim said, was a Zeke route. He had his reputation to think of. (Zeke's work was still held in some awe and if I had known then how hard Zeke had found it, or how hard I was going to find it for myself, I might have shared Scrim's reluctance.)

But I didn't know and I was keen; and arrogant. I remarked that it was really only a one-pitcher, that we could still prepare for the feast that afternoon if we got a move on, that it was our last day on Cornish rock and that I'd buy him a half-and-a-half. That did it. He told me I could lead if I wanted in a way that meant that I could lead whether I wanted it or not. He offered to hold the rope and proffer advice.

Scrim made himself comfortable, reclined on a grassy terrace and grunted the command, 'Awa ye go.' And 'awa' I went. Nothing too tricky to begin with then a thin slab and a bulge to an overhanging wall on the right, through which ran a crack, where the stains of Zeke's original aid still showed. But the pegs had disintegrated in the salt, Cornish air. It looked very hard — and as I looked very hard the rope stopped running. Scrim noticed that:

'Whit's the matter?'

'I'm just sorting it, looks hard.'

'Git a hod o' they pegs. Zeke used they pegs.'

I shouted that the pegs had gone and I was trying without. That really roused him.

'That one's ar-tae-fush-shul,' he made his Glaswegian most of all four syllables, 'so ye haf tae use them. It cannie be done withoot. Don't dae it withoot.'

He had strong views on these matters did Scrim but soon, solicitousness exhausted, conscience cleared, his thoughts turned to weightier matters — contemplation of the 'feast'.

The overhanging crack was difficult but I got a 'moac' in, and hanging hard, used it to get up. Then I was flying, head first back to Scrim, moac out, pupil off. 'Ah telt ye it was ar-tae-fush-shul, ah telt ye.' But he was wrong. It went free. A few hard moves up that crack to an edge, and then up much more easily to the top. Scrim followed free — easily — and went to the pub where he staged a very long 'lock-in' until the feast began the next day.

The parade was the highlight, a march from the village church to the village hall for a civic reception, or what Scrim called 'a cake and arse' party, by way of the five village pubs. Everyone was there, the Boys Brigade and the Rotary Club, the Women's Institute, Cubs, Scouts, Brownies and Girlguides, St.John's Ambulance Brigade; The Darts team, champions of the local league; the Rugby team bottom of the local league these last three years; the Police — both of them — a contingent from the local school, the village cheerleaders team, flags, bunting, banners and Scrim. I separate Scrim from the rest of us because, at the Mayor's own request, he marched at the head of the parade; a triumvirate, Scrim, Mayor and Lady Mayor. Scrim was drunker than any lord before or since but he marched like a good 'un and no-one would have known — well not the casual observer, the untrained eye anyway. The Mayor got as drunk as Scrim that night. Lady Mayor carried them both home.

The course went to Norway for the winter, way up north by Tromso. I loved that arctic winter and emerged fit and 'arctic trained' as RM parlance had it. A week later I was posted to Singapore; from the arctic to the tropics in a week.

The New Zealand and Menthosa adventures followed. Then, four years after Scrim's leading the 'Feast' Parade I was posted back to the climbing wing as the boss. It rejoiced in a grand new name of Mountain and Arctic Warfare Cadre. I was the proudest and happiest man anywhere. Scrim was still there, a sergeant now, his previous twenty-minute record shattered. He'd tried 'civvy street' but couldn't get the hang of it — or it of him — and he was back for as long as the Marines would have him. It was great to see him again.

Soon we were back in Cornwall playing the old game: the St. Just Feast, PT in the mornings as well as long runs in the evening back to St. Just from that day's climbing area (every year, as the

133

young Turks advanced from being last year's students to next year's instructors, the climbs got harder, the runs longer, the programme fuller — or was it that the old guard grew older!), smoking them out of Logan Rock Chimney, spam sandwiches at Sennen, Raven Wall and harder at Bosigran, some new routes too and all the old routes on the very same lovely rough Cornish holds that I had used four years before, and Marines for years before that and my father thirty years earlier. That particular romance would often occur to me as I climbed happily up 'course' routes such as Flannel Avenue at Chair Ladder, a climb that has so many holds you nearly fall off making your mind up which to use; or struggled up such as Genges Groove — always a struggle that groove — or ambled the glorious length of Commando Ridge at Bosigran, the sun setting into the sea behind. The romance: or is that sentimentality? I'll settle for either — both.

It was great to be back. Little had changed. Lucretia had left the petrol pumps, to get married, it was said; The Darts Team had fallen to third in the league but the rugby team was still bottom; The Miners Arms continued to operate inspite of the land's licensing laws, Jerome remained the village stud, sire of seventeen 'they do say', and Mr. Trelawny the village squire, sire to as many, 'they do say'. Best of all it was still 'Mornin' Captain John' and 'Mornin' Commandos' and 'ere waz on boys' in that thick Cornish accent, thick as clotted cream .

And Scrim was still Scrim. On the night before we left Sennen for Scotland, the Miners Arms threw a party. Because it was a special occasion they had applied to the Magistrates for an extension. It was granted. On not so special occasions they granted extensions to themselves. It was a nice difference, curiously important to the publican. Late on there was a crash. Scrim had collapsed, 'speared in'. He made several attempts to rise before subsiding. It wasn't that he minded being on the floor, it was that he'd left his drink on the bar.

'Pass ma drink doon. I cannie get up.' Scrim was back on form.

Next day he and I shared a Land Rover and the drive home to Arbroath in Scotland. We had a few days to spare so we stopped here and there to climb on the way. One such place was Malham Cove in Yorkshire. I knew that there was good climbing at the place; Scrim knew there was Theakstons.

134

The climb I was after was Carnage. I had read about it somewhere; had read that the first pitch was so loose that if you didn't like the holds you could throw them away. You could too; but I loved the holds, I love all holds, so I left them where they were. Scrim followed easily, as usual; indifferent, as usual. I set out on the second pitch which, like much limestone, was steep and strenuous. The top is a perfect right angle, plumb vertical to immediately flat horizontal. By the time I got both hands on the top edge the strength in hand and arm was fleeing fast. I used most of the last of it to perform what I hoped was the final pull up, grunting with effort and sweating with heat.

But I wasn't alone, not at that place nor in my grunting and sweating. There before me, as I hung, chin hooked over the horizontal for some extra support, two utterly naked bodies, *in flagrante delicto*, heaved and groaned, snarled and moaned in spectacular toe-curling abandon; those two sets of curled toes not more than a foot from my face and the epicentre of the passion not further than four urgently bent and straining legs away; gynaecologically glorious. Such was their transport that they were unaware of my intrusion. I was confused — I think that's the word — and lowered to arms' length again to consider the alternatives. I didn't want to fall. It was a longish way to my last runner and there was never any guarantee that Scrim's casual belaying would bear the test — or even that he was awake. Looking down I could see that he was in fact rolling a ciggy: a two handed job. Better not to fall. Climbing down was out of the question. So would climbing up again if I didn't get a move on.

The last of my arm strength went in the next pull-up. Great wild cries of mutual encouragement were being hurled just above and I borrowed from which advised — or was it a command? — push, push, push, while I pulled, pulled, pulled.

Chin-hook again. The briefest pause. Now they were joined with an urgency that advertised as far as the high sun that their moment was not far off. Nor was mine, I could hang on no longer and rolled over onto that grassy lovers' bed to lie inertly, *coitus interruptus* while I caught my breath and tried to think of something suitable to say. The *interruptus* was sudden and terrible. The man, by far the most embarrassed of the two — though it was a close thing between he and I — rolled to the cover of a boulder like a shot soldier, from where, keeping his head down, he reached out long arms and legs for appropriate bits of clothing. Great indeed must the passion have been for these bits were widely spread.

Try as I might the *mot juste* wouldn't come so I set about belaying as if it was the most natural thing in the world — which as every climber knows, it isn't. The girl wandered about picking up the scattered tatters of her clothes, flicking the important male garments to her mate behind the boulder, chatting the while, as if she had been engaged in the most natural thing in the world — which, of course, she had.

She asked what I was doing, a question I hardly needed to ask in return, and I tried to explain about rock climbing, about the rope, about belaying and about Scrim who'd be arriving any second. I have always found it difficult to give a purely verbal explanation of how the game of rock climbing is played, even when the audience is fully clothed and sitting comfortably. I doubt that my explanation this day left my naked inquisitor or her floundering mate much the wiser. The circumstances were unusual.

By the time Scrim appeared the lass was wandering away in her underthings, shoes in one hand, a bundle of clothing under the other arm; her mate, averted eyes alternating between heaven and earth, lamely behind. Scrim was impressed.

'See yon's a wee stotter-an' in her knickers an' that.' And I was able to say, long before President Reagan was fed the line and for reason he's never had, 'You ain't seen nothing yet!'

All the way up the A74 Scrim pressed for details. I fed him as frugally as I thought would satisfy his puritanical Glaswegian prurience.

'How come they didna hear you,' he had an ear for detail did Scrim, 'you was gruntin' like a pig.'

I tried to explain their joint enthusiasm and consequent oblivion.

'Well, you know Scrim, they were going, er, they were going — em — hammer and tongs?' The last words were inflexioned — it was more a question than answer and it was not nearly vivid enough for Scrim.

'You mean they was rutting like crazed weasels.' Scrim was a country boy at heart, and vivid were his similes.

There are other ways to make rock climbing interesting. Take this little foray on Red Wall at Anglesey, for example. Just to get the history straight I had by this time left the Royal Marines for the job of Director of the National Centre for Mountain Activities at Plas y Brenin, Capel Curig — the heart of Snowdonia and the world's best rock playground.

One afternoon in late autumn I arrived home just after five to find that a friend had called, largely, to show off his new, astonishingly fast, limmo. I admired it over the top of a cup of tea while he did a Raymond Glendenning on its virtues, not least of which were that it accelerated from 0-60 mph faster than you could say 'climb when you're ready' and that it exceeded 120 mph more easily than 'Barry exceeds 4C'. Pat Parsons was a Marine and insults his chief form of humour.

'Fancy a quick route mate?' It was an Indian evening, perfect for a warming-down route at the season's end.

'Sure. Whadya fancy?'

'Red Wall. Never done it. You?'

'Nope, but it's forty miles away — Gogarth. It'll be dark in three hours.'

'NFP in this wagon. Heading west, catch the sun. Be there before we started. Forty-five minutes at most.'

We headed for Gogarth, into the sun and an epic that would have earned an entry in Homer's diary.

Castell Helen was bathed in *alpengloh,* or a very good North Wales imitation, faithful enough to seduce us, at this late hour, into shorts and vest. First mistake. Second actually. The first was leaving Capel Curig. We decided to scramble down to the start. Third mistake. The scramble is harder than anything on the route and takes far longer than the alternative, the abseil — however unappetising that may look from above. Pat led off on the first pitch. It would be unchivalrous to describe this as the fourth mistake, but after an eternity that extinguished the *gloh,* he belayed to a rusty old peg that protruded 90% of its length. And from that peg he hung, twenty feet above the recommended belay, at the crux of the second pitch.

It was becoming cold. And dark. Very cold and very dark. As I climbed it began to hail — great big balls of them. No, I couldn't believe it either! Soon this descent, fit-for-family-viewing, perfectly pedestrian HVS was all togged up in Grade 5

137

winter clothing — which is more than could be said for the protagonists who were better dressed for a 1500 metres — and track spikes would have been a sight more useful than rock-boots on this stuff.

At the belay, I hesitate to call it a stance, Pat suggested that we could abseil off. But a night ascent of the 'scramble' down appealed even less than the merely vertical horror above. I swung up — on the peg of course — and for five minutes stood on it, while Pat hung from it, nothing else between us and rock but three inches of hail. Shorts and vest, seventy feet above the sea, wrist-deep hail, stygian dark; what a mess.

Now as every sailor and benighted Gogarth 'crag rat' knows the South Stack light flashes one second in every ten. Thus I was permitted a lighted move every ten seconds. Admiralty Chart Number 1411 says so. A grotesque disco-dance by the light of a mighty but intermittent stroke ensued; the big difference was that my own intermittency was no optical illusion, no trick of light; it was fact. Forced frozen immobility for ten seconds. A second's light; a frantic clearing of hail, a search for a hold, a lurch, a move, a foot gained. Darkness. Ten seconds of it, a recurring ten second sentence, serving time until another one second shot. Quick lit move, longer black wait; quick lit move, longer black wait; quick lit move; longer black wait. The only thing that could be said for the white stuff was that in serving as a giant reflector it made best advantage of South Stack's candlepower. For seventy feet I fancied myself in *Fame* — Leroy perhaps, *Flashdance* maybe.

'More like Quasimodo,' Pat said later as we shivered the ropes into coils of sorts.

'Flashed up that, eh.' The pun was lost in the dark.

But I am conscious that thus far I might be accused of not doing the rock climbing game justice, and that might be fair comment. Therefore, because I do love the game, even if I'm not so good at it as I'd like to be (but then, who is?) let me take one of my favourites and try to do that justice. I'll settle for T. Rex, at Gogarth again, for no other reason than that it is a very good climb — which is the only reasonable excuse, other than a laugh that may have been extracted on the way, that I can think of for writing more than a line or two at most, on a few hundred feet of rock.

Let me do the right thing by T.Rex. I'll go formal for a bit, and quote the guide book. *The Climbers Club guide for Gogarth (1977)* by Alec Sharp.

> 'T. Rex 370 feet. Extremely Severe (1969). A magnificent route up the back of the zawn. Beautiful and varied climbing in excellent positions make this one of the finest and most enjoyable (?) (my question) routes in Wales.
> Start: To the left of the rubble-filled chimney, below the over-hanging corner crack.
> 1. 90 feet. Climb the chimney then climb the crack to the small bulge. Move round this and up to a protection peg. Continue up the groove to a hanging stance and peg belay.
> 2. 40 feet. Follow the obvious traverse line right to a stance and peg belay on the slab.
> 3. 120 feet. Move left and climb the wall to the slab. Follow this to a protection peg under the roof. Climb down left to a protection peg, and step left round the corner. Traverse left then climb up to a stance and peg belays.
> 4. 120 feet. Climb up to A Dream of White Horses and traverse left along this to a protection peg. Climb the groove above and step right onto the wall. Follow the vague diagonal crack up right to the ledge in the niche. Climb up to the top on poor rock.'

And here's how that translates onto rock — a little story I'll call 'T. Rex; A song for Nige.'

Pleased as punch, I was, with my brand new, first ever chalk bag. And blizzard full it was too with the purest driven chalk you ever dipped your sticky fingers in. 'Much better than the usual stuff,' Nigel remarked as he made me a present of two great nuggets of the stuff — and himself something of a connoisseur. My own pleasure in these new toys was only slightly marred by a suspicion (since confirmed) that the gift was in the unspoken hope that such graceless antics as would surely constitute my subsequent progress (the uncharitable would say 'consequent') might be generally upwards.

There we were, eyeing up T.Rex across the Zawn. Nigel happily excited at the prospect of something 'reasonable' to loosen up on and quietly confident that, as ever, his general trend would be inexorably heavenward; I in the epicentre of an inner earth-quake beyond anything that Mr. Richter had ever imagined. As I force-fed another fistful into the already engorged bag Nigel rigged the abseil to the sea. Then he leapt, a controlled plummet and not a care in the world. I sensed athleticism of gold medal eagerness and wondered and worried for how much longer it could be caged at my pedestrian plod. In the seconds awaiting my turn I thrice checked the abseil anchors and struggled with invasions of doubt about my basic stratagem. This had been to enlist the services of a young hot-shot who knew nothing of the fear of failure or falling — let alone flying — tie on the end and enjoy the vicarious thrills of a route beyond ken or competence. Hence Nigel.

But somewhere down the A5 this plan had already 'ganged aglay'. I had been idly boasting of my 'off-width' prowess on a recent route — having only discovered the phrase the week before. 'Give me an off-width every time,' I said trying hard to impress with my trendiness — little realising that the first pitch of the thing he had in mind fell loosely into that category; or much worse, that I had unwittingly volunteered the lead. 'Wouldn't want to deny you the pleasure,' he insisted without conviction.

From the bottom of a stacatto abseil I tried to follow Nigel's gazelle gambol across the boulders to the chimney crack that is half of the first pitch. But my EBs — or their owner — lacked his seemingly cloven footed assurance and I fell into the sea drowning chalk bag and morale.

We roped up and he belayed — a bad sign. I had a look. To be sure it was a crack of sorts — almost a chimney — and if you looked quick it didn't overhang. I began. It does.

It was off-width all right. Off-everything unless you have a 46-inch arse — by which time you'd have graduated to climbing ice anyway.

Heck, what can you say about climbing off-widths? Try some technique. An arm, this way and that; a foot and a twist; a knee, a thigh, bum, back, head? They all work for a bit but in the end all the technique in the world puffs-out and you're back where you began — and knackered. So don't try to climb it. Do as Tom Patey advised years back; beat your chest, get the old jungle juices flowing and lose your temper. But lose it with care; and be sure you know where it is for you may have to find it before the belay. 'Raging Bull' all the way, no place this for 'Sugar Ray'.

Up again and fine while it lasts but 15 runnerless feet later it occurs that a fall onto something as insubstantial as Nigel would mean rather more than just a points defeat for us both. It occurs to Nigel too and he moves away leaving me to contemplate the ground and a near certain knockout. A right hook across the crack secures the torso in a clinch while a knee into T. Rex's groin takes care of all below the belt. Just above, a constriction flirts for a runner but it's a fickle feint and after a fruitless five-minute fumble it's seconds out for round two while there's still the strength to get off the stool.

Nigel, sheltering in a neutral corner, has closed his eyes. A heave, a feeble roar and a grunt bring the top of the chimney and an exquisite moac-sized slot so perfect it looks like something Michaelangelo might have knocked-off when warming up for David. The rage is spent, the bull bayed, progress punctured. I take a standing count but just manage not to lean on the ropes.

Round three is a rightwards move under an overhanging flake to the apparent sanctuary of a less than vertical groove. The flake shouts to be lay-backed but I have arrived right-arm in and so it shouts from behind. Glancing back my mind's eye weighs up the necessary moves in a fluid gymnastic sequence oozing power, grace and control. Something, says Nigel, was lost in the translation. For a moment, the entire world, or all of it that matters, is concentrated in the few square feet of rock to which I am addressing myself with enormous energy. The transfer, effected with a cataclysmic effort is, according to Nigel who, thanks to the runner, has by this time felt able to open his eyes, spectacular. Reach behind and ease out of the off-width. A scurry of feet. For a moment horizontal and feet too high, arms too tired, but a yell to fuel the fear and a mighty heave into the bosom of that groove.

At last the groove! But it's no sanctuary and I find little comfort there. Nor any rest. Fact is that it's strangely strenuous — but there's runners to be found and time to think. With token resistance the secrets surrender.

The pitch, round and fight, end in a choas of rusted pegs upon which Father Time and faltering ambition suggest I hang, there being no corner stool. Then, just as I am about to weave a belay, up pipes himself. 'Do the next pitch I'll take care of the last two,'

141

adding with the calculated casualness, 'It's the easy one.' Now there's temptation! A trade of one pitch for two much harder. But though it sounded a bargain it certainly didn't look it.

A traverse across an overhanging wall for fifty feet with no trace of grips or rest at any grade at all was about the last thing I felt like. But the chance of missing the two harder pitches beyond proved cowardice nine parts of my discretion while Nigel's mocking 'Surely you can handle that' ensured that the last tenth voted with its feet. Shame is a great motivator.

A dip in the chalk and I'd be off. The chalk! In my raging I had entirely forgotten it. Here it could work its magic and turn my traverse into a doddle. 'Chalk up,' I thought, in what I hoped was the language of afficionados, thrusting a hopeful hand into the dangling bag only to discover that the swim had turned my magic into Dulux. I had not, though, the courage left to demur and propelled on Nigel's withering gaze I crept to the traverse.

It's steep alright, and exhilaratingly exposed, but it's also all grips, rests and runners and honest VS. A dozen or so runners and forty feet later I pulled from the vertical onto a comfortinbly spacious ledge.

Hugely relieved that my troubles for this day were over, I leisurely belayed, lay back to contemplate the ocean and savoured my triumph — happy that in relinquishing the sharp end I could enjoy whatever technical intricacies that remained, 'actuated solely by the gentle moral suasion of the rope' — and, with luck, no more before a long rest No such luck! In thirty seconds Nigel had vaulted onto the stance, seized the rack and was fifteen feet up the third pitch. It was depressing to watch. He was all 'lance at rest' lissom, lithe and loose. He paused, Bolshoi-balanced, before a steepening which leads to a slab, then dismissed both with contemptuous continuous ease. Not even the decency of a grunt nor any other confession of effort. I could only respond to his poetry with doggerel — literally now, and later, when my turn came, metaphorically.

This way, that way, he ballet-it,
Every which way he a-played it,
Then all at once smooth Sugar Rayed it
Nice one Nigel.

At the top of the slab he stopped short, hard under a roof where, with the deftness of a card-sharp, a runner was arranged.

Then he started out left and, horrors, down. Down it is; some tricky stuff which elicited a reconnaissance, albeit perfunctory, even from Sugar Ray. This did little for my evaporating sense of joy. An obviously tricky pull, leftwards around a bulge, led to easy ground and the next belay.

My turn. I was unhappy. I had sold my birthright for two pitches and an easy passage but now the full implication of the downward moves were advancing upon my retreating morale.

The wall and slab extracted more than their fair share of calories but I managed to arrive under the roof still on my feet and with my wits about me — somewhere.

I found an old crab dangling from an older nut — both of which Nigel had disdained. It occurred that they had been sacrificed by a succession of seconds in my very predicament in order to afford top rope protection on the descent which followed. I toyed with the same idea but became confused in a tangle of rope tricks and, deciding that it was better to fall than to hang, I went down — climbing that is. It's the last move that gets you but you'll find the hold if you flain — and a lurch later you'll be bounding up to the belay as I was.

For the last pitch there is a choice of three. Out left along the final pitch of the 'Dream' offers a pleasantly straightforward finale. If you fancy another walk on the wild side there's the direct finish which is, I am told, harder than anything before. Or there's the original finish up steep loose rock. We, or rather Nigel, opted for the latter which turned out to be the least satisfying pitch of the climb. I'd recommend one of the others — but who cares? — you have already shared the secrets of T. Rex's soul. As Scrimgeour used to say, 'It's a wazzer.'

The doggerel drivelled on to the road;

> Then at last when he'd belayed it,
> It was my turn to essay it,
> Up I fought but bad betrayed it.
> Sorry Nigel.

> To yon peg I wildly flayed it;
> Strove to do as he'd displayed it,
> But quickly thought to 'frig' and aid it,
> Tight rope! Nigel.

Cross and down I barely made it
And up to Nige I tight-rope weighed it,
Till at last I gratefully sayed it,
Thank you Nigel.

Off he went and re-displayed it,
Bolshoi skill he lithe portrayed it
To the top at which I prayed it,
No more Nigel.

Lissom loose he quick O'kayed' it.
Gogarth's welcome don't overstay it.
But *what* a climb, sooth for to say it.
Good do, Nigel.

What follows is a tale of a climb that took two Barrys over forty years to complete. It is one of my best adventures and contains big shots of two ingredients for which I have a great, a hopelessly incurable weakness — sentiment and romance; and the story of it will be preserved for me in the sweet juices of those two things for all time. And as my father taught me to rock climb it is entirely fitting that I should close this chapter with an adventure that I shared with him. I'm not sure that it was a rock climb but it was that as well as it was anything else.

The best part of both tale and climb belong to my father and although it is a recent thing — December 1984 — it began long ago in September 1943 — before I was born. I had better explain. My father writes short stories, as will be seen, for fun. I caught him in the middle of one the other day, a story brought to his mind by the D Day landing Anniversary celebrations in June 1984. He had just told the tale of a night climbing demonstration on an Isle of Wight chalk cliff that had gone badly wrong, and as I read over his shoulder he continued:

'I can remember no comment, criticism or praise following that demonstration on Isle of Wight chalk but those who decided such matters didn't write us off for not long after-wards we were being briefed for a raid on a similar coast line in France near the Normandy Village of St. Pierre en Port, though I don't think we knew the name at the time. As

144

always we concentrated on any available intelligence, every man keen to learn every possible detail and none needing any spur to study. Such earnest application would have made scholars of us all in other circumstances and I particularly concentrated on finding a climbable line. Similar these cliffs might be but they were steeper too. They reminded me of a stretch of the Sussex coast in the Seven Sisters area and that comparison was to strike me more than once later.

I had never before attempted to choose a climbable route up a rock face from air reconnaissance pictures and to start with faces as formidable as these was something of a gamble. So when we finally decided on two apparent weaknesses in those French walls I couldn't but wonder how dependable such a judgement might be. Not that my wondering ever affected my keenness to tackle the climb, nor that there was ever any slightest diminution of enthusiasm for the operation among our party. In these times of peace it is surprising to recall that eagerness for action. By luck the two possibly possible routes which the stereoscope showed after long and careful study as the best hopes, the only hopes, were just about as conveniently far from the village as might give us a chance to make a landing undetected. And land one night we eventually did on a high tide, so high we disembarked on a shingle bank close under those lofty cliffs which then, daunting barriers though they looked and might be, offered cover for our arrival. By this time dories had engines so, needing no rowers or paddlers, could return to the parent craft. Ours disappeared into the night.

Sergeant Major Sam Broadison went immediately off with 'Smithy' (Lieutenant Smith) on a reconnaissance towards the break in the cliffs by which the villagers (as would the Germans if they were to come looking for us) gained access to beach and sea. Some of our small party stowed our gear in the undercliff while I, with others in support, went looking for the nearer and — as we thought then — the more promising of our two possible climbing lines. We were none too sure that we had actually found it for the cliff at night bore only a general resemblance to the photographs but it was, we thought, about the right place, there was a discernible weakness in the wall and anyway the first few feet were climbable. I started up.

145

At somewhere between fifteen and thirty or so feet I came on a bulge that had not showed up on the photographs, a bulge which, however slight, at first slowed and then stopped me. My hands found small holds which would have been ideal if the chalk there had not been so friable (again just like a stretch of the Sussex cliffs) that one by one they broke off as soon as I tried them. I'd climbed pitches far more overhung than that bulge just for fun. This one was seriously important. I pressed on. But steep rock can only be climbed on sound holds and the steeper it is the greater the importance of that soundness. In a few moves I was beaten, and in a position of delicate balance too, because the face arched out slightly over my head. Try how I might I could find no usable rugosity that didn't break off when I leaned on it, I hadn't much faith in those on which I stood and an overhang in the dark, even a slight one, tends to be a stopper.

Because of the bulge or the dark or both, my comrades were out of sight, and even beneath those cliffs we were loath to call out to each other in enemy territory. (Perhaps had I been able to see them I would be less vague about my height at the time.) Anyway I was beaten and there was nothing for it but to retreat and use the remainder of the night to try elsewhere. But I found I couldn't climb down either. The awkward balance, the crumbly chalk and the dark combined to make downward movement difficult and that despite all the night climbing practice I'd had. Where to put one's feet became yet another in that mixture of hazards. It was a lonely place.

I had two of the angle iron pitons. How or where I carried them I've forgotten but they were on my person somewhere and my only hope seemed to depend on fixing one in the cliff and going down a rope attached to it. Fingers as much as eyes felt for a fissure as well as balance permitted — and found one. I pushed the angle iron point into the crevice and the chalk crumbled. I tried another time or two, driving one piton into the face by hammering it with the other. It was difficult to hammer with any force while my stance was so insecure and each time the piton failed when tested. Eventually one held. It inspired little trust but I had little choice. I made fast the rope as close to the rock as possible, gently,

gently started down hand under careful hand, keeping the rope close to the cliff and holding my breath at each move — no dancing abseil, no slightest outward lean, no spectacular earthward swoop, no exhilarating exhibitionism as was often my wont in training — feet feeling hopefully for holds I couldn't see. An age later muted voices embraced me from a height little less than mine and I dropped the last foot or two. As my feet touched the ground there was a metallic sound and the piton with the rope still attached touched down beside them.

Smithy and Sam had returned. They'd been fired on where the cliff gave way to the village and I hadn't heard the shots. It might have been sub-machine gun fire lost in the moan of the sea or cliff acoustics or I might have been so absorbed in my own plight that I never heard it. Though I'd been careful not to call out to my mates at the bottom I'd made all that noise without thought (or with only thought for my own danger). To them the hammering had sounded dangerously loud.

At the bottom of chalk sea cliffs there is often a mound of debris, an accumulation of fallen rock that parallels closely the base of the cliff like a low wall. Probably the steeper and more crumbly the chalk the more pronounced is this linear mound so that a sort of ditch is formed between debris and cliff face, and this one offered a convenient hollow. In that ditch, partially sheltered by an overhang, we sheltered for what was left of the night, ate, slept, woke and breakfasted — for we'd brought rations. The night may have been warm and years of training may have hardened us for we slept in the clothes we wore without other protection. We slept well too.

In the morning all was quiet, any chance of the Germans patrolling a beach below such massive tide washed ramparts seemed unlikely and any possibility of their coming upon us by surprise, non-existent. The undercliff, the ditch between debris wall and cliff base made a good hiding place for all of us and all our gear and from it a sentry could overlook the beach for some distance in both directions while himself hidden. A couple of us looked for and found, or thought we'd found, the second of our possible routes and were heartened to find that it looked more promising than the first. It went better too so that I got as far as maybe one hundred feet of careful movement before I was stopped again.

This line went up a wide indentation, too shallow and too wide to be called a chimney but offering a perhaps possible climb in an otherwise impossible wall. From my stance on a little ledge I now faced a pitch to which I could find no answer though the rock just above that pitch looked less difficult. I dragged up a light bamboo ladder we had brought for just such an emergency and Nashy, my helper for the day, came up to my stance too. We placed the ladder against the wall with its feet on our little stance and the little Brummagem irrespressible held it there while I, delicately using both ladder and cliff, went on to another small stance. This one felt overcrowded by two pairs of feet (though Nashy's couldn't have taken up much room) but it gave my partner some security while I climbed on until I was beaten again. Although we spent the day on it we hadn't made it by dusk and were forced to descend. I drove in a piton and made fast but took the strain myself while Nashy went down using the rope as little as possible. The rope we used was too thick for abseiling but we had all grown accustomed to descending with fair speed and more than fair safety. Indeed on an easier gradient we could run down as fast as a man could abseil but now Nashy went down slowly and carefully, remembering my insecurity. Then I followed him trying not to use the rope at all.

While we'd climbed, the beach behind took on yet another likeness to that Sussex coast for as the tide went out it withdrew from a band of shingle at the cliff base to reveal a floor of flat chalk slabs, so flat the sea appeared to retreat for a great distance, leaving shallow pools here and there among the slabs. We'd seen just such a beach in Sussex but here the village men appeared, followed the tide out and searched the pools for, presumably, some kind of shellfish. Whether they also had fishing boats and were perhaps forbidden to use them by the German invaders we never learned but as the water receded so they appeared and busied themselves among the pools far along the beach and away out to the low tide line, distant black clad figures going industriously about their business with never, it seemed, a glance for the cliffs where our party hid and where two of us climbed all day.

On the way out to and back from the pools a few passed close to the section of undercliff where our party hid and they, seizing their chance, grabbed one of the fishermen who walked on his own. One of the our group, a Free French Basque, acting as interpreter, they questioned the captured fishermen who fortunately turned out to be a loyal collaborator and not, as the term usually implied at the time, a traitor to his country. Though unable to give much information himself he undertook to send someone who could be more helpful on the following day. Number two turned up as promised. He was a patriot whose first sentence was a request for a rifle and though we couldn't give him that he gave us information about enemy troops in the area. He said, too, that the narrow break in the cliffs by which he and his mates gained access to the beach was always guarded, night and day, so that we stood no chance of bypassing the cliffs by that route. Both Frenchmen kept our presence from the Germans though they passed the enemy sentry coming and going. As these contacts, compulsory and voluntary, were made when I was climbing — or trying to climb — I saw neither Frenchmen.

We renewed our assault on the wall next morning.

Some way up that shallow indentation, far enough to arouse optimism, I reached an impasse again. I could see or sense that the top was near and the adrenalin flowed. The unclimbable pitch was this time longer than the ladder when I'd hauled it up again. I cut its every rung in two so that I had two poles each with a floppy bit of rung at intervals, then lashed the two poles together with a light line carried for belays and so had a single pole one and three quarter times the length of the original ladder. Each coil of the lashing I pulled as tightly as my strength allowed for much was to depend on it, then brought up my helper (which one was with me then I can't remember) to hold this new climbing aid against the smooth wall, its bottom end resting on the ledge at his feet.

It stayed there surprisingly well and very carefully I climbed its length, one hand on the pole. It made just the vital difference. At that time I was confident that I could climb anything man could climb and by the standards of the day that may have been a justifiable opinion. In terms of nerve strain the pitch was as hard as any I had climbed, perhaps the hardest but, to my disappointment, a disappointment that has stayed with me ever since, it was not enough.

Now I could see the cliff top tantalizingly near, some ten to fifteen feet above my head but between the top and me was a pitch bearing a remarkable resemblance to the walls of my terrace home in Patrick Street. Those walls had once been pebble dashed but had been pasted with so many layers of whitewash that the spaces between the pebbles had filled leaving a surface of smooth little bumps with no break or depth between them. The cliff there looked rather like that, of similar colour and offering no hope of toe or finger hold anywhere. It may or may not have been as steep as the house walls but it was just as unclimbable.

Whether I tried cutting steps with my earth axe, which was an ice axe with a shortened handle, I can't remember but I didn't make it anyway and was forced to retreat which wasn't easy either. Did any German then or any Frenchman since ever look over, I wonder, and see my piton in that virgin chalk?

Every climber meets defeat at times if he has only an iota of initiative or a spark of daring and if he manages to retreat without a fall it is seldom a matter of great disappointment, or not for long. But the defeat I met that day has never wholly left me. It was such an opportunity. We knew there was no habitation near the top and though we'd been careful to speak no louder than necessary while climbing there was a reasonable chance that no patrol followed closely the top of what must have seemed an impassable barrier. Or if a patrol did pass that way there would probably be a lengthy interval between any two. An army with so much on its mind would be likely to concentrate on the more obvious danger points. Those ten feet or so separated us from the possibility of a piton camouflaged under a turf, from a back door into occupied France and the failure was mine though no one ever hinted at that fact.

Later that disappointment was recalled with more regret

150

when we developed a light hand-thrown, five toothed grapnel which, attached to a light knotted line, proved effective in similar circumstances and would almost certainly have been the answer to that last pitch.

Rejoining our comrades at the cliff bottom we learned that what I had begun to think of as the Barry spell was still malevolently active. We had brought ashore with us a couple of carrier pigeons as a means of communication that would not be as easily detected as wireless waves. These had been released earlier only to have the English pigeons killed by French hawks even as they soared to start for home.

The M.T.B. was coming to collect us that night so we had no more time to spend on the cliff. Major Fynn, the officer in charge of the operation decided to try an approach to the village by its front door, the break in the cliffs, or rather to redeem our failure by capturing the sentry or sentries who guarded that front door. The tide was high and still rising so that only the band of sloping shingle was left above the water and silent movement on shingle is difficult, if not impossible. However carefully a foot is lifted, however carefully placed, it makes a noise. Fourteen feet — Jack Ure stayed behind to guard our stores — sounded very loud, carefully and slowly though we moved, loud enough to be heard by the sleepiest sentry. Every few minutes we'd stop and listen and each time the silence that met our ears was a relief. Then we'd start again, the sea near and nearing on our left, the cliff on our right and shatter the silence with the crunching brattle of feet on shingle. Between sea and cliff lay the strait way. We had no option but to use that narrow aisle.

At one stop the officers in front conferred in whispers, decided that we had no hope of success. We started back along the narrow, noisy route by which we had come. It was a decision with which I had no argument. Only deaf men could have failed to hear our coming.

The dory came in about the right time and at the right place good work on the part of those responsible for the M.T.B. and in the smaller boat. We waded out. This time the tide must have been at its highest. The shingle bank at the high tide mark above that flattest of shores sloped fairly steeply as is usual in coasts open to the ocean, so we got rather wet in surrounding the brave wee boat and scrambling in. I was at the seaward end. My feet had just parted company from the bottom and I'd made a grab for the gunwale when a hand came down over the side to catch mine and help me in, no word spoken. I can't remember feeling tired or hearing any talk of fatigue which says something for our fitness. I could probably have climbed in without help, would certainly not have asked for it and have no idea who helped me but that hand coming down in the dark has stayed in my memory, a symbol of the comradeship we enjoyed in those days, the comradeship of men I can never forget.'

And so it was that I was seized by the daftest notion. Why didn't we, father and son, go back and finish the job. I put it to Dad. He was greatly taken with the suggestion but worried that if we got up easily — and it troubled him that we might — then our 1984 success would show that he had failed to alter the course of history when he held the fate of Europe in his hands in 1943. He would never forgive himself — even if history did.

'Never mind Dad,' I said, 'we still won.'

Once I had brushed this misgiving aside he was easy meat for a scheme so daft, so sentimental, so romantic. He obtained a temporary passport from the post office — he hadn't been abroad for over 30 years — and we were ready to go.

The pill box at St. Pierre en Port still overlooked the slipway. I'm not sure what else I expected but it wasn't 300-foot high, vertical chalk cliffs. They were as uninviting, as unappetising as any cliffs I have seen. The first afternoon we conducted a recce along the beach. Dad could not recall exactly how far from the village the lines of his earlier attempts lay, but he thought it could not be more than a mile. We searched for the line, I with the perspective of an '84 eye, Dad with a '39 eye and on the lookout for something that jogged his memory. He found nothing certain, although could make two or three bits fit his recollection's jigsaw. In four miles I saw but two lines that in my judgement offered any hope at all. The rest, for as far as the eye could see was hopeless — a vast white expanse of chalky hopelessness, seldom anywhere less than vertical, often overhanging, always unappealing. I told Dad firmly that there were only two possibilities and that of the two the right-hand was the more reasonable. That, I informed him was the one he had nearly succeeded on in 1943. I couldn't believe, wouldn't believe there was any other way. If there was in 1943 then either the climbing standards of the day were immeasurably higher than now or something dramatic had happened to the cliff — and since neither seemed all that likely we were going to settle for the best line we had — a sort of gully. Indeed, set in the surrounding whiteness, it looked not unlike a steep Nevis winter gully. I had to be firm, Dad's imagination knew no gravity — it soared everywhere, up anything, and would take us in its slipstream if I wasn't careful. He hadn't climbed for many years which was a considerable advantage.

I inspected the rock in detail. It was soon apparent that it was unclimbable by conventional means. Such holds as existed were flint pebbles embedded in soft chalk. They looked good but about ninety per cent of those that I tested pulled out with little more persuasion than a tug. Not very encouraging. The flints apart, there were no holds, the rock was as smooth as alabaster, and not unlike it in general appearance too. How my father had climbed upwards of 200 feet of it forty years before I could not imagine. It was inconceivable; literally that.

Dusk. We returned to the car at the slipway where I uncovered my secret weapons — ice axes, crampons — and all the paraphanalia of modern ice climbing: ice screws, drive-in ice pitons, the lot. I put on a pair of mountain boots, strapped on crampons, took up a couple of ice axes, all strangers to the shore, and addressed myself to a nearby chunk of chalk. There had been a couple of articles in the climbing press in the last year about a new climbing game — chalk-cliff climbing at Dover, Beachy Head and such — using ice-climbing gear. I wanted, needed, to see for myself how well it worked. It worked well; as long as the chalk was right. A bit like ice. There was good chalk, firm yet compliant, like névé or white ice; felt safe, felt good. There was soft chalk, too soft, so that the axes pulled through when your weight came on them — like bad, soft snow.

There was hard chalk, so hard it took half a dozen blows per axe to effect any penetration; like the hardest, the coldest of ice. This was exhausting and nerve wracking. Then there was impossible chalk; either so loose or so obdurate as to be useless — one way or the other. The recce and trials were over.

153

We returned the next day and, as soon as the tide allowed, walked along to the start of our gully. I accoutred myself for the fray, strapped a pair of crampons onto Dad, devoted thirty seconds to showing him what to do with two axes, bade him hold the rope and set off.

I was stopped short after fifteen feet by an overhang, a 3-foot roof. So far the chalk had been as good as the best Scottish white ice. I spent some minutes trying to place a 'drive-in' above the overhang for protection for an attempt to surmount it, before flailing at it ineffectively for a few seconds. Dad was not impressed with his son's front-pointing.

'Why don't you try the other side?'

Dad's eye for a line was forty years better than mine. On the other side of the gully a ramp led across to a point above the overhang — and all at a comparatively gentle angle of about sixty degrees. Returning to the beach I cramponed *pied à plage* through the shingle to the right-hand side of our gully. The chalk was névé good here too and in fifteen minutes I was hammering in a couple of good 'drive ins' for a sound belay. Pitch I; seventy feet. So far so good. Dad followed easily enough, remarking that he could feel why ice climbers frequently made mention of aching calves, to the belay, where I tied him on in the sort of one-foot-side-on-stance typical of winter climbing.

The next pitch was an overhanging groove, about thirty feet long, and composed of rotten-looking ice — sorry chalk. Ten feet; a screw for protection. Five feet more. Nothing more. I could get no higher.

'Perhaps this is where you used the ladder Dad.'

'Could be.'

I tried to climb it. Hopeless. Blocks of chalk rained down on helmeted Dad fifteen feet beneath — the world's heaviest spindrift. I tried to fight it, Scottish winter style. Hopeless. The axes just wouldn't stay and, several tons of avalanched chalk later I retreated five feet to the screw.

'Why don't you try that slab to the right?' Dad with the veteran's eye for the line again. I glanced over. Sure enough there was a wedge of a better looking substance to the right and it looked as if I might be able to follow it to the top, then traverse horizontally left, back into the gully. It struck me that although we were generally following the gully we weren't actually climbing it —

rather only returning to it for the comfort of belays.

I set off, thirty feet to the bottom of Dad's slab. It was made of the hard stuff. A dozen blows and I had two axes implanted; pin pricks. Pull up. Don't like this a bit. Down for a rest. The 'slab' overhung by several degrees.

'Hey Dad, this isn't a slab. It's an overhang.'

'Sorry Son, I'm a bit rusty on the nomenclature.'

Up again, axes in the same holes. One axe out, crampons sparking on flint, bang, whack. Left arm knackered. Too tired for a good strike. Down. Swap holes, up again, right arm striking. Bang, whack, bang, whack, bang, bang, bang. No good — no go. Down again.

'Can't do it Dad.'

'Thought you said vertical ice was no problem with modern axes, these droopy things.' I had said that but what could I say now except that I wished I hadn't.

There wasn't much sentiment or romance left in me by this stage — or fight, and I was ready to believe that our elders were our betters still.

But one more go. I'd give it one more go to try to avoid disappointment, to try to prevent a silly thing becoming sillier. And to hell with ethics — whatever they are on this sort of climb. If they'd been defined, well heck, I'd redefine them. Chalk climbing was too young a game for rules — and a fig for them whatever they were. I had three drive-ins on me and used them all to gain ten feet. Standing in the topmost I looked down at Dad. He was holding the rope loosely in a hand as a schoolkid might hold the end of a skipping rope.

'Dad, d'you think you could belay me?'

'I am.'

'No hold the rope.'

'I am.'

'No, around the body.'

He passed the rope around his back, but still no twists. Clearly that was as good as I was going to get.

The traverse left was harder than any ice climb of my acquaintance. The rock was still slightly overhanging and reluctant to accommodate my axes even when introduced by the wildest of blows. At my wits end, certainly at my strength's end, I lunged for a big flint with my left hand, axe dangling. It plopped out and

155

I swung rightwards onto the planted axe. Surely I was off; done, for. No. There was a hole where the flint had been and the left axe found it true and stuck — on something — I know nor care not what. A desperate waggle to remove the right axe, a swing left, please hold Mr axe, please stay a while; a scrabble, sparks, an across-the-body lunge with the right axe, feet in view now, angle easing, chalk softening — the gully.

I had climbed three sides of a box to get there, perhaps ninety feet to gain thirty in height. But how to belay, where to belay? I had no ice pitons of any sort left; after all five was as many as I carried anywhere, and there were no natural belays and nothing that my nuts or rock pegs would look at.

Above, the gully led to a cave, eighty feet higher. I led on hoping to find a belay, the least suggestion of one would have done. Nothing. Eighty feet of grade 3 Scottish led to the Cave. Surely there would be something here. Nothing. Above lay a chimney and after that another overhanging corner that looked as if it led to friendlier ground.

I shouted to Dad. He couldn't hear under the overhangs. I noticed it was getting dark. Then it was dark. Dad and I were lonely, separately lonely and I was afraid.

My sense of the ridiculous was breaking new ground. I had to get to a bar to reconsider this whole thing, get it into some sort of perspective, historical or otherwise, invent some new word for dafter than daft, a word to equal this lunacy. But how to get to that bar? The nearest one was a mile away. It may as well have been on the moon. And there was the moon. Oh the romance of it, the bloody moon!

Feeling around in the dark I found a sturdy flint — a couple of clouts told me that. I daren't test it any harder in case it failed. There might not be another. I clove-hitched a sling to it, clipped in the rope and abseiled into the night trying to weigh as light as possible.

Free in black space I thought, 'what the hell am I doing here, we're forty years late anyway.'

'Ah! there you are Son. I was getting worried.' Soon the ground and a moonlit boulder-hop back to the car.

In any other circumstances I would have felt fully justified in calling it a day and going home. But there were peculiar perhaps unique, psychological forces at play. The sentimentality, romance if you like, a terrible fear of disappointing and that half-realisation that surrender would make this crazy thing crazier. And anyway there's 'No Surrender' in our part of the world.

Back the next day to jumar up to that chicken-headed flint — I'd left the rope in place. Perhaps I knew all along. A quick lesson in jumaring for Dad and between us we just beat the lapping tide. Dad was not impressed by the flint.

'I'm glad you didn't tell me about that last night.'

I wished I had, we might have gone home — an abandoned rope would have been small tax on sanity. The chimney was OK. Flints stayed, flints went, but enough held firm — usually the ones at the back that seized on loops in the rope and folds in clothes and held tight until you had ripped free or plucked them out. The overhanging groove above was rotten — grade five and no mistake. Then a lovely big grassy arete and a grass-plod for a hundred feet to the top. Forty years in the climbing — forty years late.

Dad said, 'That was much more frightening than the real thing.'

'Real thing, the real thing?' They've some strange standards these old timers.

There was a pillbox nearby. It reminded me. 'How were you going to get the prisoner down?'

'Arm over arm down the rope with him on my back.'

'Did it occur to you that he might not want to go?'

'No, never thought of that. I was a strong lad.'

Dad is now a lad of 67. Over 100 years between us. Really! We were old enough to know better. Mum said that.

157

5

Britain

SLICES OF SNOW,
CHUNKS OF ICE

I wish to dedicate this chapter to Scrimgeour, without whom much of it would not exist. There was, of course, no such soldier; and yet there was. Happy Scrim, sad Scrim, loveable Scrim, hateful Scrim, Corporal Scrim, Sergeant Scrim, round and scamp Scrim, lean and mean Scrim, hag and hungry Scrim, scrag and scurrilous Scrim, svelte and silver-tongued Scrim; he is the personification of all that I loved about the Royal Marines and its fine soldiers; and of the Mountain and Arctic Warfare Cadre in particular. He is everyone from Ginger Allen to Tosh Macdonald; Don MacLeod to 'Chopper' Young — the whole lovely alphabetical lot of them.

If I told you that every winter, as the police, the Rescue Services and AA are issuing radio bulletins warning of arctic conditions on the hills and atrocious road conditions, and as 99% of the population reach for blankets, salt, antifreeze and the central heating switch — that at the very same time the other 1% are rubbing their hands, sharpening crampons and honing axes in gleeful anticipation that the event will be at least as severe and as long as the predictions, you'd be inclined, though in this case without justification, to suspect that I'd taken leave of my senses.

And doubtless it would be stretching the limits of your credulity, if I went on to suggest that some of that 1% will tumble into their cars come finish of work on Friday, that they'll drive through the night, to places as remote as Glencoe or Fort William where after an hour's sleep, or two, they'll stumble through bog and wind and weather for up to a further three hours, fight their way up an unseen gully on some northern arctic scarp for anything up to another ten to an as likely as not benighted summit from where a viewless descent leads — with a little skill and a lot of luck — back to the road, the car and, if there's time, a pint. More of the same the next day and a long crash back for work Monday morning.

And if you believe that you'll never swallow this: that those of us who pursue this brutal pleasure love it, think of little else those long winter months, spend most (sometimes more) of their money in its pursuit, go back for more each year and — strangest of all — can't really understand why other folk think it all a bit odd.

These British winter pleasures are esoteric indeed. Sometimes they are purely retrospective too — and sometimes, even then, only with assistance of copious alcohol! Which may be the reason why winter climbers have so much difficulty explaining the reason why.

My own winter climbing career began in 1973. I had been appointed to command the Mountain and Arctic Warfare Cadre in December of the previous year. It was the best job in the world; I thought so at the time and have done nothing since that has caused me to change my mind. The Cadre was under the command of 45 Commando Royal Marines who were located at Arbroath, Scotland. I reported to my new CO Lieutenant Colonel Sir Stuart Pringle Bt. (later to suffer the loss of a leg in an IRA bombing). He knew me well from Singapore days. This was a pity — though after two years of luck and largely undetected crime I had made up most of the lost ground.

'Good to see you again, John.' He lied with considerable grace and near conviction.

'Good to be here, Sir,' I said, truthfully

'We're all off to Norway for two months in January — I'm a bit worried that your arctic skills may have rusted in Singapore,' he stated truthfully.

'Oh don't worry about that, Sir, I'm on the ball and right up to date,' I lied.

Somehow I got by, that first winter in Norway. The next two winters were easy by comparison. But at the end of the first winter I suffered a reverse that could have brought a premature end to my soldiering career. At the time many opined that it should.

We, the M & AW Cadre that is, were based at a part-time Norwegian Army barracks at the little village of Bjerka, more or less in the middle of nowhere — the nearest place of note being

159

the Arctic Circle. It was a great time for a philistine. All day —
and some nights — on skis, mountains to live on, snow to live in,
Lapps to linger with; whisky (duty free 15 shillings a bottle) and
£6 a day Local Overseas Allowance to cover the added cost of
living in this expensive place. Major Nick Vaux, who was later to
distinguish himself in the Falklands with a DSO, was our local
boss. He was Bonaparte reborn, a slave driver, a big wee man.
We feared him — and loved him. In his ferocious and tender care
— if you knew him you'd realise that it was a perfectly simple
matter to be both at once — we worked hard and long; played
short, sharp and almost as hard. The result: we were a happy
few, a band of brothers — though fraternity wasn't always the
most obvious feature of our daily intercourse.

One morning Nick summoned me. He was in a foul temper.
No particular reason — it was morning — reason enough for the
big wee man; and our Boney being a warrior, none of us were big
enough to think that unfair. Besides, as I have said, we loved
him.

'You sent for me Sir.'

'Yes. There's an important Norwegian General visiting next
week and a whole bunch of civilian hangers on — MPs and
buggers like that. It's all very sensitive, us all the way up here
and the Ruskies up the road. We are to entertain them. I want
you to lay on a 'demo'. Something interesting; something they
won't have seen before. What's it going to be?'

There was no use protesting that two seconds was scarcely
time enough to think of something suitable for so sensitive a
visit, but it happened that we'd been working on a way to escape
from frozen lakes and rivers in the event of the ice breaking
under us as we crossed. This was always a worrying possibility in
winter warfare especially in Norway where the temperatures
could fluctuate between $+5°C$ and $-30°C$ in the space of a
week. No other European army seemed to have an answer — we
never thought to ask the Russians — so we had been devising one
for ourselves. It was a pretty simple drill but I thought it might
impress. Nick thought so too, adding, unnecessarily given the
fond fear in which we held him,

'It'd better be good and spectacular — and no cock ups.' This
was Nick's little *pour encourager les autres*.

Spectacular it was most certainly. Good it was certainly not.

160

I briefed the boys and we set to with a will. After two full days of frozen practice the nearby lake was pocked with holes that the Cadre's more senior members had hacked for the more junior to ski into.

Slowly and, for the victims painfully, we worked up a drill slick enough to impress the most hard-nosed of Generals. Trial and error was the style, or 'trial and terror' as one young Corporal, a frequent 'volunteer' described it.

Time came for a dress rehearsal. It was the day before the real thing. By this time we were well organised: a fresh, unswum lake, a red-taped dais for the dignitaries, a warming tent for the victims, a loudspeaker system for me to pronounce upon and all kinds of signals — radio, semaphore and everything in between to ensure clockwork precision. Nothing had been left to chance; we had even pre-split the ice the night before to ensure that the demonstration patrol would break through. Then we had sprinkled the whole area with loose fresh snow to cover cracks, tracks and damage. The dress rehearsal went beautifully until the patrol reached the pre-split spot; one by cringing one they skied across it without so much as a quiver of recognition from the ice. It had frozen hard and solid over night. But what to do? We couldn't risk this happening again on the day. Repairing to the Cadre store, we held a council of war. It was far too late to dream up an alternative demonstration — and anyway I wasn't prepared to face the Austerlitz such a confession would have brought forth from Nick.

It was Flames who saved it. Flames O'Toole. Flames was our storeman, a Glaswegian of Irish descent and wilder than anything on either side of the water. But his heart was in the right place, which, in truth, was the most that could be said for him. That and perhaps the fact that he was given to large gestures. Flames; he had earned this nick-name in an attempt, piqued at what he felt to be unjust punishment of some minor misdemeanour, to set light to the Officers' Mess and thereby gain entry to the bar stockroom. When I'd expressed my disappointment at his lack of loyalty — I was sleeping in the Mess at the time — he disarmingly assured me that it was nothing personal and he hoped that we would continue to be friends. Which we did. I do not recall his punishment but it was miraculously light and would certainly have had the 'wettest' Home Secretary baying for blood had he known. But the thing was that everyone liked Flames and after all, pyromaniac or not, his heart was in the right place and he was given to large gestures.

And, as I have said, it was Flames who solved it. PE was the answer he said, PE; Plastic Explosive. He was 'all about', an expert and just happened to have some in his possession. It was handy as a fire-lighter these cold arctic nights. 'You sure, Flames?' Flames was sure. Couple of pounds. No, double it to be safe (safe!); a few yards of D10 cable, a radio battery and just give him the word and he'd guarantee a hole where and when we wanted. I showed him where and explained when. He worked half the night on it. It had to be ready for the next day so that there was no time to rehearse: anyway when it came to destruction, Flames could be relied on. He laid his charges under the ice, through augered holes, drank half a bottle of whisky against the cold (his recommended treatment, not mine — but Flames had a metabolism and physiology all of his own), did some malt arithmetic, half doubled the charges again, laid his wire, concealed it and took his battery to bed to keep it warm and working. He said the cold did terrible things to batteries. I wish it had been colder.

The great day came and somewhere around eleven the cortège — a General, his staff and a clutch of MPs. Nick met them, fielded them with ease and escorted the lot to the lake that was my stage.

I was ready, more than ready. I had an area reserved for them, red-taped on the lake's frozen surface and well away from the spot designated as the epicentre of the forthcoming explosion. In front of their little box stretched full ten acres of pristine frozen lake — and as it had snowed an inch over night it couldn't have looked better; Constable couldn't have made it look better. This *was* the driven snow. In the pine forest that came down the hill to the lake's edge I had concealed a section — a patrol of nine. They too looked just fine: camouflage suits, whiter than the driven snow; rifles and webbing in camouflage tape; skis new from the Quartermaster's store; a purposeful, professional look on lean young faces. I thought them the best sub-unit, in the best unit, in the best army in the whole wide world; which I reasoned, made them the nine best soldiers in the whole wide world. (If you spot a flaw in my logic I don't want to hear from you. Don't forget

these were the fellows who knocked spots off Galtieri's boys —
and whilst you have doubts about the justification of that series
of battles you can't argue the result.) I wore my pride
uncamouflaged. The signals section had erected a loudspeaker
system so that half of Nordland would benefit from the demo. A
warming tent and a Medical Officer stood close at hand, clear
evidence of British efficiency and our solicitude for the welfare of
our troops. Evidence of heat, there was little: a primus roaring
bravely against the all-conquering cold; it's the thought that
counts.

Yep, I was ready; Flames too.

He was ensconced in a sleeping bag and hidden deep in the
snow, there being no other convenient cover, a brand new radio
battery cuddled to his chest and a barely discernible cable from
there to the explosive charges. Only a River Kwai eye could have
spotted them. At Flames' end one of the wires of the cable was
attached to a nail and already implanted in its terminal hole.
Flames held the other wire in another nail in his hand, ready for
the signal to plunge. Nick, as a last minute thought, had invited
the local press; they as ravenous for news as any other in the
world.

'Might as well advertise the fact that we know a thing or two
about cold weather warfare. No harm in the Russians knowing
either — all good deterrence.' I thought that Flames was probably the most effective deterrent in the Western Alliance, a few
more like him and the Russians would think twice about the
Northern Flank.

Nick nodded. I was on. I gave them some preliminary spiel
about the hazards of patrolling across ice on rivers and lakes and
the potential dangers of such an attractive short cut — stuff
they'd have heard before, a dozen times from a dozen armies. But
when I announced that they were about to witness a patrol falling
through the ice to their front — and extracting themselves — an
expression of morbid curiosity replaced one of polite patience. I
blathered on, the best military flannel 'when the tactical situation
allows... assuming air superiority or at least air parity... a
local decision... when speed is of the essence... Finnish *Motti*
tactics notwithstanding... a thickness of ice of two inches is sufficient...' — it all fell soft and obfuscating as snow on more
good military flannel.

163

On the word the patrol appeared to our front, well spaced, in perfect arrowhead formation, skiing at an effortless lope. It looked good, the VIPs were clearly impressed. I lowered my guard in early confidence and went on,

'You will observe, General, that the section commander has signalled his men to loosen one rucksack strap; he is clearly worried about the ice.'

That 'ice' was the key word. It should have set Flames plunging with his nail. The leading skier should have been sinking gently out of sight; but there he was large as life, not nearly discomforted enough for my comfort. I looked at my script, momentarily thrown, got the next line and looked up prepared to brave it out.

The lead skier was no longer to be seen, nor anything of the rest of the patrol, nor anything besides; even the sky had been obliterated in a great spume of snow, smoke, water and ice. A deafening loudspeaker-amplified explosion rent the air. The world had ended; my world anyway. I stood and hoped; it was about all I had left to offer. As the wake of the explosion subsided I was surprised to see that the patrol was still heading purposefully to the far bank, not a hair out of place, the look on their faces, if anything, more purposeful, more professional. At least they were unhurt. Perhaps the loudspeaker had given a false impression, I thought, feeling dismayed that they hadn't been sunk. But that dismay was as nothing compared to the feeling of abject horror I experienced as I turned to the General, an ad-lib half way along the tongue. He, his staff, the MPs and worst of all Nick were up to their waists, right up to their very senior waists, in the coldest water in all Europe, the ice about them, like my career, shattered. The press scribbled and photographed — the scoop of their lives — the winter of mine. Flames claimed it was all to do with ripple effect and stress-fractures and other things that lay men couldn't be expected to understand. I was unhappy — and very unpopular. Even the Sergeant Major's 'if they can't take a joke they shouldn't have joined,' brought scant cheer. This was Flames' largest gesture; history has not recorded what the Russians made of it.

It was with some relief that I quit Norway and returned to Scotland to pick up the tatters of a once promising military

164

career. We had two days at home. The boys' joke was always 'and the second thing I did was take my rucksack off' — and I bet that was not always so. Then we were off again — the Cadre and me — twenty of us, to the Western Highlands of Scotland for training in snow and ice climbing. We based ourselves in tents on the shores of Loch Laggan by Aberarder Farm and the start of the path that leads to Creag Meagaidh. It wasn't so much the blind leading the blind as the purblind leading the partially sighted. Some of the boys had had a scrape and maybe a scrap on Scottish ice but I had never so much as set foot on the stuff, or hand or crampon or axe either. Apart from my New Zealand exploits, a snow plod on Menthosa and some easy early alpine seasons, I knew little about winter climbing in Britain — and nothing of the sort of technical ice climbing we were soon to embark upon. Yet here I was, to run a course on the subject of snow and ice; my dubious qualifications, a passionate interest in the subject, a falsely professed knowledge of it and about thirty thousand feet of snow plodding. My presence at Loch Laggan that day was a co-incidence of rank, of the whim of the Major responsible for Royal Marine Officers' postings and of the absence of anyone better fitted for the job. But I had learned some useful stuff in my Marine apprenticeship. Amongst it: never let the truth spoil a good story; never allow total ignorance to silence the profession of an opinion; confidence covers confusion and bullshit baffles brains. I had nineteen brains to baffle, nineteen separate confusions to cover with confidence. I bought a magazine, *Mountain World*, I think it was called. It advertised an article on ice climbing and sure enough, inside there it was telling of the simplest things like fitting crampons, use of ice axes, techniques of holding a slip, of braking with an axe, of cutting steps, of belaying and other good things. I read it, devoured it and regurgitated it with brazen confidence.

Then I pointed my lads at Coire Ardair bade them follow me and followed them — they were hellish fit — the four miles to the coire which sits snug in Creag Meagaidh's lap.

Here and now, before I reveal that winter's excitements, I ought to state, in case I am losing your confidence, that I am indeed competent to tell this tale. Ten years of adventure, blunders and luck have combined to allow me some judgement in these matters, and if you have stuck with it this far, you deserve to have a better picture of this curious game painted for your edification. Not easy though — it's an esoteric game, remember. However, now, ten years later in 1984, I can state with authority that should you ever find yourself on Lochnagar's Eagle Ridge — and if you are any sort of mountaineer you assuredly will for it is one of the very best — then you'll probably have to cause to ponder the gear you're toting. Chances are that you'll be booted, spurred and accoutred with all the latest in ice climbing paraphernalia — two shortie axes, 12-point crampons, footfangs even, at least three varieties of ice-screw, pegs, nuts and if you're really unlucky, a deadman. And there's about an equal chance that, somewhere near the top of that fine route, you will begin to ask why you bothered with the half of it. Indeed, you may have formed the opinion that your crampons have served you rather badly your axes scarcely better and your ice-screws not at all.

Am I serious? You bet. I know that crampons can usually be relied on to turn unfriendly ice slopes into companionable mates. But though Eagle Ridge is a winter route it is not an ice climb. It's that special sort of winter route — a mixed climb; a modest summer severe in a wolf's winter clothes of snow and ice which conceals without offering alternatives, unlike the sheets of sparkling névé that bedrape your typical Scottish gully. And so far mixed routes have spurned the advances of the 'gear revolution' of the early 70s, a change which has had such a dramatic effect on the ice climbing game. This is why such as Eagle Ridge Direct, Black Cleft (at least the hard bit), Raven's Gully, North East Buttress, Tower Ridge and Route II on the Carn Dearg will, for my money, always give better value than your Zero's or Point Five's which are basement bargains at Grade 5. Modern gear has reduced those once mighty gullies to mere icicles of their former stature; a more or less exciting exercise in front pointing — though it's true that the scenery and situation can often compensate for the mindless boredom of the gait. But for the most part the great buttresses and ridges have escaped unscathed; not for them the rape of a half-hour solo.

If you haven't tried it, front pointing that is, give it a bash — it's deliciously simple. And if you really want to enjoy your ice, outside whisky, it's probably as well to avoid textbooks which manage to bestow such obscurities as 'Piolet Traction' on a

166

simple quadrapedic plod whose greatest advantage is that it comes naturally, like walking and makes about the same demand on the co-ordination. 'Piolet Traction!' 'Front-pointing' will usually do, 'Piolet Bludgeon' if you are in earnest and, *in extremis*, 'Piolet Attila' is all-conquering.

Grab a couple of axes. Almost any length will do so long as they have drooped or well-curved picks, a couple of teeth and a wrist loop. Stick a crampon on either foot and away you go. You have a runner-cum-jug in both hands and always just above your head. Properly placed in anything from half-decent névé to water ice you can pull, push, hang, swing, pendulum, belay, rest and bivouac; all from these wondrous sons of the ice revolution.

And anyone can do it. It helps to have biceps like Brian Boru and calves like the Parthenon but if you haven't and you get puffed you can clip in and sit down for a blow. (There are those who say that this is cheating but the logic of such a claim defeats me — what difference does it make whether you hang by your arms or your arse.) I saw a lass once struggle with the stile to the Allt a'Mhuilinn which, at the time, looked to be the limit of her physical ability. Several slow and patience-sapping hours later she mustered at the foot of Comb Gully, her first-ever ice climb. On her feet a pair of perfectly ordinary 12-point crampons, in her hands a pair of modern axes, two of a species several hundred strong. Then without a second's hesitation she showed that fine gully, even the steep bit at the top, to be an easy day for a lady who had hitherto, with quite unnecessary modesty, placed such as Crib Goch at the summit of her ambitions. (Before I am attacked by every 'responsible' instructor in the land I'd better add that a day's play, dance and movement — with and without crampons and axe — on ice boulders, from flat to vertical, is a very good thing; but that's not the point.)

Back to Eagle Ridge and her sisters who are the point. Halfway up, somewhere near the crux, it occurred to me that I'd have been as well off in boots nailed with tricounis, which was how many a good Scot was shod right into the sixties and how Patey tooled up for the first ascent in 1953. And apart from once hooking an axe through the eye of an old ice-peg which lives in the rock thereabouts, both axes spent the entire climb dangling noisily and uselessly from my wrists. This because Eagle Ridge is a ridge-and-buttress route, a mixed climb — a pastiche of ice, snow and rock and everything in between. It is graded V. No ice revolutions, super-drooped axes or footfanging crampons will make a ha'pence worth of difference to that; and never to be devalued or downgraded it will remain a grand climb. Axe flailing ice sprinters beware! This is a route to wrestle, to savour — to climb.

Folk spend hours arguing about the grade of particular ice-climbs: is Point Five still a 5? Was Elliot's Downfall a 6 while it lasted? Who cares? How can an icicle be graded, does it need a grade? Steep ice is, as all the world can see, steep ice. If your axes stay then so do you. If they don't then you're down. What else? Nothing. Only the under 30s could really care whether they had climbed a 4 or 5 or 6. Not that there is anything wrong with ice climbing. Gullies, especially, redeem themselves by changing their grades daily. Hourly in some cases. I once encountered a very frustrated star of American ice and screen standing disconsolately in the rain at the CIC hut having failed miserably on Zero. 'Goddam it,' he whinged, 'that mother was coming down faster 'n a man could get up.' Next day he romped up on perfect white ice. 'Goddam it, how can you grade that shit?' The answer is that you can't really. And why bother? Steep ice holds no technical intricacies, conceals nothing before the fact, will reveal not much more after it. What does the grade tell you that your eye can't see? Nought. Interesting that Eagle Ridge Direct whose first winter ascent in 1953 predated the first ascent of Point Five (then considered impossible) by six years. Nowadays most would agree that a Point Five in good nick is an easier proposition than Eagle Direct in similar conditions. Interesting too, that Bill Brooker, who shared the first winter ascent of Eagle Ridge with Patey and Taylor, told me just the other day, that the very conditions which would now make it easier — sheet ice and névé — would have rendered it near impossible in 1953. All the work of the 'gear revolution'.

Now, show me the pure ice climb where this sort of excitement is to be discovered.

Professor Norman Collie after the first ascent of Tower Ridge in 1894: 'And what joy, think ye, did they feel after the exceeding long and troublous ascent? — after scrambling,

168

slipping, pulling, pushing, lifting, gasping, lurching, hoping, despairing, climbing, holding on, falling off, trying, puffing, loosing, gathering, talking, stepping, grumbling, anathematising, scraping, hacking, bumping, jogging, overturning, hunting, straddling — for know ye that by these methods alone are the most divine mysteries of the quest revealed.'

How little all that technique has changed — on a buttress route.

Or nearly a century later, but with no apparent advance in style:

'I hammered an ice-peg into the one surviving lump of ice. It hit rock after two inches and I tied it off. I glanced down at Netti, belayed to her axe 30ft below. She was hidden inside her hood... I moved up using the peg as a handhold, feet scratching, then catching, on something unseen. Suddenly I was mantelshelfing on that absurd peg, standing on it, wildly thrusting my axe into the snow only to find it soft, useless. Frantically, I packed the snow into the semblance of a handhold and launched myself sideways on to it. It held.' (from Rob Collister of Scorpion, Cairn Etchachon, Cairngorms.)

Or:

'I was soon standing precariously on top of a rock spike, clinging by a side pull to the overhanging wall above. Round the corner to the left was a groove full of loose snow... I performed a disturbingly thin layback move and managed to get an axe placement round the corner. My feet followed reluctantly finding rock under the snow.' (Alan Rouse on the Central Buttress of Ben Eighe.)

Rouse again this time on Route II, Carn Dearg, Ben Nevis:

'The snow would not support our weight unless, by chance, crampons bit on a rugosity beneath while sloping handholds allowed only leaning moves to clear the next few feet ... standing on sloping footholds in crampons needs precision and some luck!'

169

Or Carrington on Raven's Gully:

> 'Scraping a couple of flimsy footholds in the thin icicles
> allowed me to jam the shaft of my axe in a crack I feverishly
> grabbed the axe and with legs threshing wildly...'

Can you say any of that about a pure ice climb? True in the old
days of hanging on with one hand and of cutting with the other —
of 'howking immense jug handles' — you could at least say just
that, a hundred times over to the top. But these days you put your
right axe in, you put your left axe in; then you can shake it all
about for as long as you need. Modern axes have devalued the
currency of ice which used to be index-linked to doggedness, per-
severance and plain neck.

Look what's happened. Smith's Gully, once 'formidable and
unrepeated' and long regarded as one of the hardest of Scottish
gullies, is now soloed in half an hour. The Appendix, five years
ago a contender for Grade 6, soloed in 1982 in an hour. Point Five
and Zero — routes with a world reputation — soloed by all and
sundry in minutes. All because modern axes have beaten them.

This was not the psychological and physiological breakthrough
of the 8000-metre peaks without oxygen, nor a spiritual triumph
such as the first ascent of the North Face of the Eiger or luck,
without which nothing is gained, like the South West Face of
Everest; but a pure and very simple technological ploy. In the late
60s, and early 70s MacInnes, Cunningham and others in Scotland
(and at about the same time Chouinard in the States), began to
droop the picks on their axes after playing around with daggers for
a few years. They found that when used with a wrist loop (held
like a ski stick) it was possible to hang on good névé, white ice and
water ice. (As with all the great inventions, it is so simple you
wonder why no-one thought of it years before.) With two you
could hang forever and teamed with 12-point crampons (which
had been around since 1932) ice became your compliant friend and
the brutal art of step cutting almost died overnight, though some
recalcitrant Scots fought a rearguard action and clung
(precariously as always) to traditional methods. They may be there
still. Good luck to them if they are — they'll not be squeezing in
many routes — though they may argue that they'll be squeezing
out more satisfaction.

170

I remember only eight years ago heaving my way happily past a pair of step-cutting Scots on Hadrian's Wall. We finished in an hour and fitted in a couple of other routes that same day. The Scots cut steps for ten hours and claimed great satisfaction in a report in the SMC Journal, and I'm still not sure who was the dafter.

The most difficult bit about ice climbing these days is choosing your axe. Yesterday, there were a dozen different sorts of axes in the local climbing shop. By next week there'll be half-a-dozen more. It helps to have made your mind up before you embark on your route but it's not always easy as I realised recently when, fifty feet up a piece of steep ice, I was still deliberating which of three axes went best. Don't worry it's not that important. Terrordactyls are still hard to beat on mixed routes and the adze version is a winner on névé when it is too soft to hold a pick. Interesting here to note that as late as 1971 John Cunningham, ice doyen of us all, was saying when asked about the then very new Terrordactyl:

'It's yet to prove its worth conclusively. To my mind it isn't sufficiently versatile.'

Just two years later there must have been a thousand Terrordactyl-wielding ice climbers who might have dared to differ. For pure snow or ice a longer shaft seems sensible — giving a certain mechanical advantage in the swing. Many continentals prefer longer shafts not having to contend with the confines of Scottish gullies or the intricacies of our ridge and buttress routes. I tend to change my mind every year.

Vultures worked perfectly one winter — a good droop to enable them to hold without too many teeth — which make them stick. Humming Birds sing well on water ice (for which they were designed) but warble unhappily on the average British winter route. Last year I had an affair with a couple of French lovelies, the Chacal and the Barracuda. Both are long in the tooth and in their virgin state impossible to remove from the ice. Filing their teeth to half original length sorts this out and the Barracuda has the only adze which can hold a candle to the Terrordactyl — and it's far better made. Next winter? Who knows?

The winter game never was about balance, delicacy or intricacy, nor was it ever about subtlety or technical nicety. It was, and still is, about the weather, wildness and fighting the good fight, 'a frozen waiting in icy torrents of thundering rubbish, a fight with the green rockless wastes of the last 400ft of Scotland while the sinister dark clutches at your ankles, a world where to spend your last time and where only the bold stroke will suffice, where victory is celebrated not with a shaming glow of smugness but with great baying whoops of triumph and relief; a world of primitive delight.'

Or as Milton, who may have known more about winter climbing than any of us had ever supposed, put it:
'wild above rule or art — enormous bliss.'
New gear has changed none of that; it all remains — and more.
And as great games always do, winter climbing is already compensating for the technical advances in axe design. Climbers are moving away from the gullies and their ice — even if a handful of frozen waterfalls still offer strenuous excitement — back to the buttresses and those hard summer rock climbs that wear enough winter clothing to become winter climbs — though it's not always easy to judge when a summer rock climb becomes a winter route. The best definition I have heard is that if it's easier in crampons, then it's a winter route. Joe Brown, I think, was the author of that Solomon-like judgement, and if it appears to contradict Patey's preference and all I have been arguing in this piece, so what. The game has no rules.

Perhaps Boysen's winter ascent of Black Cleft on Cloggy in 1963 shows that the fashion for winter ascents of summer rock routes never really died in the first place (though at 5A this was years ahead of its time). Certainly Braithwaite's winter effort on Bloody Slab in 1979 also on Cloggy, shows the way for the future. Or does it? Who knows where's next as mountaineers search out adventure somewhere beyond that technology. The game goes on. Get out there, boy, and get amongst it!

But 1973 was early days and I knew nothing of all this erudite stuff then. Let's get back to the Mountain and Arctic Warfare Cadre, Aberarder Farm and Creag Meagaidh.
Among my charges were 'Scrim' and young Lochinvar — except he hadn't earned that name yet, so I'll call him Nicholls. Nicholls was being groomed to replace me in due course, an event that was likely to occur sooner than either of us had anticipated judging by

my recent record. For the moment Nicholls was a student following the same course as I had some years earlier.

The one thing that *Mountain World* article hadn't told me was that two grading systems were current, one numerical — 1 to 5 — and the other adjectival, Difficult, Very Difficult, etcetera, up to Very Severe; the very system that was traditionally used for rock-climbs all over Great Britain. I grabbed Nicholls; he would be my student, my partner. He readily agreed — not that he had much choice — I was the boss, a captain by now and he was a student, a lieutenant still.

Together we consulted the guide, one that employed the adjectival system. We agreed that we ought to begin with caution and go for a Very Severe; that we knew we could handle easily on rock and we presumed that it represented roughly the same order of difficulty on snow and ice. In our simple faith we hadn't spotted that, unlike most rock climbing guides which even then nearly always allowed at least two full grades above VS, in our guide that grade represented the highest order of difficulty. This isn't to say that VS *was* the grade of the hardest climbs, but rather that the hardest climbs were graded, by a conservative and idiosyncratic author, VS. Get my drift?

Smith's Gully caught my eye. It carried three stars, was deemed by our conservative author to be one of the best climbs in Scotland — something of a panegyric from him. And it was a mere VS. Go for it.

We went for it and, because it was raining all the way up to Creag Meagaidh, we were the only ones who went for anything that day. Somewhere, just after the start of the second pitch as I recall, it turned on us; went for us. An avalanche over us, a leader fall, an avalanche between us, a cornice collapse, another fall and the top. It was still raining.

'Up hill that for VS,' Nicholls suggested, 'did you notice those avalanches?'

I assured him that I had; not only noticed them but felt them too; touched them. We made a wet way back to Aberarder Farm, somewhat chastened by the experience and resolved to drop a grade and try our luck there.

That night in a pub we met a civilian mate who knew all there was to know about Scottish winter climbing — or so he assured us.

173

'Poxy conditions,' he said, 'don't suppose you got anything done.'

'Not much,' I said, 'went up to Meagaidh to have a look at Smith's.'

'Waste of time, eh,' he meant the walk up.

'Yeh, not much fun.' He nodded all expert accord until I added, 'except the last pitch, the ice was better up there, colder. That was OK.'

I looked at him. His jaw had dropped open, aghast, incredulous. I wasn't sure which.

'You're kidding.'

'No really.'

'Come on.'

'No really.'

'What was it like?'

'Piece of duff.' Nicholls — it was his favourite grade — retrospectively.

'Come on.'

'Really,' Nicholls again. I was saying nothing, trying hard to effect an air of knowing nonchalance.

In his next garbled paragraph, our friend set us firmly in our ice climbing tracks, gave us a huge shove into the seventies and dispelled many a myth. He told us that he reckoned that ours was only the third ascent of Smith's, that it was reputed to be one of the hardest winter climbs in the country, that it was certainly harder than Point Five Gully or Zero Gully. Point Five! Zero! These were climbs, hardly more than names to us, and only in our wildest dreams did we dare as much as think them. The climbing of them! That was for others. But his iconoclasm had done it for us and I owe my ice climbing to him — and the inability to read a guide book properly. See what I mean about books?

The week that followed remains the best climbing week of my life; our mate had given the psychological barrier a heft; we trampled it underfoot and so far it hasn't got up again. We moved straight to Ben Nevis and on successive days climbed Point Five, Centurion, Zero and Sassenach; the first and third with crampons and axe, the second and fourth in EBs in the sun and with a glissade down No 5 Gully to end: an unusual, perhaps unique combination for late March. On the fifth day Nicholls and I went back to the Ben looking for a fight. We had a great day and by the time we had returned to our tent at Corpach I was so disgustingly pleased with myself, so utterly chuffed, so brim full of beans, that I grabbed the back of Nicholls' Course Report, thus far blank, and wrote the following in twenty minutes. The speed of it may show, the smugness too; but that's what I did and this is what the back of Nicholls' snow and ice climbing report said (the front remains confidential and the substance of some dispute):

'Jeez, they were arrogant, those lads. All the arrogance of youth and more besides — the arrogance of those whose vaulting ambition has yet to stumble on a pair of front-points.

They were mighty pleased with themselves too. After all, they had just climbed Smith's Gully as their first-ever Scottish winter route. True, they had been fooled by MacInnes's adjectival winter grades into thinking it was akin to a summer VS. But even so, hadn't they just romped up it, one short axe between them, through the rain and a couple of respectable avalanches? And hadn't a hastily convened Clachaig tribunal declared this debacle to be the third direct ascent? They were pleased with themselves all right.

What about Point Five? They zoomed up that in a couple of hours, and Zero the next day before swapping crampons for PAs to scamper up Centurion and Sassenach. All this in one week... of course they were arrogant. Why, this very day they had scratched about for the new route they now felt was their due, and pounced on a little line somewhere right of Glover's which, with rare modesty, they graded 4. (It is doubtful whether their arrogance would have been dented one whit had they known that Raeburn had done the route fifty years earlier, and graded it 1.)

When they thought, which wasn't often, they saw themselves as young gladiators, or a self-appointed Praetorian guard to winter climbing. Too lucky in their narrow experience to need the crutch of romanticism; unbeaten, unbattered, unthinking, they could climb mountains but were not yet mountaineers.

Despite their brand new Grade 4 it was still only 10 am so they cast about for something else to occupy them till opening time. One of them, I can't remember which, and it hardly

175

matters now since they were both fools, found that Comb Gully was just down the road. Neither the route-description nor its star-rating excited much interest, but their attention was caught by a note: 'Since Dougal Haston climbed it solo in 20 minutes, its reputation has declined.'

To arrogants such as these this was a Dachstein thrown down in challenge. Not that they knew much about Dougal Haston, or cared. Nor did they care that Comb was a little gem tucked away amongst the castellated towers of that part of the Ben. No, they cared only about the challenge, and they knew a race when they saw one because they were young and, oh! so arrogant. . .

Helter-skelter down No.2 Gully to the foot of the Comb. Toss for position, set a watch and off again. Go! A gallop up the first snow slopes. A canter to the bay where a startled team were belaying. A trot to the final bulge, where their presumption gave best to steepness and they climbed for a minute or so before a final idiotic charge to the summit plateau where they collapsed, feeling ever so slightly silly. 'Seven minutes,' gasped one to the other.

Why? 'Dunno. . .' one said. 'Why not,' said the other. If they had reflected then, as they have since, they might have argued that since the game of mountaineering doesn't bear rational examination for more than a couple of minutes it wasn't worth thinking about. They might have done, but they didn't.'

They are wiser now. Slower too, ten years on. And sorry. Sorry because they treated a great wee route badly; sorry because they remembered little of it; sorry because seven minutes is too quick to savour any gift that the goddess of all mountains dispenses as a favour; sorry because they're less daft now.

That was years ago. Since then they have been back to do the decent thing. Climbed it, that is, with all the accoutrements of modern ice and in more decent haste. Enjoyed it too — and found it, here and there, rather less than straightforward. Best of all, they arrived at the top several spindrifted hours after 'go'.

Wise men, they now know that climbing on the Ben belongs to a tiny élite of games best consumed in a slow passion with the conscious accumulation of pleasure as insurance against that day the passion, or the power, deserts — 'speed passions's ebb as you greet its flow — to have — to hold — and — in time — let's go!'

Do I know these lads? Sure. We all do. There are two at every crag still vying to bear that standard for the Praetorian guard. I know. I tried to carry it once myself, for seven daft minutes.

In the years that followed, between then and now, I grew up — but not too much. I fell in love with winter climbing; it fitted me better than other bits in the climbing wardrobe. I tried to write articles about this wild thing I loved — an arrogance, I admit. I wrote with quick pulse and pace. I couldn't help it; the thought of a wild winter climb quickens my pulse, precipitates my pen; it is not a game for the singer of an empty day. My style has been criticized; there's no space to rest they say. That's fair. Nonetheless, I can't help it, the fight gets me and if I think at all it is before, not after.

'Think first, fight after — the soldier's art.'

I'll try to slow down with Scrimgeour. It was easy to go slowly with him, that was the pace he liked the best. He didn't like this winter climbing, this snow and ice business, much, he told me so himself.

'Well, Scrim, what d'you think of this snow and ice climbing game?'

'Utter shite.' His considered and unequivocal reply.

I considered that he would be best employed teaching and revising basic snow skills. I was particularly keen that at an early stage we covered the business of braking and stopping a fall with an ice axe properly, I briefed Scrim carefully to that effect, and asked him to lay on a demo and a period of instruction the following day. A scan of a text book or two and Scrim had all he wanted about stopping with an ice axe. What he needed now was the right terrain, not necessarily text book-terrain, you understand, but terrain for what he had in mind and he was a master of the science of practical jokes. High and low he recced, sedulous beyond normal measure or previous effort. We should have all been suspicious of that but we were too busy enjoying ourselves. On a perfect sunny day, as the rest of us climbed Tower Ridge or Glovers Chimney or Green Gully, Scrim could be seen dashing all over Coire na Ciste assessing angles, measuring distances, lying prone to gauge what was dead ground, occasionally making an entry in a scruffy note book. Never before, in his wildest enthusiasms, had Scrim made written note in anything, with the possible exception of his 'Posby' book — clearly something had caught his imagination. When I met him at the CIC hut on the way back he declared himself well pleased with the day's work.

Next day I watched with interest, intrigued to see what the product of all this industry was to be. Scrim lined up the lads on an innocuous-looking slope of about 30 degrees where, from his mount, he delivered a sermon, all guts and glottal stop, about the need for a speedy self-arrest when victim of a slip. Then in dramatic demonstration he threw himself bodily off his mount and hurtled with alarming acceleration toward the students. They were impressed. He hunched over his axe and stopped. They were more impressed. I was impressed. 'Obsairve. Now yon's an aisy wee slope,' Scrim said, 'too aisy tae waste more than a demonstration on. Over here,' he waved his axe toward the other side of the mount that only he and I could see such was the lay of the land — not for nothing had Scrim got the feel of every fold hereabouts, not for nothing that diligent recce, not for nothing those notes and all that hard work.

'Over here,' he continued, 'ut's as steep as a witch's tit. Ut's the only decent area I could find. An' there's a terrible big cliff at the bottom so when I launch you hold yersel' ready til I shout, "brake". Then brake as quick as Christ will let ye — afore ye plunge over yon precipice (Scrim was warming to his work). But. But if any of yoos brake a second afore I say ut'll cost ye a dram. Who's furst?'

There was a scramble. These lads were an élite, keen to run Scrim's gauntlet, eager to the breech.

'Wait a minute, one at a time. Corporal MacIntyre, you furst.' Scrim was sergeant again and thought that a touch of formality might lend some clout to his carefully rigged melodrama. He had Corporal MacIntyre lie on his back head down the hill, from which position, Scrim adjudged the prospect to be the most daunting. Scrim held the man in place by standing on his shin while he, still on his mount, squeezed out the last drops of drama. The students could see nothing of MacIntyre, the slope on which he lay and down which he was to be propelled, or anything of the ground on the other side of Scrim's carefully selected mount.

'Now don' forget, nae braking till I say, then quick as Christ'll let you or yu'll be over yon cliff — Ut's nae sae far awa tae start with.' Note the carefully timed, carefully measured additional information. Hitchcock could not have squeezed a drop more drama.

'Go.' A shout and a big shove. Scrim turned to his audience who could only guess at MacIntyre's progress.

'Remember lads, nae braking till I say, OK?'

He spoke slowly, casually, as if the precipice and MacIntyre didn't exist. The students began to worry how far Mac would fall if Scrim didn't turn back and give the 'stop'. You could see their concern. So could Scrim.

'Let's have a look,' Scrim said looking back. And raising his hands in horror,

'Stop, stop for Chrissake stop,' a pause then, 'shit, too late, next.'

The next lad went no less eagerly to the breech, well not by much anyway, but, Scrim's superb stage management notwithstanding, the farce could not be maintained much longer. As Corporal Stewart breasted the mount he looked down on the far side where he saw a gentle slope, soft and smooth, no trace of a precipice or the least step and a puzzled but relieved mate picking himself up unhurt at the bottom of a long run out. His grin flashed what he saw and the curtain came down to laughter. Scrimgeour was well pleased.

The next day was the last of the course. We went to Stob Coire nan Lochan in Glencoe. The lads had requested a short day in order that justice could be done to the festivities that Scrim had organised that evening. The Imperial Hotel, Fort William was the target; Scrim had made it his local these last two weeks creating such an impression, equal on customers and takings alike, that Jimmy, the hotelier, would have moved heaven and earth to meet his request. In the event both, it is reported, suffered some adjustment.

Fate and the Assistant Military Secretary had decreed that I was to be an adjutant, fate worse than death for a man with his heart and his boots in the mountains; and that at Poole, in Dorset, a pleasant enough place, but about as far away from my beloved hills as it is possible to be on this island.

'Scrim, this will be our last chance to climb together — how

179

about a winter route with me?' I thought he was going to cry; the rougher cut the diamond the easier spring the tears. And Scrim was rough; and the tears, soldier's big splashy sentimental salty tears never far behind.

'Aye, sure Boss,' he readily agreed — though not so sentimental that I got to choose the climb.

'Let's dae Y Fork Gully.' It was the easiest he could think of quickly enough to get his in first. That was fine by me; I had romance in mind, not the climb. For the two hours from the road to the snow basin below the cliff, we talked about old times, hopeless romantics the pair of us. Reminiscing — the old men's backward glance — a sweet pain, unrewarding happy hurt, Springsteen's 'glory days', Browning's 'one draught of earlier, happier sights'. We sang, listened, laughed at them all.

An easy snow slope led up to the foot of the gully which in turn led easily for a hundred feet to the first steepening. Here we uncoiled the rope, tied on and sorted out some gear. As Scrim scratched about for a belay my attention was caught by a scraping higher up. Looking up I saw the backside of a climber about to disappear up and over a bulge fifty feet above. He was generating a fair flurry of snow and I thought it would make a good photograph — bum and flying snow against the blue of the sky. As I focussed, he zoomed in. He'd fallen off. He'd landed on me. He'd embraced me; stuck fast. Fortunately Scrim had me tight on belay a split second before or I think we, the 'bum' and I, would have quickstepped a downwards dance. A shout! Again I looked up. There, plucked clean as goosedown from rock and, presumably, belay, by the 'bum's' tight rope was his partner, stark against the blue sky and a good way towards it. But he came down, crashing down; plucked such a twang that he passed over us, some way out, and skidded to a landing on the easy snow slope beneath. One hundred and fifty feet beneath. But not to a stop — which is what saved him. He skidded on, de-accelerating imperceptibly, what Scrim later called the 'Holmenkollen effect' (after an Olympic ski-jump near Oslo over which, Scrim claimed, a mate had slid on a tin tray — to a new world record). As the lower man skidded, the rope between he and 'bum' stretched its full elastic stretch. 'Bum' looked at Scrim; held on to me. Scrim shrugged at 'bum'; held on to me. Good and tight please Scrim.

Scrim held fast. I held fast. The other fellow clung with drowning puppy eyes. Oh those eyes, the things they said. Twang. Whang. 'Bum' was off again, torn from our grasp. And so they travelled, yo-yo, full three hundred more feet until a scoop stopped them. They lay inert, surely dead. I untied and ran down. They were stirring, groaning. I, dreading the inspection — the damage surely bends, breaks, holes, rips, tears — arrived, it must have been only thirty seconds later, hardly daring to look. They were standing, feeling, squeezing, easing, brushing; miraculously unhurt; speaking!

'Eh,' said the one, a Yorkshire lad, 'I wish I could get the hang of this front pointin'.'

'By,' said the other, also a Yorkshire lad, 'that were exciting.'

Scrim had had enough. We went to the Imperial Hotel. Half way through nothing in particular, Scrim rose and announced that it was time for speeches. He had a rogue's love of unctuous propriety. And since he knew that none had been prepared (nor were they wished by other than Scrim) he had himself composed a poem. Well, Scrim called it a poem. It barely qualified as doggerel but, to my amazement, when I bumped into Jimmy in Fort William last winter it was remember this and remember that and remember Scrim's poem — time earns promotion. I replied that I could, vaguely. Jimmy had it pat and sent it to me on the back of an Imperial Menu. But it was better the way Scrim slurred it, solemn, earnest, deaf to his own drivel and chuffed to his Glaswegian bits — though on those formal occasions he inexplicably talked in what he thought was a 'correct' English accent. But it's a long way too from Sauchiehall Street to Sloane Square. The result was near unintelligible as the spoken word can be but the doggerel was proof against the assault of any tongue.

'The Imperial Crew,' he coughed a commanded silence.

'We don't half get around a lot — we're a mighty
                              itinerant few,
An' we makes a lot of friends — an' a couple of enemies too,
An' as we don't get 'ome much then an 'ome from 'ome
                              must do.
So Jimmy, Jeanie, Jauntie, Betty — in fact the whole
                              Imperial Crew,

'We 'ope you don't mind it if we say we've made an 'ome from
    'ome of you.'
Scrim was pleased with his work. That was evident. So pleased
that he extemporised another stanza, if doggerel can be so divided.
'An' we've supped some ale an' some drams an' a pint o'
    Guinness or two,
An' many's the night we tackled those stairs when more than a
    little fou,
An' lived it up and lived it late an' turned the fresh air blue —
So Jimmy, Jeanie, Jauntie, Betty — in fact the whole Imperial
    Crew,
We 'ope you don't mind it if we say we've made an 'ome from
    'ome of you.'
Then another —
'To the girls we've said our own thank-you's — or some of us
    'ave tried,
(Tho' don't forget we came to climb; 'tis climbing get's us
    high.)
So Jimmy, Jeanie, Jauntie, Betty — in fact the whole Imperial
    Crew,
We 'ope you don't mind it if we say we've made an 'ome from
    'ome of you.'
And another —
'So here's to all at the Imperial, the girls an' the fellows too.
I'm not sure where, an' I don't care, what next 'otel will rue
That they took us on an' made a bomb — well at least a bob or
    two.
So Jimmy, Jeanie, Jauntie, Betty — in fact the whole Imperial
    Crew,
We 'ope you don't mind it if we say we've made an 'ome from
    'ome of you.'
And another —
'An' so we say to the Imperial, Jimmy, Missus and the team,
We 'ope you'll accept this wee bauble, a token o' our esteem;
An' so we say to the Imperial, Jimmy, Missus and their
    friends,
Don't laugh too soon, you never know we might be back
    again.'
— five verses and I think that that tramp most royal would have
made it a sestina had he not grown thirsty. All this recitation

stuff was interfering with serious drinking. He grabbed his glass and raised it. The applause alone could have won a Nobel Prize.

'A toast,' Scrim said — that old drunken formality again.

'Here's tae us,
Wha's like us;
Damn few.
And if there's ony left
They're a deid.'

Scrim's war song. I don't know where he got it, nor am I certain what it means, but I like it.

It was two years ago, 'depressed at the enervating march of civilisation' and in a morbid angry mind, that I wrote a letter. It was never posted. I lacked the courage and was unsure of the wisdom. I still am.

'I gave my heart to know wisdom, and to know madness and folly: I perceived that this also is vexation of spirit. For in much wisdom is much grief' (Ecclesiastes i).

I'll take the courage, if not the wisdom and post it now.

You Blew It

Six people were killed on the Ben on the Monday, 22 February 1982. The next day I bumped into Ian Woolridge of the *Daily Mail* up to do a bit on winter climbing. It was in a bar; he seemed to be a good bloke. I implored him — 'do mountaineering a favour and get it right.' He'd do his best he said and he was talking to active mountaineers involved with a BBC ice-climbing live broadcast. Great, there's some hope, I thought.

Sure enough he chatted to Brown, Nicholson and Nicholls. And between them they blew it. They lost what was perhaps a unique opportunity to explain to a first-class sports writer the esoteric nature of this game we play.

Look at what they did.

Dave Nicholls, dear friend of mine, said, or is reported to have said, 'You must always remember that if you fall in a lonely place half-a-dozen climbers are morally committed to face the same dangers to come and get you out.'

High falutin' stuff and sententious nonsense. 'Moral obligation'. I'm not aware of any and if you disapprove of the victims being out in the first place that surely releases you from any moral obligation, whatever it means, that you may otherwise have recognised.

Moreover Dave, when did you ever consider would-be rescuers?

Not that time in the Lyngenn Alps, lonely though it surely is, when we were avalanched out of a powder-filled gully, climbing on a day when no sane man would have been within miles. The day we got up out of the snow, shook ourselves like puppies and laughed all the way back to the tent. Not that day on the Leschaux when a cornice collapsed on us half way up a route that was idiotically dangerous. Not those two attempts on the Eiger in the rain, not on Smiths in more rain, the avalanches and a peel. Nor on a score of other occasions.

(I know this man well. He's as brave as a lion. That's what gets him up.) Why didn't you have the 'moral' courage to tell Mr. Woolridge what you really think? Why were you stage-struck into some daft pseudo-philosophical drivel? Climbers rescue one another because they *understand* why they climb even if they can't explain to Woolridge *et al.* Anyway what sort of climber goes to his mountain with an eye to the rescue? He may live forever but he won't see many summits. Take Nicholson. 'I often sit in the pub listening to some of these climbers saying what they are going to do. It makes me weep. You know that if they get up there it will only be by sheer luck. You know that if they keep on trying to get up there it will only be by sheer luck. You know that if they keep on trying to get up there that luck has got to run out.' What valedictory arrogance. Sounds like he's sat in that pub too long. How does he know that these lads are not better than he? And has his ambition, perhaps in his younger days, never outstripped his ability? And was he never lucky? When you begin to talk about young climbers like that it's time you stopped climbing. (And 'that a man's reach should exceed his grasp or what's a heaven for?' Well what is it for?)

Take Joe Brown, great man and hero to us all that he is. 'I'm alive now because from the very start I've always been cautious and have never worried about what people will say if I turn back. I've been in dozens of dangerous situations when you know that if you make one mistake you will fall off and get killed.'

What caution were you exercising when you fell out of Point Five, Joe? And it must have been a very incautious sort of caution that allowed you to get into all those scrapes. Trouble is he's too modest. He is alive because he was (is?) brilliant. We lesser mortals sometimes have to rely on luck.

Why all this hypocrisy, why this idolatry to the myth of the sanctity of human life — the most dispensible commodity on earth? The same day that 6 died on the Ben dozens drove themselves and others to death on the roads. Society accepts this; it would be inconvenient not to use roads. Hundreds die of booze each year. Society accepts this; we like boozing. Hundreds more go up in smoke. We advertise it, the Exchequer depends on it, sport thrives on it.

It gets worse. The producer of the BBC film told me the programme had to be live. A documentary would be no good; no-one would watch it because they would know that it was to end happily. But live they would watch it for the same reason that folk watch Grand Prix racing — the uncertainty of the outcome. And what can that mean in mountaineering? The sanctity of human life?

Why didn't our stars say something truthfully simple like 'Six people died on Ben. That's a shame but it's just acceptable and certainly more acceptable than any of the alternatives. If climbers didn't die, climbing would.'

The non-climbing public stand little chance of understanding such a sentiment but they'll not make much sense out of the other utterances either.

Climbers should stick together, take their risks singly or with their mates, resist the trap of off-the-cuff philosophies to the press, rescue each other and tell the plainest truth.

Robin Smith may have got somewhere near conveying the message with 'It is a world where only the bold stroke will suffice, where victory is celebrated not with a shaming glow of smugness but with great baying whoops of triumph and relief; a world of primitive delight.' Unfortunately he died climbing and six dead climbers have been betrayed by colleagues.

185

Strong stuff. I am never able to see what is so especially tragic about a death on the mountains (as long as the climber was there of his own volition — wholly different principles apply to people on mountaineering courses or in guided parties). If we choose this game and its dangers we should not complain if we, our friends or others of the same persuasion fall victim to 'the fell clutch of circumstance'. Poets, men to whom the gift is given to say these things better than the rest of us have already said, and will most like again, a dozen times what I feel, but cannot or dare not say. I lean on a handful:-

W.B.Yeats:
    'A lovely impulse of delight
    Drove to this tumult in the clouds;
    I balanced all, brought all to mind,
    The years to come seemed waste of breath,
    A waste of breath the years behind
    In balance with this life, this death.'

or Graham:
    'He either fears his fate too much,
    Or his deserts are small,
    That puts it not into the touch
    To win or lose it all.'

or Emerson:
    'Tis man's perdition to be safe,
    When for truth he ought to die.'

Or Clough, less seriously:
    'Thou shalt not kill; but need'st not strive
    Officiously to keep alive.'

Or Scrim, very seriously:
    'What the heck is it all about anyway?'

Strong stuff indeed. I may live to regret it — I hope so.

Back to better, less angry days. This is my favourite story. In 1976 I moved to Royal Marines Poole as adjutant. I sat behind a desk, the biggest danger boredom or the threat of an avalanche of paper, and dreamt of mountains. I began, at last, to read mountain literature; a vicarious thrill was better than no thrill at all. One day in a magazine I saw a report about an organisation called the Association of British Mountain Guides. I had never heard of them before. They were advertising an assessment of winter climbing skills for entry into their ranks to be held on Ben Nevis. It sounded impressive. My Commanding Officer thought so too and let me off for a week to attend. I applied; the Guides accepted. (They were hard up then but no more, there has been a flood of talent in recent years.) A few weeks later I arrived by train in Fort William, the happiest man ever to have stepped off it.

I enjoyed the assessment. Few of the others did. I had the advantage of coming from a job I hated, anything, assessment included, would have been fun after that desk. It was during this week that I met Peter Boardman. He was the British Mountaineering Council's National Officer and was attending in some sort of 'observer' capacity. This meant he should have been neutral. To begin with he was unfriendly. He distrusted soldiers who claimed to be mountaineers — his prejudices were not entirely misconceived and he had every reason to distrust my reason for being in Fort William that week. He said so. Years later it was still the rudest thing he ever said to me — and ruder than anything I ever heard him say to anyone else. He harboured some strange ideas about the military and soldiers. I was used to that. They have been a persecuted minority since 'Tommy this and Tommy that' — probably for far longer. We climbed a fair bit together in the next few days (Tower Ridge, the world's best climb amongst others), got to know each other, got to like each other. He saw that despite my khaki hide I was pure mountain inside. Wind-assisted by mountains and a few beers, we became good friends. After that he was never neutral.

The assessment ended on a Friday. I passed, just, thanks to Pete's forsaking his neutrality. Saturday was free, but what to do? Conditions were bad on the Ben, the forecast worse, but Friday night was Jacobite night and beer decides routes like nothing else; like sweet reason never did.

'How about Raven's,' I suggested, but no-one seemed to hear.

'How about Raven's,' Pete said thirty seconds later. Everyone heard, he was the famous one, and a great, great mountain day was but a hangover away.

Raven's Gully, Grade 5, Buchaille Etive, Glencoe. Raven's and the Great Man, here goes.

We parked by Altnafeadh and bundled out, six of us, in a welter of gear. Then the boot door was hoisted skywards, triggering an avalanche of equipment. The accoutrements of modern ice are awesome. I watched the Great Man with interest — and some nervousness. After all, here in our very midst was one of the glitterati, the embodiment of *jeunesse dorée;* and BMC National Officer to boot. We would watch and learn. I knew little about the Man except that he had climbed Everest whilst still a virgin, was reputed to be a nice bloke, and like all nice blokes was popular with grannies.

The five of us waited, respectfully allowing Pete first shot at the mountain of gear that lay strewn half across the A82. If, as I think we did, we expected him crisply to gird himself like some latter-day gladiator we were to be cruelly disappointed. Indeed he paraded woefully ill-equipped, lacklustre even, standing before us sporting not much more than odd stockings, two very pedestrian axes and a supreme indifference to the arsenal which lay all about. 'Don't forget the ropes,' he said and set off toward Great Gully, a painfully thin sack flapping in the wind.

That wind! It was a wild day even down here and Raven's did not look friendly. See it for yourself on one of those raw Rannoch days and you will assuredly agree. This is the Buachaille's bad side; black, malevolent, and the slit of Raven's blacker still. Not friendly. No flirt here with a fine lace of chantilly ice, nor any smile of firmly compliant, sparkling névé beckoning to a summit altar. No, Sir. Black walls and a black-eyed gully trapped in a bleak embrace between Slime Wall (what horrors that name conjures for the PA-shod) and Cuneiform Buttress. Hobson's choice. But Raven's was one and we were six, so we had the advantage of her.

Then the wind did for two of them. The wind and an escape ploy that would have graced Patey's pages: 'I live here,' protested Allan, 'I can afford to wait for better weather. Do it any time.' His partner quickly clipped into the same gambit and they turned with the wind and ran goose-winged back to the car. I envied their sanity, admired their courage, looked askance at

Pete. The Great Man, his face set in an expression of frozen insouciance, resolutely plodded on, lugubrious to the last but betraying no sign of the hangover that should have been beheading him while I suffered for all four.

In an hour we gathered at the foot of a gully of steep, soft snow that drowned the first three (summer) pitches and led straight to a chockstone roof which forms the summer crux. Pete surged forward. If I half-expected a Red Sea parting of the powder to allow him unimpeded passage I was, for a second time, disenchanted. The Great Man flailed, grunted and swam — the last a badly co-ordinated butterfly stroke — in a distinctly mortal fashion to collapse in a terrible wrack of panting just below the chockstone. We three followed easily up a well-bulldozed trough. Here Martin Burrows-Smith, who instructs these things, suggested that it might be a good thing to rope-up. He joined with Pete, I with Paul Moores.

Pete, now recovered, went at the crux, the wall to the left of the chockstone. It spat him back. Obviously there was even more to Raven's than met the eye. 'My dad did this in 1945 in army boots,' I observed trying to sound helpful. Whether Pete believed me (and it's true) I have never discovered, but it goaded him to a fury, galvanised him. He charged full frontal to the breech and squeezed up the full 5a of it, axes and crampons sparking where his bludgeon laid bare the rock. The rope ran out at an alarming rate.

I followed, leading my half of the team. It was hard. Jams for the right arm and foot, left axe anxiously searching skyhook incuts. Left front-points despairing a lack of ice, and crampons complaining cacophonous on bare rock. Just when I thought I might be off downwards — a careless knot in Pete's rope caught between my left front points and lent me that tiny tug which measures the mile between up and down. Such was the Great Man's surge up the easy slope beyond that he was unaware of his 12-stone parasite.

I joined him at the mouth of the cave below a second enormous chockstone. It was wilder here. As wild as Smith or Marshall could have ever asked for. Wilder than we wanted, 'wild above rule or art'. The moor had been rough, but this was something else. A vortex of omnidirectional, supersonic spindrift that numbed the senses and stung the flesh. Straight to the vein like Stones' chords or Sibelius' crescendoes — go to Raven's on a wild day and you will feel what I mean.

The four of us crawled deeper into the cave and found an eerie haven. Martin produced a flask of coffee, Paul a great nugget of chocolate, I a packet of biscuits. Pete, without so much as a noblesse oblige, tucked into all three simultaneously. 'The sports plan is this,' he said at length in superstarspeak, 'there are three or four gigantic chockstones at intervals above this one. With luck they'll all provide a cave just like this. One of you will lead and fix the rope so the rest of us can use it to save time. I've already done the crux for you so you should be OK now. Anyway, I'm a greater-ranges man myself.' Sips of coffee then, 'Now you go first Paul.'

Paul steeled himself and crawled back to the maelstrom. He had not gone ten feet before we lost sight and sound of him, but thirty seconds later he was back, gasping like a pearl diver.

'What's the problem?' asked Pete, into a mug of coffee.

'Can't breathe out there, or see a thing either.'

'Take a deep breath and just keep going upwards — the line obvious,' advised Pete through a biscuit. 'And give the rope a couple of tugs when you want us to come up.'

Poor old Paul. He huffed and he puffed and he puffed and he huffed; and he hyperventilated. Then over the top. Pete kicked a dozen coils toward the entrance. 'Enough for him to be going on with.' The minutes ticked by as we chatted comfortably over our coffee and biscuits. From time to time one of us, following the Great Man's example, would foot a few yards of rope to the void, scuttling quickly back to the sanctuary and a sip. 'Much like this on the summit push on the Big "E",' Pete observed casually, adding with equal nonchalance, '28,000 feet higher on Big "E", of course.' Difficult to follow that, and though I struggled for a riposte none came within 20,000 feet.

At last the rope went tight and two tugs signalled an end to our coffee break. Out we went, Somme-style. The weather was daunting; this surely was Armageddon. The wind tore at you. Tore into you. Snatched the breath from between your teeth before you'd barely tasted it. Buffeted the brain insensate and knocked at the heart and challenged 'Climb me if you dare'. And where or what are you? What pleasures are the draught of this moment? To be sure there's no space, no freedom, no grace or joy in movement. The world ends three inches in front of your face and limbs go where they can, where they will stay — and you seldom see where that is. Can this be the same game that we play in the sun on those slabs, a few miles away around the corner? That gambol in shorts with chalk and rubbers. The one a series of narcissistically-deliberate moves, like physical arithmetic; the other a blind, wanton struggle — a gravitational gamble. Can this be the same game? The brain says, 'No, not at all.' But the soul shouts to be heard — 'Yes it is!'

Martin's turn. Out he goes. Out come the coffee and biscuits. And so we went on. When my turn came I struggled upwards for twenty minutes with little idea where I was until I found myself in the lee of an enormous chasm, 100 feet deep. I cast about, looking for the gully continuation which refused to reveal itself, fixed the ropes and tugged. The others quickly joined me, Pete looking greatly exercised:

'This is the Direct Finish,' he said, 'Chouinard did it. Chimneyed it, and he's even shorter than you.' I didn't believe him. Still don't.

'Got to do something for the second half of your pitch.' The comment chided me down and across left to where I found the groove of the original finish. The climbing was steady, pegs here and there and an occasional glimpse over the left shoulder through to the storm to Slime Wall and an evil-looking Shibboleth. A winter ascent of that lot? From the imagination springs such sweet horror! I hugged at my groove and fought back the images that shivered involuntarily across the inward eye, sowing a seed in the sub-conscious. It lingers yet, barren, I hope.

There's a landing fifteen feet from the top, where we joined. Then a convoluted corkscrew of a problem pitch and it's all over. We were out. Out of the vortex, gone from the maelstrom, with nothing worse than the scraich of the wind and a scoot down Great Gully to worry us.

The Great Man spoke and I waited for a leg-pull: 'That's the best day on the hill I've ever had.' His face creased with pleasure and four huge smiles exploded far wider than that Direct Finish. Raven's had beaten badinage.

Postscript. I wrote this on the bus coming back from Chamonix. A few minutes after I had put down that last full stop we pulled into Victoria where I bought a newspaper. Peter Boardman, it told me, was dead on Everest. Stricken, I returned to this story and hacked at all that now seemed in bad taste. Daft of course, but understandable, I hope. Most of it is back now, as it should be. As he would have wanted.

We were close friends and that friendship was based on badinage — our Anglo-Saxon backgrounds allowing nothing outwardly closer. I recall a fatuous argument we had one day while stumbling up the Allt a' Mhuilinn about the importance of physical courage (of which he had more than most). I loosed off schoolboy Kipling, *Henry V* and Macaulay. Pete's counters were weightier by far: Grass, Eliot, Lawrence, until the CIC Hut brought a truce. Then a climb consumed our energies.

Well, I could never make much sense of your writing team, Pete, so in Kipling's words, 'Here's my best respects to you'.

There was a time when I expended all my winter energies in Scotland, in search of snow and ice and something to climb. At that time, like most Scotland-based climbers, indigenous or not (and most are not) I would have scoffed at any suggestion that Wales might be worth my winter time. Then in 1978 I left the Royal Marines and moved to work at Plas y Brenin, the National Centre for Mountain Activities, a move that did little for my soul (I left most of it behind in thirteen tangled years in that old and honourable profession — but it did a lot for my climbing) and since it is climbing that I am presently about, the move was no bad thing within the confines of this book.

Within a week my conversion to Welsh winter climbing began. A year later it was complete.

The first disciple of my Paul-ine conversion was Western Gully on The Black Ladders in whose evangelical clutch I was soon embraced. I'd gone out that first weekend with an open mind to give the Welsh winter a go. I returned from the road to Damascus (which in Wales is called Bethesda) with nagging doubts. If there were many more climbs like this in Snowdonia then my prejudices were in trouble. There are; and they were. The crunch came the next year on a route called the Devil's Appendix. In summer this is a 300-foot waterfall that spatters over Clogwyn y Geifr at the head of Cwm Idwal, not more than forty-five minutes from the road, a stone's throw by the average standards of Scottish approach walks. In winter (some winters), the spatter freezes into a spectacular cascade of ice. It froze in

192

1978 and was climbed for the first time. It froze again in 1979 — which had us all wondering how regularly it had been freezing in the past waiting, daring someone to have a go. As always in climbing, the first ascent opened the psychological floodgates.

In 1978, the year of the first ascent, Joe Brown had stood second in the queue while two upstarts stole the route from under his nose. Joe's partner was Davey Jones of Ogwen Cottage — and though the Appendix grew like Jack's beanstalk out of his backyard — yet still they were beaten to it. It was a terrible thing. Mind you, as the upstarts would doubtless be the first to point out, folk, including Joe had been sniffing at it for fifteen years, dogs round the Devil's Lamp Post. And for fifteen years the 'out of condition' ploy had given best to the physical and psychological barrier of 300 feet of very steep ice. How strange, then, that the route has been in 'nick' for three or four years since that first ascent. A new ice-age, or new ice-tools. . .? Full marks to the upstarts. (Mick Poynton and Phil Kershaw; their feat deserves better treatment than the tenor allows.)

Brown and Jones followed minutes after and then everyone was at it, the word had got about — the Appendix did freeze, it could be climbed, had been climbed. Farther afield it spread on the climbers' bush telegraph, there's this frozen waterfall of a thing down in N. Wales. . . the word got about. Waiting for the Appendix to freeze became the game and when it did, in 1979, I was there with Martin Boyson, but not quickly enough. The rumour that the Devil had bared his Appendix was already rife; there was a queue. And Boysen was impatient. He nearly always is. We were fourth or fifth in line, which wasn't anything like good enough for him. Wasn't it sufficient frustration that the first ascent should have been snatched by two unknowns without so much as a credential between them whilst he, doyen and co-creator of the Black Cleft and a dozen other Welsh winter horrors, hungered impotently in Altrincham?

After its fifteen years of growing into climbers' consciousness, The Appendix aged rapidly. First climbed by two unknown Englishmen; second ascent three minutes later by an indigenous instructor and an ageing rock-star. Shortly afterwards a Scot declared that his country had nothing like it, which is as close as those north of the border will come to admitting that they found a climb south of it hard. In 1981 an Irishman soloed it for Christmas.

Martin stomped about, all sulphurous vim and vigour, for two minutes or so before exhausting what passed in him for patience and charging off to find another route. I followed reluctantly in his wake. After all, it was a grand day, and a couple of hours of Appendix-watching suited me fine. I lived just down the road and could nip up in a minute on any of the next two or three times this century that the Devil obliged us with his route. But Martin, fraught from the teaching of biology to fifteen-year-old recalcitrants, needed his climb and needed it quick.

He selected an improbable line and shot up it to snatch the first winter ascent of the Devil's Pipes. Ten minutes later we were back at the foot of the Appendix where the queue was scarcely diminished though a man-and-wife team were abseiling off the climb. While wifey froze at her belay, hubby had struggled manfully to the top of the first pitch, at which point, extended beyond the call of marital duty and his own ability, he abseiled off muttering that it was 'too hard for the wife'. Surely the most unchivalrous 'climbing down gracefully' ploy of all time.

Martin set about the rest of the queue with the same galvanic energy with which he had cleared out the 'Pipes'. I could but wonder at his nerve. Aspirants five and six were despatched to a 'much better route' around the corner. Lamely they departed, only, as I later discovered, to fail on this improvement. Numbers three and four were plainly told that the route was far too hard for them and, relieved of their burden, they wandered happily away in search of easier ground. One and two, made of sterner stuff, held their ground and prepared to launch themselves at the first pitch with Martin, outraged at this intrusion into the Master's design, castigating their temerity. I marvelled at the hauteur of the great.

And even as I marvelled a second energy registered somewhere in the subconscious. The atmosphere was suddenly gravid with matters of great moment. As though drawn by some psychic power (or on reflection it might have been those awful animal grunts) our heads were turned as one, our gaze rivetted by an unforgettable display.

Just across the 'Kitchen' an instructor frontpointed with fastidious precision to the upper rim of an ice cliff, where he paused, Piolet Gibbon, in order to demonstrate some arcanum to assembled and awestruck tyros. Extracting his dues in gasps of

194

assembled and awestruck tyros. Extracting his dues in gasps of admiration he disappeared from his charges' view and pounded up the ensuing 40° snow slope in search of a belay. He was 150 feet from the ground but still 10 feet short of his target when the first victim, assuming a tight rope signalled his turn, set off with prodigal energy.

The pupil flailed upward for 15 feet or so, Piolet Attila, discovering in those luminous seconds that ice-climbing was more biceps than brains. Meanwhile, the instructor sedulously embraced a boulder with a textbook belay, consuming the rope, as chance would have it, at precisely the same speed as the victim climbed. Awesome though the latter's energy was it was also human, and at 30 feet his quadrupedal threshings wilted fast until crampons and axes, lacking power or accuracy, ricocheted to nowhere. Weaker still he grew. A search in the engine room of his soul found a final calorie which fired some terrible grunts and a last convulsion; and then that calorie was thrown, with his axe, to the wind. With no more to give, not even the energy to fuel a yell, he sank into his harness, slumped into the rope, hung free and limp and dangled, as if from a yardarm, 30 feet from the ground — utterly spent. Boysen, numbers one, two and I stood in mute admiration, too stunned to salute. Had I been alone I think I might have wept.

A split second later this stunned silence was shattered. The instructor, having double-checked his belay, squared his gear, fixed feet firmly, checked it all again and found no fault, sat smugly and called with the measured, practised sonority which is the hallmark of those who ply that trade: 'Come-up-when-you-are-ready'. The command, for such it was, reverberated about the cwm and one by one, separated only by the speed of sound, a dozen spectating teams collapsed in mass hysteria.

Martin pitched forward, face into the snow, clutching at his throat and convulsed in apoplectic laughter. The other Appendix team did much the same while hoots and howls floated up from all around. The whole Kitchen was aboil with laughter.

At last numbers one and two tumbled off, no longer capable of mustering the necessary aggression for an appendectomy; which left Martin and me. One of the departing climbers offered me a shot with a pair of Hummingbird axes: 'Perfect for steep water-ice,' he said. I had never seen them before but thought to give them a try and left my own axes on the floor. Looking up, the flesh of the Appendix was plain to see. A trunk of water-ice rose 120 feet to a ledge and belay. At mid-height there was a painful-looking swelling, then a comparatively benign groove led up and left for a second 120 feet or so. The belay was not obvious. On Pitch 3 a horizontal traverse sneaked rightwards to an angry, vertical chunk festooned with malignant icicles, each a huge anti-climber missile as long as a lance. The full breadth of the upper face was hung with these, often grotesquely contorted like the grasping fingers of Hokusai's waves. Some Appendix! I briefly pictured myself picking a way through such a canvas, but here at base the imagery escaped me and levity ruled.

I giggled my way up 10 feet of steepish ice, where I attempted to lodge a Hummingbird in a vee formed by two converging icicles. They would have accommodated my own axes happily, but for some reason rejected this new-fangled tool. As I fiddled, an enormous tug on the rope plucked at me, and glancing quickly down I saw my second pulling on the rope with truly satanic fury. With a levity-shattering splat I landed at his feet, where the Hummingbirds were snatched from my wrists. Martin, angry again, cursed my time-wasting.

'Balls to those bloody parrots — use your own gear — and get a move on!'

I did as I was commanded, fearing Martin more than the Devil — they seemed to be sharing the same pair of horns. Ten minutes later I belayed about 100 feet of steep ice. I recall nothing of that first pitch. Martin sprinted up the next and spent all of twenty seconds engineering the worst belay imaginable — an axe loosely jammed across a groove of rotten ice. Faith and his left hand held it in position while he managed the rope with the right.

'Quickly!' he snapped, as I eyed it.

Quickly I went. To the traverse, exposed, exhilarating and 300 near-vertical feet above the floor. And then the final bulge, as exciting as any chunk of ice I can remember.

Not so much to tell about a great ice-climb, you will say. Not much indeed for, though it is a great climb, I still remember the laugh we had better. Anyway what can you say about steep water-ice? If the axes stay, so do you. And they did; biceps not brains, see! On the way down the lines of a song occurred to me: 'Now I ain't saying we beat the devil,' but we laughed at his joke for nothing — and then we climbed his climb.

British Winter climbing — good game, great game; got to play it 'fore you can say it. And then they go together — with gusto.

6

Nepal

GAURI SANKAR: NO RESTING PLACE FOR THE IMAGINATION

'In wilderness is the preservation of the world'
Thoreau

'Mountains are not chivalrous; one forgets their
violence. Indifferently they lash those who venture
among them with snow, rock, wind, cold.'
George B.Schaller

This is about a failure; a personal failure — the hardest sort to
bear.

And so it will be the hardest tale to tell. I am not sure if I can
tell it truthfully; or if I want to. There are difficulties. I want to
keep it short, to tell it quickly so that I don't dwell on the bits
that hurt. The mind is mended, the body nearly. Do I really want
to dredge up that past grief? The answer is no; I don't. The mind
heals with purges, the details may no longer be there. My
memory is hopeless anyway. Sure, I kept a diary, but often not
for days so that when I caught up, my recollection sometimes
failed the detailed test. Pete Boardman certainly thought so when
I loaned him my diary to supplement his own when he was
writing *Sacred Summits*. 'You've even got some dates wrong,' he
told me, shocked. I shrugged. It didn't matter much to me then,
matters not at all now. Nor am I sure that my diary was entirely
honest. I knew Pete intended to write a book of the climb. I
cannot claim that it did not influence what I wrote, even what I
said. What a terrible admission. If then, you're after the defini-
tive account, the history, of the first ascent of the South Summit
of Gauri Sankar, read it in *Sacred Summits*. I may myself one
day. For the moment I prefer, if I must look back, to use a dark
glass. Pete's glass, his clear, sharp glass, might show me more

than I dare to see, might prick this sentimental eye with stubble truth. Then would scrag and precious fun perish in truth's famine. I would rather nurture whatever fun I found that autumn.

There is another problem. Pete died on Everest three years later, which is nothing now for tears but nothing for prickles either. I used to call him, in jest, the Great Man. He wasn't a great man, he was too young for that (and so took himself too seriously; was concerned about his image), but I think he might have been in time. But his death will be a restraining influence; I want to leave Boardman where he has settled in me — and anyway, 'speak as they please, what does the mountain care?'

Within these constraints, I'll tell the story as best I can and if my 'quick heart quickens from the heart that's dead' you'll have to skid across some sticky patches with me — or seek the Great Man's version. Or take the next chapter.

'Come on lads,' Pete would exhort us as our efforts to subdue the delicately corniced West Ridge began to falter.

'Come on, it's no worse than the Midi/Plan traverse.' Now I thought about that a bit at the time — and a lot since — but try as I might I can't bring myself to agree with the Great Man. As I remember it the Midi/Plan traverse is a doddle; sunkissed and festooned from dawn to dusk with all manner of Euro-citizenry and whilst we had our fair share of sun, even Boardman's massive presence and gentle scoldings scarcely served office for that voluble crowd. No sir, this place was altogether less friendly.

But to the beginning. It had all started nearly a year before with a 'phone call. 'Want to come to Gauri Sankar?' 'Yes,' I replied, flattered to be invited personally by the Great Man himself. 'We've had a late drop out,' he continued, 'and you were the only bloke I could think of who could get the time off.'

I did some homework. Gauri and Sankar — it is a twin-summited mountain — were two of the remaining unclimbed 7000-metre summits in the Himalayas. The mountain has deep religious significances for both Hindus and Buddhists. Sankar, the North Summit, is the Hindu god Shiva, and is married to the goddess Gauri, the South Summit. The Buddhist Rolwaling Sherpas, living south of the mountain can only see the South

Summit. They call it Jomo Tseringma. It is the most holy mountain of the Sherpas.

Photographs showed it to be a spectacular looking hill with razor ridges and precipitous faces. It was the Himalaya's 'last great problem' and more than forty expeditions had applied for a go since it came back on the 'market' in late 1977. It had been out of bounds since 1968 because the Chinese and the Nepalese couldn't agree on whose land it lay. Before that it had repulsed no less than six worthy efforts including one by Whillans, Clough and co; the Swiss Guide, Lambert, had deemed it impossible and it had become known as the Eiger of the Himalayas. All of this made it very attractive.

We had permission for an attempt in the autumn of 1979 whilst an American/Nepalese team led by Roskelly were a step ahead with a shot in the spring. Naturally, in the true spirit of mountaineers we hoped they wouldn't get up. But they did, damn them. A fine effort it was too. Hard and direct up the centre of the West Face of the North (and highest) Summit. You'll have read of it in *Mountain* and elsewhere. All good stuff, but it left us in a bit of a quandary. There was little point in repeating their route and all the other probable lines seemed to rise from Tibet — forbidden territory. Gauri, however, remained virgin and two obvious lines beckoned; the South Ridge tortuously long and blocked near the end by a vertical-looking cliff hundreds of feet high, or the West Ridge, a fine-looking line, steeper over all, but still very long. Perhaps we could bag the traverse between the two summits as well. Perhaps. After weeks of speculation we decided that no decision could be made on the poor photographs and scant information at our disposal; we would have to wait until we saw the real thing. Which is what we did.

Kathmandu was a disappointment. I'm not sure what I was expecting, but here in full measure was the perennial paradox of the East; the beauty of most things old, the vulgarity of all things new. But the paradox no longer assailed me — my senses had been inured by years in Singapore and by extensive travelling throughout the East. It was old hat for Pete too, but Tim Leach, our youngest member, was fascinated, as is anyone of any sensitivity when confronted with the East for the first time.

We had to spend more time in Kathmandu than the necessary

administrative chores demanded for when they were all done — the kitting out of Pemba Lama, our Sherpa sirdar (who we had asked to join us on the climb as a member of the team), the sorting out of a Liaison Officer, Sankar Pradon, the hiring of porters, visiting the Ministry of Tourism, obtaining visas, trekking permits and insurance — after all that was done, a week's worth on the Eastern scale, Guy Neithardt was still absent. Guy was a friend of Pete's, a Swiss mountain guide from Leysin. He often worked with Pete at the International School of Mountaineering at Leysin of which Pete was the Director.

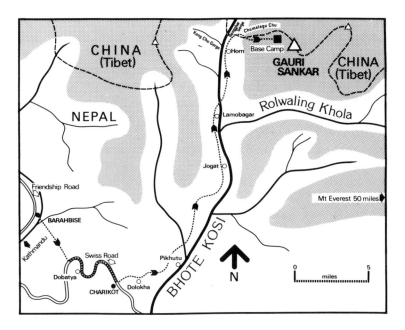

At last Guy arrived and about a week later than we had antici-pated we had the whole expedition at Barahbise, a dusty four-hour road journey from Kathmandu and the point at which our ten-day walk-in was to begin.

The walk-in was an idyll. A ten-day mobile geography and sociology lesson. Much has been recorded of treks through the Himalayas and ours was unexceptional, though it served us well. It gave us a chance to get to know each other. Pete and I were old friends but I had only met Tim once or twice and had never climbed with him. I had never met Guy before I collected him at Kathmandu airport. In fact Pete was the only person who knew everyone. We began to get to know each other quite well in the next ten days — and better in the following thirty — though, as always in the half-world of mountaineering not as well as we each deserved. The walk-in was useful training and acclimatisation too though ten days to base camp at over 16,000 feet was quicker than was ideal.

Pete and I talked together a lot, probably because we knew each other best and were, in any case, close friends. And like many close friends we were very different. We would argue about the daftest things. About words, about whether the modern and increasingly accepted meaning of 'disinterested' was a good thing, about what had happened to the word 'chauvinism' and about what Fowler would say about it — which since we didn't carry a copy of *Modern English Usage* was pure conjecture; about Kipling, about politics with a big 'P' and about climbing politics which should have no 'P' at all. Pete would describe himself as a working class boy when he was comfortably and substantially middle class. I could not understand why it was better to be one or the other and told him so; told him too that it was time he grew out of it. One day I quoted Kipling's *If*. Pete hit the roof. These were the middle class values that I held dear he said — and he used 'middle class' in a pejorative way. In fact I did hold *If*'s values dear but I came from a far poorer background then he. The irony was that Pete was the walking, talking personification of *If* — and yet I bet he's angry with me now for saying it.

He would say that I was politically naive — which I am. He meant it as an insult, I took it as a compliment. I would say he was politically astute, meaning to insult. He was flattered. Yet I was the man of the world, had travelled the world, seen and done things Pete wouldn't dream of and he, the astute politician, was still a country boy, a gritstone boy, at heart. But we got on like a house on fire and we made each other laugh — which was to be important. A last thought; we knew that it was Pete's intention to write part of a book about this trip. I can't say how much that knowledge affected what we did or said — but I have to confess that I was conscious of it and it must, therefore, have exercised some influence over my action, decisions and statements. Now there's food for expedition thought!

The paradox of the East nibbled at us most of the way to the bottom of the mountain.

One night, at the end of the day's trek, we camped at Pikhutu, a beautiful place on the banks of the Bhote Kosi — 'the river that rises in Tibet'. Pete was playing a Blondie tape and caterwauling with her as she sang. Guy and I decided to have a splash in the river. We found a quiet spot, stripped off and plunged into an invigoratingly cool current. A few minutes later some women came by and were greatly offended at our nakedness. They screamed what I interpreted as abuse at us and gestured angrily in our direction. I was saddened that we had upset them. I remembered learning while staying with Ghurka soldiers in Borneo, that they did not go naked before one another and even when showering they wore pants.

'Still the world is wondrous large — seven seas from
                                                marge to marge;
And it holds a vast and various kinds of man;
And the wildest dreams of Kew are the facts of Kathmandu
And the crimes of Clapham chaste at Martaban.'

The same lines, in a far far sadder context came to me again, later that night. I wrote it in my diary:

'Tragedy. A couple came in at dusk with a baby — looks about 3 years old with boiling water burns over at least 30% of his body. They ask for help. Forcing myself to look, I consult our medical book and realise that he must get to hospital soon. Ask when this happened — 4 days ago. I cover the child with some clean linen ripped from my sleeping bag liner. We give them 200 rps and pack them off to hospital. The nearest one is at least three days away. I fear there is little chance. How can they do nothing for 4 days? I am deeply saddened and for the first time in years pray — not a very respectful one I'm afraid but nevertheless a prayer — 'Lord if you're up there, do something for this child — please'.

The expedition makes little sense for a while, but then nothing does. Billions of dollars being wasted around the world and Nepal needs hospitals. But strangest of all was the parents seeming lack of concern. Do they accept tragedy and death more readily than we do? Did they not realise the seriousness of it all? Why do they not help each other? We

203

showed great concern but none of the locals moved a finger to help. Are they tougher and harder than we? The mother and father have gone off into the night with their son — what a pathetic sight they make.'

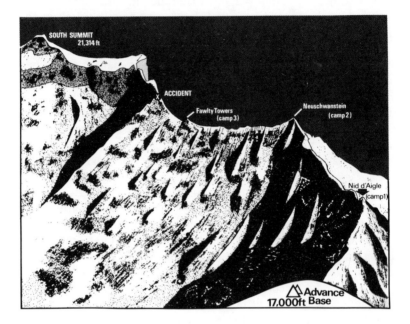

We first saw Gauri Sankar clearly from a rope bridge the next morning just above the village. It looked magnificent and it was easy to understand why for years the locals thought it to be the highest mountain in the world. It rises, seen from that bridge at any rate, right out of the jungle with no other peaks at hand to compete or compare. An orgy of photography ensued with longer and longer lenses contesting the prize-winning shot; to be sure it was an inspiring sight. As an Ulsterman I felt enabled to wax fairly lyrical about it all. Guy, a *French* Swiss, also permitted himself a superlative or two. Tim Leach on the other hand had his Yorkshire heritage to restrain him and allowed only that though it looked 'interesting', it wasn't nearly as exciting as the Caley Boulder near Leeds which apparently boasts both the hardest and the most exposed climb in all the world. Pete, great man that he was, was still betwixt Kangchenjunga, marriage and

204

K2 (or was it the other way round) and was heard, so modestly, to say to Pemba Lama, 'You should see Kangch'. Pemba could only gaze in awe, first at the hill and then at the Great Man.

The West Ridge was looking favourite and we pressed on to a base camp at 16,000 feet which had been used both by Don Whillans and Dennis Gray way back in 1964 and by the Americans this last spring. A blazed trail led us pleasantly through Dennis's 'thickest jungle in the world' and six days after leaving Pikhutu, ten after Kathmandu, we arrived at Base.

The site was barren, rocky and a shade inhospitable, but what made it even more unsatisfactory was that we could not see our mountain. Nor any other come to that. Pete and Guy seemed to acclimatise immediately — Pete had 'Kangch' to thank and Guy had spent all summer trotting, clients in tow, up and down the Mitteleggi. Tim and I suffered; Tim so much so that after a week even his Yorkshire stubbornness had to call for quarter and down he went to the jungle. As we helped him down the hill to a lower altitude we thought we would see no more of him this trip.

In the next few days we found our mountain again — and it looked bigger and better and even more beautiful. We sited an advance base at the foot of the West Ridge upon which, in vague discussion since Pikhutu, we had decided to concentrate our efforts. There ensued a week or so of lugging stores from Base to Advance Base. I found it hard work and any strong ethical feelings I had ever held about the use of porters or sherpas quickly evaporated. But it was too late for we had long since despatched our forty porters leaving the five of us for the hill and a small team for Base Camp. In any case the others were made of stronger stuff — and Pete had his reputation to think of.

At last we had ferried our entire stock of food and kit to Advance Base and now remained there ourselves ready for the next stage. There was no science attached to all this — no computing of provisions or rationalising of gear. It was much simpler than that. We simply took all we had and hoped it would suffice. And a fond hope that may be considered when we could count only a dozen rock pegs, a couple of ice screws and a handful of deadmen between us — though we had cassette tapes to spare.

From Advance Base the West Ridge looked terrific — collosal. We were at about 17,388 feet which left roughly 6000 feet and all spread over a mile of interesting ground sporting snow ridges, cornices, faces, buttresses, all sorts. The plan was nothing if not simple: get on to the ridge and keep on it to the top. Guy dismissed a kilometre-long horizontal looking bit in the middle with a gallic shrug. 'One hour, maybe two, step cutting,' he pronounced and as if to show that he knew none of the rest of us had ever cut a step in our lives he elegantly described a graceful arc with his right arm — which is apparently how it is done.

Before the sun set that evening we as good as had it in the bag. All that remained was the climb. The next day brought new ground and great excitement. Gaining the ridge proper turned out not to be absolutely straightforward and it took a full day and several mild contretemps to establish the best way. In fact we disagreed on this right to the finish and it was not unusual to see us set out together for the ridge, split after a hundred yards, only to rejoin on the ridge itself. Nor was it rare for us to do the same on the daily return trip.

Our tactics, democratically selected by Pete, were euphemistically dubbed 'modified alpine'. This is a useful expression which embraces a wide range of ethical weaknesses in an ever-degenerating spiral towards traditional Himalayan strategies. We opted for fixing ropes as we went on all the difficult bits (this turned out to be the entire distance), abseiling back to camp at night, returning to jumar to the previous high point the next day, pushing on for as many days in this fashion as was necessary to exhaust either our seventeen fixed ropes or ourselves. Then, find a camp site and lift and shift the gear over as many days as it took until we had established the higher camp. Next, recover all the fixed rope, leaving bright orange abseil loops where we could for the eventual retreat and repeat the whole performance from the new camp — until we got to the top or ran out of food or energy or enthusiasm. In the event we ran out of the lot in precisely the reverse order.

The climbing was constantly interesting, often exciting and sometimes quite tricky. At last three or four pitches of Scottish 3-ish led to a point where we had no more rope to fix. It was an unlikely looking campsite but Pete decreed it, a mite traditionally, 'Camp I', and Guy, less prosaically, *Nid d'Aigle* (The Eagle's Nest). It was short on space, long on exposure and boasted what must be one of the world's most precipitous lavatories.

The load carrying followed: a long jumar from Advance Base to the *Nid d'Aigle,* collapse; shed the contents of rucksack — and occasionally stomach too — and abseil home. Even Pete was seen to puff a bit while Guy's *Nom de Dieu*s increased in frequency and volume, power and range in direct proportion to load and altitude. Then just as we were about to take up the ropes for the next stage who should hove over the horizon but Tim, half bent double under an enormous 'sack and eyes set fast on the summit. (We had reckoned without his Guisely grit.) I barely managed to stop him; but when I did he accepted an invitation to join the team. He was a wee bit scornful of our pedestrian tactics and would, I suspect, have much preferred a bolder approach, taking in every obstacle direct and stopping for breath, only on the summit and then but briefly, before glissading back to the Caley Boulder.

We all welcomed Tim's arrival but none more than I. You see I had been responsible for 'organising' — I use the word in its loosest possible form — the food. Already, only a third of the way up the route it was looking distinctly sparse and Tim's unexpected arrival brought me the perfect excuse of an extra mouth to feed. I hoped the others wouldn't notice that he hardly ate at all.

Domestic life at the *Nid d'Aigle* was a bit fraught. Three were squeezed into one tiny tent whilst the two in the other cooked for all five and did a sort of meals on wheels around the campsite. Moreover, Guy, being Swiss, could not entirely divest himself of the trappings of civilisation and insisted on clean cutlery, pristine pots, cordon bleu cooking and no farting. All of which was asking too much. In the end he declared us 'animals' which seemed to make us all feel happier and we soldiered on — a team once more.

With an expansive wave of the hand Pete indicated the next campsite some 1500 feet above at Point 6000 (actually Point 6037m, 19,800ft) and atop an improbable looking ice cream cone. By now we knew better than to argue. The standard reply began 'On Kangch. . .' — in any case he was always right.

Off we went with lots more of the same. A few hard rock steps fell to Tim's Caley cavort, the ridges to Guy's Gallic gyrations, the plods to Pete and the rest, whatever it was, to me. Point 6000 was reached after some pleasantly exciting climbing up steep exposed snow slopes and sharp, equally exposed ridges. The last few hundred feet of fixed ropes were precarious but they survived the days of load ferrying that followed. Two small platforms, each no bigger than the groundsheet, were eventually chopped in the 45 degree slope immediately under Point 6000 and we braced ourselves for the next hurdle. Guy christened this place *Neuschwanstein* after mad King Ludwig's Bavarian cloud castle — he said he kept hearing Wagner's *Lohengrin*.

Looking along the ridge from our new camp Guy's 'one hour maybe two' looked as if it might consume rather more of our time. Guy was still contemptuous — I, rather sceptical. The next day, a rare stormy one, Guy and I were put to the ridge while Pemba, Pete and Tim ferried some last few stores and began to pull up the fixed rope. In yesterday's sunshine Guy's optimism had carried the day. Today shrouded in cloud and windy and cold my scepticism dealt defeat. Together we crawled out two cringing rope lengths before retreating to the tent with our tails between our legs — and mine promising to stay there. It was my worst performance on any route anywhere. True I had seen little evidence of Guy's promised prowess at the step cutting but it was my own abject defeatism that rankled then, and still does. Pete, arriving late from his toil, was less than pleased though he took it all with his usual stoicism.

The next morning it was clear again. Things looked better, not just prettier, but more friendly too. The exposure was still stupendous but there were soft comforting shadows, curves and folds could be seen, and ledges, places to rest the mind and eye, discovered. The trouble yesterday had been that there was no resting place for the imagination.

The following day I was sacked from the front and sent off on my own to bring up the remaining three or four fixed ropes. It was sunny again and, abseiling down, I enjoyed the experience of being absolutely alone on this big mountain. About midday I regained the tents at Point 6000 and looked along the ridge. There was no-one to be seen. Assuming that Tim had galloped along it I concluded that he may need some more rope and set off with the few that I'd recovered. I found them about one and a half pitches beyond our previous 'high' point and having a hard time of it. Tim was easily the best technical climber in our team but this was no place for technique. I dumped the rope and sat to watch — there being nothing else to do. My very presence — I suppose I looked smug — seemed to provoke Pete who seized his axe and the lead and set off up the next section whirling his axe like a dervish, demolishing cornices with two handed claymore blows, the repercussions of which soon had both us and the ridge shuddering. He covered 150 feet in about a minute and a half and left behind an M1-like footpath along which you could have wheeled your grandmother. In fact Pete claimed his grand-mother could have done it on her own. (I have met her. She is a remarkable woman but I have my doubts — no disrespect.) As a gesture it was cataclysmic, as a demonstration galvanitic, as a piece of climbing artless — but it didn't half do the job. Unfortu-nately he was now exhausted and flaked out *à cheval* over the ridge. I ambled up the footpath he had left and led on emulating the Great Man's 'piolet bludgeon'. It worked. A couple of pitches later and with honour restored we went happily back to Point 6000 with the key to the route in our pocket. The sunset was unforgettable.

The next campsite, at the end of the horizontal section of the ridge before it steepened considerably, was the most precarious thus far. We perched on it beside a small rock tower so we chris-tened the place 'Fawlty Towers'. One night Tim vomited into his sleeping bag and then all over Guy who broke the world *Nom de Dieu* and *Bordell de Merde* record at once. At dawn the offend-ing bag was put out to air. (Guy would have aired Tim too if he could have found somewhere to hang him.) Shortly after, a slithering sound, the sort nylon makes on snow, reminded Tim of where we were. Too late. Tim's bag was on its way to Tibet where it may now be keeping some surprised peasant cosy. After that Tim spent some cool nights huddled between Pete and me, but never complaining — not that it would have done him much good if he had.

Back in the lead again Pete and I were fixing what we hoped was the final buttress — 1500 feet of it. It was getting late in the year and some strong gusts were beginning to catch us on the ridge. I was feeling great. My earlier scepticism had vanished and with the end in sight a new optimism and energy emerged. On about the fifth pitch of the day a particularly fierce gust caught me and I had to cling hard to the mane of the ridge with hands and feet to stay on. It lasted only a few seconds and then subsided into comparative calm. Higher up I ran out of climbing rope but on seeing a friendly looking buttress 50 feet ahead and easy ground between, I untied from the climbing rope and called to Pete that I was continuing on the rope we were fixing. I quickly reached the rock and placed a good peg — so good that I stood back to admire it — just as another gust whirled in, stronger than the last and with a hellish sound I'll not forget. Off I came and in what seems upon reflection, slow motion, down, down, down I tumbled. The slope was steep, 60 degrees or so, and I was soon hopelessly out of control with no prospect of stopping before the glacier some 5000 feet away. Rather like your toast, which falls buttered side first, I fell to the north, into Tibet and the shade. I was puzzled — I felt no fear. I have since wondered if fear is generated by the mind to fuel a life saving effort. Here it was clear that no effort under the sun could help. There was no panic either, perhaps because there was no fear. My thoughts were clear and, for once, rational. The rope would break. I was sure of that for it was not designed for shock loading. (When we had collected them from the factory the old lady who had made them warned us maternally, 'Now don't you go falling on these'.) No, my life did not flash before my eyes in an instant but I did experience some deeply personal thoughts and then realising that my head was taking a battering I hoped that I might be lucky enough to be unconscious before much longer. 'Really blown it this time. I'm dying. There's nothing to it. No big deal.' Then I stopped. Pete had held and the rope hadn't broken. He said later that he realised that if he stopped the fall too quickly the load was likely to break the rope so he had let some run through his hands, burning clean through two pairs of gloves in the process. It was clear thinking and I hope I remembered to thank him for it.

A day later at Fawlty Towers I recorded the day of the incident, the whole truth only slightly tainted by twenty-four hours hindsight. Later thoughts are in parenthesis.

(Looking back through my Gauri Sankar diary I have noted a paradox: the more serious the situation, the harsher the environment, the more uncomfortable the business of writing the more reliable, the truer the record grows. It is as if in the low valleys there is too much detail to record faithfully; and although there is plenty of time for consideration, that time is spent in decorating plainness, dressing simpleness, embellishing ordinariness instead of simplifying, clarifying or just carefully setting down that plain record. Up here life is too precious, too good, to mess with. It is difficult to be smart-arsed on a knife-edge ridge at 20,000 feet for twenty days. The truth shines easily through at these rarified altitudes, it's hard to miss — there is nothing but.)

5th Nov. Awake at 4.30 but Pemba falls asleep over brew so we don't get away till 8.00. Tent very cold with masses of frozen condensation. Goretex cover on sleeping bag very handy for keeping the wet out. It's a cold and windy morning as Pete and I set out for a big day. Jumaring up ropes I feel really good except that I drop a glove which infuriates me. No problem though — have a spare. Reach previous high point at about 10.00, feeling strong. Sort out ropes and I lead off on first new pitch of day — great feeling — no man has ever been here before. The wind is strong but the climbing, a little snow arete, not hard. Ropes snag somewhere beneath Pete and I am preparing to wait while he sorts them out when a hideous shriek sounds above, followed by an incredible blast of wind that nearly plucks me from the arete. I hang on tight — it only lasts a few seconds. I consider going back down to Pete to try to find a less exposed alternative but decide to carry on. See rock belay about 50ft above but can't reach it on the climbing rope so tell Pete to untie and hold me on fixed rope only. (Our practice was that the lead climber would climb on a standard 150-ft climbing rope and tow behind a non-stretch rope for fixing. These had been cut, for no reason that I can remember, about 40ft longer. The second man would jumar up the fixed rope once the leader had anchored it at the end of his lead.) Reach belay, put in peg and am just about to tie on when another shriek and blast of wind unbalances me. It is a good stance so I do not worry overmuch until I find myself out in space. A frantic grab at the rock does no good and down I go. Over and over hitting rocks and snow and seemingly falling for ever. I am dead I am sure of it. There's thousands of feet to the ground and I hope that I am knocked unconscious before I get there. I distinctly remember thinking of Kath and Little J. Then I stop — a rope has held. I am alive and little J. has a

211

dad. I seem to have broken my left wrist and twisted my left knee but I am alive. I behave irrationally and shouting 'I will not die, I will not die', I grab my jumar and start jumaring like a mad-man up the fixed rope which has held me by snagging on the arete. I have fallen about 200ft. I am cold, alone and feel rather sorry for myself. I shout to Pete, who I cannot see, that I am OK — more or less. He apparently is shouting after me but the wind prevents us communicating. At last he sticks his head around the arete to see me still slightly below him. I must look a wild sight having lost my hat and bleeding from the head. He is wonderfully calm as I reach him and burst into tears at the relief of being alive. (But I remembered the story of Shipman and Tilman so forgetting themselves as to shake hands and quickly pulled myself together.) The descent begins. Pemba, who was bringing up more rope is very shaken and calls the other two up to help. I cannot help myself much since my left hand is useless, my left leg shaky and my brain bemused and concussed. But foot by foot, the lads get me, helping myself where I can, back to Fawlty Towers. As soon as I get in the tent I feel better and bemoan the fact that I can't climb any more. Pete tells me I should be thankful that I am alive. He's right and I am consumed with thoughts of little Joseph.'

At Fawlty Towers a general retreat seemed prudent at first, but as I recovered from the concussion I had sustained, things looked better. After a discussion we agreed to leave the final decision to the morrow. When, sure enough, I felt better. Guy, suddenly a learned medical man, pronounced the leg and arm but bruised. The pain told me more, but in my head, as the Americans say, I felt fine.

I had plenty of time to cultivate my diary over the next four days. And because these are four days that I have succeeded in quite erasing from my memory, I give you the extracts from my diary unmolested save for parenthesised afterthoughts again. I accept that this device, the use of diary extracts, lays me open to the charge of taking the easy way, perhaps even of indolence. But I have thought hard upon it and have decided that this is the way that I prefer to treat this unhappy chapter of my climbing time.

'We discuss a plan of action and I eventually persuade them that I can look after myself while they continue to try for the summit which I feel is within our grasp. Eventually they agree to move out early tomorrow in the hope of getting a view of the final difficulties. It breaks my heart that I won't be with them but I'd rather they got up than gave up on my account. Getting down with one arm could be interesting but at least I'll be rested by the time they have had their summit bash. Take some pain killers and try to sleep, but it's not easy — the wrist hurts in every position I can think of trying.

6th Nov. Pete and Guy off early 6.30ish followed by Tim with ropes at 9ish. Pemba left behind to look after me! Wrist hurts like hell but leg not too bad — walkable just. Watch with increasing envy the progress of Pete and Guy along ridge — how I wish I was doing that leading. Still I have had some good pitches. The weather is really good and there's less wind. They made good progress — it all looks so near and yet we know the summit is still some distance. Can hear them shouting in still air. We are very short of food so I don't eat. I can hardly justify it, lying on my butt all day. Feel very groggy — aching all over (notice windsuit is torn in several places) — feel as if I have gone 15 rounds with Marciano and lost every one of them — wrist hurts like hell. (Sorry to whinge so but I did say unexpurgated — the wrist must have been on my mind.) Await return of team to hear the news. We have to be quick — there's only about a day's food left and that's skimping. Sad at missing my big chance when I was going really well, but have to get the thing in perspective. I am alive and lucky to be so.

Lads return late after long day. Guy and Tim think we can hack it — Pete more pessimistic and realistic — I suspect. Guy's opinions always ridiculously optimistic and unrealistic. Plan is that the three of them will spend tomorrow fixing new ground then make summit bid from here day after. This pleases me — I hope that if my hand is less painful I can jumar to end of fixed ropes and then plod easy snow slopes to summit. Hand less painful already tho' still swollen and unusable.

7th Nov. Tim and Guy off early to fix new ground. Pete follows with more rope a few hours later. Pemba and I loll about in heat (it could be warm at midday out of the wind — which although strong, was intermittent) — no room to stretch out and sunbathe tho'. See Tim 1000ft above having problems on new bit he had thought to be easy. No food again. Lose sight of leaders in cloud and snowfall. Await their return with considerable interest. Not sure whether my hope to get to top is realistic — hand still useless. Still I can give it a try and come back if it doesn't work.

8th Nov. In discussion last night it was obvious that none of them thought I had a hope with one hand. They will be lucky to make it anyway. I said I would stay behind — then sulked with disappointment. But I believe it to be for the best — I would hold them up badly — and it will already be touch and go for time. I keep trying to persuade myself that the hand is getting better but I can't hold a glove in it — no hope to climb. I awake this morning bitter and review my disappointment.

Being positive I have much to be grateful for. I am alive and will see my family again. It's been a great trip — not over yet and I have seen and learnt much. The mountaineering has been fantastic and I have had more than my fair share of good climbing. I suspect we will have an epic getting back. The others will be exhausted — there is no food and I can hardly climb, and we have taken up all the fixed rope.

Pete and Tim left early this morning, followed an hour later by Pemba with pot and stove, and 2 hours later by Guy looking very tired and moving slowly — I have doubts that he will make it. I watched as they traversed the ridge to previous high point, then went out of sight. I have watched all day, waiting for them to appear on the col — so far no sign. I think they will be out all night at this rate. How I wish I was with them but I gave myself a quick try out just after Guy left and it was soon obvious I had no chance at all — in fact getting down will test me to the limit.

9th Nov. Watched anxiously all yesterday afternoon and evening for a sighting which I think I am bound to get if they make the South Summit. Have heard voices — seemed quite close perhaps from the notch and the end of the ridge, but so far now about 0900 have seen nothing. Last night was very windy and very cold and it is difficult to believe they are in

214

good nick.— especially Guy who looked on his knees before he left. I hate to panic but I can't help but feel that something is wrong — what I don't know — but they must all have suffered last night.

I'm trying to make a plan — it's not easy. Even if I solo to Base Camp — 3 days in my condition — it will be at least another day before we can reach the radio in Lamobagar. Even then I doubt whether a helicopter could do anything at that height (22,000ft +) and a fixed wing will be able to do nothing more than look and perhaps drop food etc. I wonder if it could land at the col? (Did I really wonder that? What a ridiculous thought!) Anyway if they are still there after 3/4 days they really will be in poor shape — no bags or food. So if I go down will it help? May be better to wait here and help them when they descend. If they are in good shape they can help me! I'll make a decision tonight. Seems clear now that I should have gone down when I first hurt myself — with Pemba. Trouble was at the time I thought it may heal and still give me a chance of the top and also we had promised everyone we would try to get Pemba up. Easy to be wise after the event.

At this stage I was a worried man and was reasoning my way in and out of all sort of possibilities. I simply could not work out what to do for the best. It wasn't so much that they hadn't returned but that I hadn't seen them. As far as I was able to judge I should have been able to do that easily on the last 500ft to the summit which was an easy snow slope — and in full view. In an effort to make a good decision, how rational I was I didn't know and couldn't trust, I wrote an 'appreciation'. This is a systemised process of reasoned thought that military staff colleges attempt to teach to their officers. I never had much faith in them, partly because I wasn't very good at them and partly because we were taught that Nasser had said in 1956, 'I did an appreciation of the situation from the British point of view (he had been to a British Staff College) and came to the conclusion that they would not attack.' I realise that this could mean that Nasser was as bad at appreciations as I, or that indeed the British should not have attacked — but Nasser's statement served well in reinforcing my anti-appreciation prejudices and justifying my reluctance — they are very hard work — as clear thinking always is. Anyway, the point is that here I found myself before my own Suez. I had nothing else to do so I tried to squeeze the 'appreciation' process out of my memory. That in itself was not easy — I had never been an attentive pupil. I fear that the result will hardly rank as a classic of its genre. But it might stand as the highest ever written appreciation (some can arrive at the correct conclusion in a twinkling of an eye — they, if the system is right, become Generals, chairmen of companies, judges — anything, it seems but politicians).

For what it says of the condition of my mind, I copy it here.

An appreciation, 20,000′+ on Gauri Sankar to decide whether I should stay 'up' or go 'down'. 0900 — 9th Nov. Written in an attempt to bring some light, reason and logic to this convoluted Irish brain.

SITUATION Pete, Pemba, Guy and Tim left yesterday 0700-0900 for summit. They expected to be back that night by light of full moon. They took downsuits and gaz, pot and tea for bivvy but no bags. I watched them along ridge until they went out of sight. They should have reappeared several hours later on the summit slopes — or back on ridge in retreat. So far — over 24 hours later they have done neither. Last night was very cold and very windy — it will have been a hard bivvy, Guy was tired before he set out.

AIM To get out of this mess alive.

FACTORS

1. I have broken wrist.

2. There is no food here — they have none. I can subsist on water but will need some strength to get down.

3. There is not a lot of dead ground and yet I have not seen them for over 24 hours.

4. Team not strong. Pete and Pemba probably OK. Guy exhausted and Tim young and likely to be tired.

CONCLUSIONS

1. Moving very slowly or not moving at all; in either case, something is wrong.

2. They can't exist long on gear and food they have at that altitude and these windy, cold nights.

3. Even if I stay here I can't help them.

216

4. I will delay their descent from here with duff wrist and knee.

DECISION

To go down to Base tomorrow at first light (will need all daylight). Will try to get aircraft to shed some light on mystery. And then before I reasoned myself completely round the bend:

9th Nov. cont'd. I see them! they are all there and coming slowly down. Great they are safe — and I am spared an epic of a lifetime. I get the story. Bivouac last night — very cold — Pete said 'It's cold in November at 7000 metres with no gear' — arrived summit this 9am — somehow out of sight from me. They are all exhausted. Full story later. Pete said 'There was only one thing wrong — you weren't there.' I couldn't answer.

All we had to do now was get down. Again I remember little of it. Indeed, I can state with utter honesty that I remember not a detail of anything we did that night — which wouldn't have been much, especially as there was no food to cook. Nor can I recall a single word of any conversation — and I'm sure we must have had a debrief, a story of the climb to the summit, something. I remember nothing, not even the fact of the last night at Fawlty Towers. I have no clear idea why this should be. I have admitted to a poor memory elsewhere and happily confess it again. But this is forgetfulness of an extraordinary completeness. Could it have something to do with the healing process of the mind? I think it could — though knowing nothing of the mechanics of the mind that is only a guess. I must also confess that until I came to write about it, this loss has concerned me not one bit. I have a thousand climbing memories, sad and happy to fill my head; I have never been conscious of this loss until today. Now I am curious, no more.

Of the retreat (and I do not use that military metaphor carelessly, it was a retreat and it was orderly only by the skin of anything we had left), I remember only the most general things: the pain, the quiet desperation; the determination to stay cool, to not lose my temper, to not let my mates down — or myself, to screw the last ounce of fight out; the fight, the hanging on, hanging on, hanging on.

And curiously I remember fairly clearly the best thing that

217

happened that day, the discovery at Neuschwanstein of some marmalade, butter and peanut butter. We scoffed it, licking blobs of butter off fingers swollen from toil. Even Guy, whose veneer of civilization had been easily the thickest, joined in. The retreat was life reduced to its simplest form; the struggle to survive. That is not a cheap form; it cost us nearly everything we had left (and it's cost me memory though that is a small price). I wouldn't have missed it for the world but I would for anything less. We wanted to get back to the 'burden of life that is a live-long tangle of perplexities' a phrase that could only be written by someone who is well away from life's edge with time to indulge the pat thoughts of idle moments.

My diary records that day:

> **10th Nov.** Thought we could move back to Advanced Base or even Base in one day. Set off at about 9 am and I soon realised we were in for a struggle. Pete, Guy and I moved on one rope. I nearly fainted every time my hand touched anything and my knee kept collapsing on me. Guy was tired and Pete was so close to collapse with exhaustion, that I didn't hold them up at all. We tottered back along the knife edges of the ridge — if one had slipped he would have taken the other two. Had to concentrate as never before. Waves of nausea. Pete kept going to his hands and knees for a rest. At last we got to Neuschwanstein (Pt. 6000) where we found half a tin of butter, ½ a pot of marmalade and a pot of peanut butter which we scoffed neat. (Only hot water for breakfast.) Then abseiling and the rock ridge to *Nid d'Aigle*. Agony. I have never been in such pain. Arrive at *Nid d'Aigle* at 2100 in total darkness, crawling along on our hands and knees. Tempers frayed. Concentrating on holding myself together. Only warm water that night and again for breakfast on 11th. Think we'll make Base Camp easily. Very cold abseiling back to col — takes longer than we think. The walk up to Advance Base a nightmare.'

And here, as the struggle diminishes, as life looks a certain promise again, my memory returns.

I reached the tent at Advance Base about five minutes after Tim, Pemba and Guy and ten minutes ahead of Pete. Pemba was going more strongly than anyone, but then, and I don't mean this unkindly, he had done the least. Guy and Tim were coping better than Pete or I. I learnt later, it must have been later because I remember it, that Tim's mighty technical talent had been brought to bear on some hard mixed pitches near the top on the day before the summit. Not bad for a man we had written off a month before as a non-acclimatiser. Guy too was doing well; I had doubted he would make the summit when he left Fawlty Towers on the 8th.

Pete was in a terrible state. I am not sure what it was that made him worse than the rest. A combination I think of several things. He was the acknowledged leader, a role he was unhappy about but performed magnificently; he was worried about his father who was dying of cancer and though he never voiced this worry once on the climb he told me of it later in Kathmandu; it was his second Himalayan Expedition that year, and Kangchenjunga at 28,208 feet without oxygen, was not the best warm up for Gauri Sankar. Pete was never sure how much that trip had taken out of him, or how quickly he could expect to recover. As he staggered up that slope to Advance Base I think he would have agreed that both the toll and the recovery period were greater than he had been prepared to admit.

As I watched him approach from my slump in the snow I recalled an episode a month before at this same place. We had been carrying loads from Base to Advance Base. One day when I was suffering from diarrhoea Pete had reached the site of Advance Base some minutes ahead of me, dumped his load and coming back to where I was struggling, offered to carry my load. I said no. And I meant it. Pete teased me for what he liked to call my 'warrior virtues' or my 'Boys Own' ethics. All this came to me as I watched my friend struggle that last 100 yards — and I could not resist it, the cost to my weary body notwithstanding — anyway this effort came from the soul. I got up, even that seemed a big effort then, and plodded slowly — and I hope smilingly, for it was a joke — to Pete.

'Want a hand, mate?'

'Do you mean it?'

'No.'

A draw; the perfect points draw. We had sparred in the friendliest of rivalries all through the expedition. That was the last round. I'm not at all sure that it makes any sense.

219

'O foolish one to roam
So far in thine own mind away from home!'

We found some tins of spam. We ate them, drank some melted water and rested for an hour. I told the others that I envied them on the descent for having the thought of the summit to succour them. Pete replied that being alive was no small thing to be thankful for. Right he was.

It was late afternoon before we quit camp. There was one low col to cross before we gained an easy snow slope that led for 500 feet down to Base Camp. Moved by a common, but unspoken feeling, those who reached the col first waited for the rest so that we could all descend that last easy slope together. Everyone waited except Tim. The no-nonsense Yorkshire man had not been moved. I couldn't begin to understand why; nor could begin to explain why he should have been. Pete shouted angrily after him but an evening breeze soothed that raucousness away. Tim didn't hear and Pete was quickly glad. We (the romantic ones? the foolish ones? the old ones?) strolled down to Base Camp together in the honest glow of a good fight, narrowly won and an exquisite sunset. Now the climb was over, the climbing done, the thinking could begin.

At base we conducted a stock take on our bodies; lank, tangled hair, ribs — all of them — and two stones lighter apiece; stockings filled with dead scales of skin, fingers raw, faces burnt, blistered and old; the accepted price. We had reason to agree with George Schaller 'Mountains are not chivalrous'!

The walk-out should have been bliss. It was between autumn and winter and the way lay softly russet and pleasantly warm. But a bitterness crept in through my wounds and I was nagged by the fear of permanent damage to my wrist.

At Pikhutu we enquired after the baby. It had made a complete recovery. We were happy about that. Pemba procured some *chang* and we celebrated. That night, around a camp fire, the *chang* still flowing free and fast, Pete asked me why, when I had fallen I hadn't shouted or screamed. I loved to kid him along and here was another opportunity,

'Well mate my Dad used to say that if you're going to die you should die quietly.' (I did hear him say that once but now I was taking him very much out of context.) Pete thought that fitted his image of my self image perfectly and made an instant entry in his note book. I'm prepared to bet that 'die quietly' is in *Sacred Summits* somewhere. Better lines have occurred to me since. I might have said, borrowing from another, something to the effect that most of Shakespeare's characters get their dying done with an economy of words: Hamlet ('The rest is silence'); Romeo and Juliet, Antony and Cleopatra; Arthur ('Heaven take my soul and England keep my bones'); Caesar, Cassius and Brutus. I might have said that but I didn't; the best lines always come too late. Perhaps it's as well, he was tickled pink at the answer he got — and it amused me to play my part, to amuse him.

On the plane from Delhi Pete showed me the expedition report that he had been working on. He invited me to comment, to make suggestions. The report was fine. I had one comment. When describing the descent he had written of me as being in 'some pain'.

'That's understating it a bit,' I said.

'Better to play these things down,' he replied. I agreed but joked,

'Christ! Who's playing the Mr 'If' now?'

We both had a laugh at that.

I was late back; later than my employers, The Sports Council, had given me leave for. I had missed an important Plas y Brenin Committee Meeting and thought I would be in trouble. The day I arrived in England the Sports Council were beginning their annual conference at Crystal Palace. I sought to make amends by getting there as quickly as possible. I went home to Wales, collected some clothes and travelled, beard, limp and broken wrist, to the conference. After two days I could stand the pain no longer and went to the nearest hospital, Kings College. It was the first time I had ever been to a civilian hospital and I was unsure of the drill. On entering, a sign said 'casualty' which I considered accurately described my condition ('walking wounded' would have said it in the old days) and followed the signs to where a limp and bent queue sat disconsolately under a hard neon light. I took my place and waited; two hours.

'Hm, when did you do this?'

'Two weeks ago.'

'Why didn't you come earlier?'

I tried to explain. It was X-rayed.

221

'I'm sorry,' the doctor said. 'I can't make head nor tail of this, but don't worry we have a wrist specialist in today. I'll get him to look at it.'

Ten minutes later I was ushered into another office where the wrist specialist and a group of his mates were poring over my X-ray with ill-concealed glee.

'My dear chap. Your wrist. Marvellous. Really marvellous.'

My hopes soared.

'This is the worst wrist I have ever seen; absolutely marvellous.' His colleagues nodding vigorously. They clearly shared his enthusiasm.

'What do you do for a living?'

'I'm a mountaineer.'

'Hm — I'm afraid you'll never be able to climb again.'

He was wrong. They nearly always are. He has only himself to blame; he performed the operation. The wrist is ninety per cent now. OK on ice and mountains, a bit stiff on rock.

That was five years ago. The wrist and all those hidden wounds have healed with hardly a scar; the mind and body have seen to that. But there is one thing that the mind has not been able to expunge from the memory; the cold virginity of the wind of high places. And I still believe that 'the code of the warrior is at the heart of the mountaineer'.

7

Alaska

MT. DEBORAH:
A RIBBON ON EDGE

'If there were dreams to sell,
What would you buy?'

Thomas Lovell

'This is Alaska man, you don't like it, you can go!'
Drunken Alaskan, Downtown Anchorage

I think, I hope, that this will be the easiest story; because it is the most recent, because it has been distilled and matured but not yet gone stale and because it was as near to perfection as any adventure can be — which is not to say that it was perfect — but it wasn't far off. Judge for yourself.

It all started — as it so often does — with a photograph: in this case a grainy black and white job showing the East Ridge of Deborah. Deborah? I'd never heard of it, but it looked good. And the title of the photograph? 'Defeat' — the dejected figure and battered tent lending spice — vicarious safe-in-the-kitchen spice: tastes good at home, loses something in the climbing sort of spice. In a flush of the first enthusiasm I found out a few things about Deborah. It had been climbed first by Fred Beckey and Heinrich Harrer; vintage enough. They had described their route, the South-West Ridge as the 'most sensational' ice climb of their lives; testimony enough. Since then the mountain had been climbed but four or five times in twenty years; warning enough. And the East Ridge, my ridge, still challenging me from the book as I read and researched, had already repulsed two, maybe three attempts, had earned a book on itself and had achieved 'Last Great Problem' status; caution enough, spice enough!

But cosy at home, no closer than a photograph, no colder than the kitchen, vaulting ambitious doughty dreams, shed of the lead

223

of reality, are free to climb anything, anywhere — and often do. So they should, for of such dreams are climbs made — sometimes. That's how I first climbed the East Ridge of Deborah — in my dreams. Photograph in hand, a dozen times I dreamt the up and the down of it. I dreamt the hard bits, the easy bits; I dreamt it was easy and hard, quick and slow, two days or a month long. I dreamt of little else, I really wanted that ridge, especially after my failure on Gauri Sankar. I wanted it badly. It never became an obsession or anything like it — my attitude to climbing is too frivolous, too dilletante for that — but I was working up a blood lust for a good scrap and that ridge looked as if it could provide one. At first glance, it was hard to trace a line on the photograph but I took it into 'the labyrinthine ways of my own mind' until I persuaded myself that I follow a line from bottom to top. A blink got me up the bad bits, and I could steer a course through grain and cornice. No obsession, but the mountain did become a feature on my mental landscape. It remains there, for healthier reasons now.

Deborah is in the Hayes Range in Central Alaska, about the same latitude as McKinley 100 miles to the east, though at 12,339 feet, a dwarf in comparison with that distant neighbour. This much I found in the family atlas. I visited the Royal Geographical Society to find out if they had a map of Deborah, or at least a map with Deborah on it. They had maps of the whole world, and in half a dozen different scales, but there were gaps here and there and in one such gap stood Deborah — poor reward for an honest attempt to plan. It didn't really matter. Alaska is easy to get to and the logistics of the trip were alpine rather than himalayan, and since I was a much better dreamer than I was planner, that suited me just fine. A rucksack, a plane ticket, a spare pair of socks; this was more to my taste than the welter of paper — letters begging, letters inquiring, permissions, payments, receipts and all the rest, that Gauri Sankar had generated. My temperament was better suited to things 'whose plinths are laid at midnight and whose streets are packed at morn.'

I recruited a team — easy enough at Plas y Brenin with so mighty an adventure as bait — though to be sure an appetite for the bait was about all the team had in common. Rob Collister, man of culture, of peace; a renaissance man, all the good bits from *Chariots of Fire,* arrow alpinist and as fit as a butcher's dog (a deliberately inappropriate metaphor for a vegetarian by conscience). Roger Mear, a fine arts man, twice before to Alaska, our local expert whose querulousness hid a terrier determination; also a vegetarian — though not by conscience — he just hated the taste of meat (that at least I could begin to comprehend). Collister — well he was a hopeless case — but I envied him his moral armour. Malcolm Campbell, gibbon-limbed rock ape, Shergar sinewed, computer whizz-kid; and rapidly going off meat. In truth they were a disgustingly couth and cultured lot; two Corinthians and a Greek god — Campbell was 'way honed'; or three wets (as Mrs. T might have it) and me. Redneck, getting redder. Philistine, Goth, Vandal; all three. I regarded them with a mixture of awe, affection, and a pagan distrust of things only half understood. Beside them I felt riven with the flimsiest of human failings: I think I could have hated them if I had tried.

On paper we didn't look bad. On the ground we looked awful. Campbell had a chipped ankle bone and a surgeon scalpel-keen to operate; Mear was already in hospital for an operation on his knee, with less than two weeks to our flight, while Collister and I had children with mumps — and we both mumpless — so far. And all intent on a ridge about which Dave Roberts (whom I had by now completely forgiven) said in his book *Deborah. A Wilderness Narrative*:

'In a glance that lasted a few moments the expedition seemed to end... what I saw... was a serpentine wisp of snow, like the curl of a ribbon on edge... I could see the double cornice — the whole of the little (snow) bridge was undercut incredibly on both sides, so that it looked as if a strong wind might topple it. It was only ten feet below me and thirty feet long. The last ten feet of it were impossibly thin. Next, I saw the face of the mountain beyond. The crumbly brown rock towered, flat and crackless, a few degrees less than vertical. A thin, splotchy coating of ice overlay most of the rock. Where the rock overhung, great icicles grew. A few vertical columns of plastered snow, like frozen snakes, stuck to the coating on the ice. And above, blocking out half the sky, was that terrible black cliff, the six-hundred-foot wall we had once blithely... allowed three days to

225

climb... I had never seen a mountain sight so numbing, so haunted with impossibility and danger.'

What he might have been moved to say if he'd seen the team of decrepits that now had design on his 'ribbon on edge' hardly bears thinking. Why I wasn't frightened away (mindful of what I have said earlier about the power of the written word on a climber's psyche), I am not sure. Perhaps there was a greater psychological strength in four compared with the more usual alpine two; perhaps it was too far away, both in space and time, to cause immediate worry; perhaps, and this I think is more than a perhaps, I was actually attracted by those words — they held a deliciously fearful fascination, a fascination too fearful, too delicious for me to risk examining very closely lest I discovered truths about myself and why I climbed. Maybe. If so it was well to leave that last thought unmolested, it was cutting too close to the bone and I have always been a better ostrich than philosopher.

For whatever reason we were undeterred. I say 'we' because I had naturally shared with the others this fearful thrill — shared and quartered — there's no room for selfishness on a mountain. Only my mother showed concern. She found the book open at the page, saw the photo, read Roberts' prose, and worried a mother's worry. I assured her that I would double my life insurance (I did) and that, not to worry, the Americans were masters of overstatement (as I am of generalisations — sometimes more useful than the truth and always cheaper). But not this time. About a month later I was to learn that Roberts was spot on — more accurate, more truthful than I have ever been, or found it necessary to be.

Our collective physical dilapidation? We did the sensible things. Mear shed his plaster early and took up a crutch; Campbell evaded his surgeon, Collister and I stopped worrying about our balls and we put the flight back one week. Then we went for it.

Roger was Our Man In Alaska. On previous trips he had succeeded on a new route on Mt. Huntingdon and on the Cassin Ridge of McKinley in winter. Those efforts made him an Alaskan expert by most standards. It was he who had suggested going in April, arguing that though it would be colder than the usual June-July season, the weather would be more settled. We took his word for it; and I still don't know if he was right or wrong — I have only the evidence of one visit and nothing to compare. But when it came to what gear to take, we were all experts, or so we thought. No-one would take another's advice. Roger's advice was that it would be like the Alps in winter and whilst that was, as it turned out, a very fair comparison, it triggered a different signal in each of us — mountaineers are hopelessly idiosyncratic. To Collister, near ascetic, it meant a spare pullover and an extra pair of socks. To Mear himself it meant painstaking vapour barrier systems — which he carefully explained to me and which I, foolishly, pooh-poohed. To Campbell it meant acres of goretex of the most lurid hues and the foresaking of his beloved chalk bag and shorts. To me it meant scrounging as much warm gear as I could persuade anyone to part with. Of hardware and technical gear we all took our favourite bits and pieces so that despite several of Campbell's computerised mind's 'rationalisations' we arrived in two heaped planes-full on the glacier beneath the East Ridge of the mountain with about three times as much gear as we needed. But that was not yet.

Debbie Taylor, friend, co-worker (Brenin's Domestic Bursar), and saint, volunteered to drive us to Heathrow. We left Capel at three in the morning and arrived nicely on time, about an hour before take-off. Campbell was the lad for figures and had been appointed the Expedition Finance Officer. His accounts showed that the Mount Everest Foundation had generously donated £800 and the British Mountaineering Council £200; his bulging pockets confirmed this. But at the airport our Finance Officer looked crestfallen; he had forgotten his cheque book, so that his evident solvency notwithstanding, he couldn't buy his own ticket. I was pleased that there was someone else who made these blunders.

We dragged our gear across to the check-in desk; two rucksacks apiece and a tightly packed gargantuan grip — about the size of a small car, and stuffed much fuller than its dimensions recommended. A customs lady of equal bulk commanded us to unpack the grip. We protested. She responded by ordering us to unpack and display the contents of every bit of baggage. Princess Anne, she promised us, was sharing our flight and she was running no risks with her Princess Anne.

The flight passed without incident, but was noteworthy for two things. The first was the food. In-flight catering makes no allowance for vegetarians, serving only fare for carnivores; fare's fair. This meant that I, a carrion omnivore, dined hugely of scavenged meat leaving limp lettuce and the odd cold pea to my mates. The second was Roger — something he told us about the interview by the MEF Screening Committee that he had attended. We'd sent Roger to represent us because he knew about Alaska. We thought that this intelligence would be of advantage. It was wasted. The Screening Committee, Roger said, appeared to know nothing much about Alaska or mountains either. We could have sent a blow-up rubber doll. Roger related how he was questioned about this and that, his general mountaineering experience and good common sense earning points and pounds (sterling) all the way. A last question from Denis Gray, General Secretary of the British Mountaineering Council, might have stumped him had he not been so guilelessly honest. How was it, Denis wanted to know, that Plas y Brenin could spare four members of staff to go to Alaska at the same time? Roger answered truthfully that he felt that was none of his (Roger's) business, that as an instructor he had merely asked the Director who had said fine, no problem. Another Committee member asked who was the Director. Again Roger answered simple and true, 'John Barry'. 'But,' a third demanded, 'isn't he going too?' 'Yes,' Roger said. 'He's the leader.' That had them beat and they coughed up, generous to a fault, £800. It is worth adding that I was only the leader on paper, literally just that. MEF grant application forms require a leader to be nominated. A four-man team of friends to an alpine peak needs no leader — and this team had none.

We flew to Anchorage over the Pole. Like many boys I had a globe at home when I was young. I knew there was a place at the top of the world painted white and called the North Pole and that it was an ice cap. I had no idea of its vastness, its sheer unremitting barrenness. It was chillingly spectacular, chilling even in that warm aircraft. We flew over not far from the Pole itself then headed south into Alaska. After some hours, looking through a port window I saw some good-looking mountains, 40,000 feet beneath. Was it? It was. Deborah! That a flight of many thousands of miles should take us within free falling distance of the mountain of our dreams! It seemed the unlikeliest thing; but there it was, more clearly now — there was no mistaking it. On the starboard side, farther away, stood McKinley, Foraker and all sorts of good things, figments fit for future imaginings. Then the descent to Anchorage. Eight and a half hours.

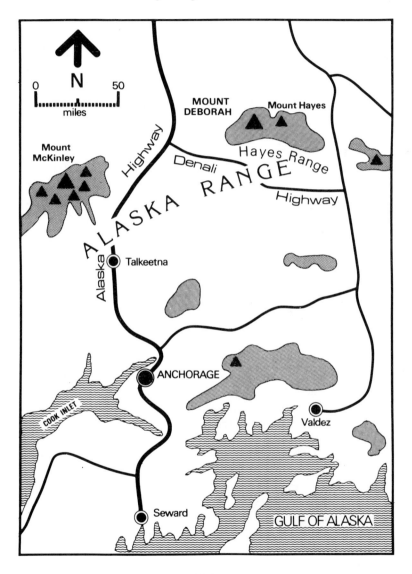

Anchorage 22nd April; we were in Roger's hands. He said we'd need a car. We hired one and went shopping for food.

We found a supermarket, a Safeways several acres square, where we tottered around the shelves in desultory jet-lagged apathy. It would have been far more sensible to have got some kip and returned the next day fresher and better organised, but there wasn't a demi-zombie among us who had the wit to say so. Roger calculated that we needed provisions for twenty days of which five were designated 'Base Camp' rations, the remainder 'hill food'. Into the Base Camp trolly went all sorts of treats — cheesecake mixes, freeze-dried scrambled egg, tins of peaches. We debated the hill food problem at some length. As the Veggies saw it *I* was the hill food problem — how to cope with the carnivore. They had unearthed a 'special' — hundreds of packets of vegetable stew, reduced to a fraction of the original price. I was suspicious of the reduction but it was eagerly seized by the Veggies, who, happily surprised at such unwonted largesse in this capital of capitalist lands, pronounced, heedless of their truculent carnivore, a diet of vegetable stew or cheese and biscuits on alternate days. I complained that meat was cheap at twice the price but there's a piousness about the vegetarian argument against which plain likes and dislikes are embarrassingly bereft of righteousness — so I went along with them with as much ill-will as I could manage, consoling myself that an indiscriminate, omnivorous, general-purpose, multifuel engine was far better kit than a finely tuned, selective, discriminating, singlefuel job that clogged on meat, cholesterol and greasy chips. These thoughts were unspoken — indeed, unspeakable. It was clearly going to be an expedition of high moral tone. (We never got to the famed Anchorage strip clubs either. That was Collister's fault. He is the only man I know whose claim, that he had only been in a strip club once in his life and that by mistake — upon which revelation he fled — is universally accepted without the slightest demur, indeed with sympathy. It is just not possible to tear the arse out of a red-light area and then, in all conscience, to tie onto the same rope as such a man for a soul search on one of nature's finest hills with any hope of deliverance. Roger, no vegetarian when it came to flesh, made great advertisement of the wares of night clubs of his previous acquaintance, but probe as we did, there was no chink in that moral armour; a lusty wind blew great gales through mine. So no red lights; Collister's fault.) Anyway, vegetable stew it was to be.

We soon ran out of enthusiasm for the shopping — which was just as well or the result would have been a greater shambles than our purchases already represented, and having amassed nearly $600 of groceries we approached the Manager confident of a discount. It was about an average Friday night family grocery collection he said. No discount. We drove to the house of Mark Skok, a friend of Roger's who had generously agreed to put us up while we were in Anchorage. Here, bleary eyed, we sat in the pale April sunlight and tried to make some sense of our shopping — but none could be made. Somehow, despite the fact that four brains had helped to compute the sum (including Malcolm, a piece of software and hardware rolled into one), we had come away with over 600 bars of chocolate of one sort or another. That, as even I was capable of working out, was more than seven bars per man per day — a dentist's nightmare. But it was calories, and I noted with sugary insincerity that at least it wasn't meat. The best I'd been able to do was secrete a bottle of Tabasco sauce into the provisions. I had intended that it should liven up ten days of vegetable stew. Unfortunately the others found it and decided they liked a 'sharpener' in their stew too, declaring Tabasco to be idealogically sound. And it was only a small bottle.

That night there was a party at the house to which our host had kindly invited us. A friendly lady from a local radio station addressed me, half small talk, half interview.

'Tell me why exactly are you English in Alaska?'

'We are going climbing,' I answered.

'Mountains?'

'Yes, Deborah.'

'I ain't never heard of no Deborah but I went to go up a mountain once. When I was 'bout half way up, I looked at the summit an' I said, Mary Sue, there ain't nothin' you need up there, so I went right back down.'

I thought her very sane.

The next day, after a third sleepless night to add to the first two, we went shopping again. There were things to buy like snow shovels, and bamboo wands for marking safe routes on glaciers; and things to correct, like the previous day's shopping. Alaskan climbers use grain shovels as snow shovels; they are bigger and better. We bought one at an agricultural supplier. It had a blade that was at least twice as big as any shovel I had ever seen. Most of the rest of our problems were solved in REI — Recreation Equipment Incorporated. Again this was bigger and better than any climbing shop I had seen before and its staff were better informed and more helpful than any of my acquaintance. Browsing through the book section, I came across this in a chapter on the simple skill of abseiling — which the Americans (and the French) call 'rappelling'.

> 'Ah rappelling. . . the programmatic answer for adventure oriented programs that seek a sure-fire, grabby, comparatively inexpensive, easily protected, sometimes spiritual, gutsy, enjoyable, physical commitment activity that provides good copy, positive parental reaction, excellent photographic possibilities, enthusiastic administrative support and a sense of personal achievement that transcends validity.
>
> Is it any wonder that everyone wants a rappel as an integral part of their program? I mean, can you afford not to rappel; "Have you rappelled?" becomes less a question of interest and more an opening statement of fraternal affiliation.'

I was reminded why I was less than enthusiastic about American English.

That afternoon we swapped our car for a truck before returning to Mark's house to load our kit into it. He had thoughtfully traced a copy of Dave Roberts' book, *Deborah. A Wilderness Narrative,* which he said we could take with us. The next day we set out for Talkeetna. The scenery along the Alaskan Highway was marvellous; it so captivated us that we forget our map reading and took the wrong road (not bad with only two to choose from) — and it was two hours before anyone noticed. We arrived in Talkeetna at about 2 pm. Roger took the truck back to Anchorage — it had to be returned to the hire company and Roger needed to have the stitches from his knee operation removed. Apparently he fell asleep as this was being done. The nurse was impressed.

Talkeetna looks how I imagine all wild west towns looked in Wyatt Earp's day — with its side walks, swing-door saloons, hitching rails and cowboys — though, as far as I could tell, no cows. The town was emerging from winter and the snow was thawing its annual mess. The locals were friendly to a degree and though I wouldn't say the place was pretty it had a scruffy charm — and a sense of humour. Above a pile of derelict cars, awash in snow melt, a painted sign read 'Welcome to beautiful downtown Talkeetna'. All ten houses and three bars of it. We spent the night in a sort of bandstand. I read Roberts' book. It was good, and very frightening. The passage that begins,

'In a glance that lasted a few moments, the expedition seemed to end'. . . and finishes, 'I had never seen a mountain sight so numbing, so haunted with impossibility and danger', thrilled and terrified by turns. Was this really how I wanted to spend my annual holiday? I knew that the answer was yes but it has to be asked all the same. But, though I was now a fan of Roberts' prose there was, for my taste, still too much soul searching, too much exposing of thought, motive and argument, too much of what it is fashionable to call group dynamics, too much equally fashionable interaction; I thought it unhealthy to be so honest. By all means the truth must be told, but it wasn't necessary always to be telling all of it. And to commit it to paper — I had my doubts.

'What needest thou? — a few brief hours of rest
Wherein to seek thyself in thine own breast;
A transient silence wherein truth could say
Such was thy constant hope, and this thy way?'
'O foolish one to roam
So far in thine own mind away from home!'

The next morning Roger returned. He had hitched up rather more quickly than we had driven. We secured the services of an Air Taxi. Talkeetna is a road head and jumping off point to most of Alaska's mountains. Air Taxi firms are the staple business and I would guess that there are more aircraft in the town than there are cars. Cliff Hudson, a veteran of mountain flying, agreed that his son would fly us the 100 miles to Deborah. The little Cessna could only manage two of us at a time. Rob and I squeezed in sitting on about half of our gear — the seats had been taken out to make enough room. The interior of the plane had the appearance of a vintage car, spartan, draughty and just about operational — and our pilot treated it as he would a runabout. He instructed me to hold the door, apparently it had the habit of flying open during take off, and we lumbered along a muddy unpaved runway towards a pine forest at the not so far end. It seemed unlikely that such a crude looking machine could fly and inconceivable that it could do so with three adults and several hundred pounds of climbing gear on board. At last, when an arboreal arrest looked a distinct possibility, back came the stick and up went the plane — as it had hundreds, perhaps thousands of times before.

'Which way?' the pilot asked.

'Deborah,' Rob said.

'Yeah, Deborah I heard of but ain't been to, which way?'

We showed him a map and he set a course to the north east. Below were forests, iced lakes and snow, a road, the Denali Highway, frozen tundra wastes and then the magnificent mountains of the Hayes Range. Rob and I identified Deborah and excitedly pointed at the glacier we wished to be put down on. We flew in close to the East Ridge. It looked horrifying. The plane banked to turn, tilting the mountain with it. Now the East Ridge looked worse. The pilot circled the cwm of our glacier two or three times before descending for a bounce along its surface to test for flatness, firmness and angle — there being no ground relief in the bright shadowless light. A bounce, three or four hops along the glacier surface and up into the blue sky again, mountains looking down from all around.

'OK this time.'

Down we went. A perfect landing about 2½ miles short of the East Ridge. Rob and I hopped out, unloaded our kit, helped the plane turn and watched it take off for Talkeetna to pick up Malc and Roger and the rest of the kit. By the time he returned we had half finished an igloo which was to be the communal eating place — galley I would have called it once — and had erected the tent that Rob and I had agreed to share. The other two had a tent apiece.

Roger and Malc were as impressed as Rob and I had been with the situation — and Rob and I no less impressed now than two hours earlier.

As the Cessna roared off again, with a wave and a 'see you on the 16th May', leaving the world to the four of us and Deborah, I recalled the pilot's reply to our first inquiry. 'I can fly you to

Hell, Deborah — both.' Was this transatlantic aphorism, North American hyperbole — or did he know something we didn't?

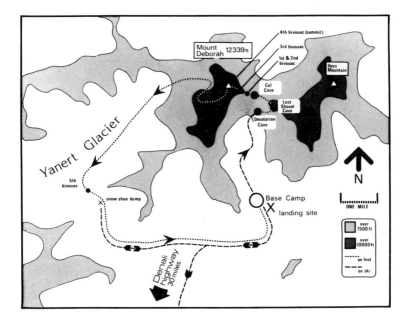

Now there's photographs that don't lie and photographs — the mountain variety especially — that do. I had hoped that our little monochrome was lying through its teeth — at least that it was concealing more than it revealed — and that fact would denounce the picture fiction. But somewhere in circling the glacier for a landing site, which had the effect on our perspective of tilting the camera most cruelly, somewhere I lost that faith. It was weeks before it returned. From the glacier the East Ridge looked improbable. I could trace no line, fake no confidence, spring no hope. Cliffs loomed, cornices arched on cornices as I had never seen in the Alps or Himalayas; as Roger had said they would and as I had discounted or forgotten. The snow lay feet deep and I was cold and concerned.

But we were four to share our misgivings and diminish them in our various ways, by debate, discussion, half-chewed reason, food and friendship and, at least in my own case, by those two imposters, bravado and bullshit.

235

That night we gathered at the snow hole for a meal and a 'council-of-war' as I loved to call it and as the others could scarcely bring themselves to hear. The meal over, a big brew in hand we fell to discussion of the next day's tactics. Soon it was clear that something was wrong. Every suggestion provoked an argument and not one argument were we able to resolve. Whether it was something to do with the dynamics of a group of four generally, or this group of four particularly, I don't know, but if it continued there would be a lot of argument and not much climbing. To ease the situation I decided to drop out of the decision-making process (something I found hard to do; it was alien to my nature) but we had come to climb the East Ridge and I didn't really mind if I did it the next day or a week hence — or very much how we did it — so long as we did it. Rob fell silent too. Some days later I learnt that he had reached the same conclusion, and made the same decision. My experience of working with committees since leaving the Services had given me little faith in them as a means of making decisions. I had attended hundreds and my impression was always the same: that one reasonable man can do the job of twelve more cheaply, more efficiently, more fairly and more quickly — and if he can't, he should be replaced with someone who can. Here at the foot of Deborah I was happy that the combined best of Roger and Malcolm, who were still discussing the last detail of everything, would result in as acceptable a decision as the combined best of all four and that two would be quicker in direct proportion.

At length a plan emerged. Months earlier while studying photographs of the ridge it had struck me that even if we got up, getting down might be the bigger problem. A better bet, though not by much, seemed to be to descend on the west side, perhaps by Harrer's original 'sensational' ascent route. The problem then might be a twelve-mile plough through knee-deep spring snow back to base. I had borrowed some snow shoes from an old Marine mate who wasn't too anxious about having them back. We decided to pre-position them at the foot of the west side of the mountain in case we came by that way. It was also decided that we should establish ourselves and our kit on the col immediately at the foot of the East Ridge. Since this was 2500 feet above us, and more than 2 miles up the glacier, there was clearly some hard work to be done.

236

It had been a strange day. We had breakfasted in a 'wild west' saloon and dined in an igloo; two meals separated in conventional perceptions of distance and time by 100 miles and less than twelve hours, but in other ways by a million years of tundra and several ice ages. I looked up at the East Ridge silhouetted now by moonlight and felt a quick stir of wonder — clean, pure, virginal — a stir I had not felt since sitting on that hot hut roof all those years ago in New Zealand. Thirteen years is a long time and the Southern Alps a long way away but these mountains were closer than that; one soul spanned them, they were beats in one heart; they both loosed that elemental wonder, a frisson, part joy part fear, with no telling which is which, until it is too late. Then it can be all one or all the other or both in varying degrees. Only one thing was certain, we were in for some adventure!

The next day (26 April 1982) in a wonderful sunny six-mile swoop of a ski we dumped four pairs of snowshoes, ski sticks and some food on the west side of the mountain at a little col about four miles short of the foot of the Beckey/Harrer route. It was a day to remember; not a living thing, nor trace of it; a wild white world.

Then a hard hump for a day or two led toward the col, the col from which the East Ridge sprang, 2500 feet above our little base of tents and an igloo. We built a cave at the head of the glacier, 2000 feet hard under the col, where Roberts had his 'Desolation Camp' (it wasn't a happy place for him). We adopted the name but only for sentiment; here in a well-appointed cave, roomy and warm, there was no desolation. A short steep ski led up to the *bergschrund* and the 2000 feet of alpine AD to the col. We spent a day carrying gear upwards and tucking it in piles all over the mountain before returning to Desolation Camp for the night. Next day we crossed the *bergschrund* again. To me, perhaps lacking imagination or sensitivity, it was just another *bergschrund*, a nuisance, nothing much more. But to Malc, whose ankle was behaving badly, it was a Rubicon: a river he could not cross for beyond it the path lay uncertainly upward, uncertainly inward, and after it there could be no individual turning back. As he skied back to base he must have felt lonely and sad. As we climbed on we felt his loneliness and our own sadness. The physical burden was not difficult to rearrange, but climbing is no simple sum; the bigger share of anxiety was unwelcome, there was damage below the waterline and we were poorer in spirit.

Approaching the west end of the col late that evening the weather turned and we decided on a cave there and then. We might have christened this one Desperation after the desperate energy of our digging, the instinct for shelter being a fairly primitive one, but called it 'Lost Shovel' instead because in my enthusiasm for warming work I threw both shovel and snow down the mountain, about 2000 feet of it, to where it would not be recovered. Fortunately we still had the big grain shovel to work with and a cave, small but home enough in that storm, was won. Inside, despite the cold, and there only being room enough to pit-wriggle one at a time, we were chuffed. The 'crack' between us was good and as we traded repartee above the roar of the stove, I was actually looking forward to the first vegetable stew of my life. A good one it was too — that first one.

Next day was clear, blustery and cold — about alpine winter cold. We moved across easy slopes to a point 300 feet above the col to find our way down blocked by a 100-foot serac. An abseil from a mushroom, magic enough at the time, solved that and we spent the day shunting loads to the projected site of 'Col Cave'. Here the Goth gained points, stunning the Veggies with a bit of alternative technology fit for a Green by loading up a bivvy tent until it bulged with kit, lowering it over the serac and sledging into the col with devastating, but entirely natural efficiency, minimal environmental damage and not a fossil fuel in sight. As far as I recall, and admittedly my powers of recall are notoriously fickle (and anyway why let the truth spoil a good story?), it was the single idea of the entire enterprise that met with general approval.

We dug, with our grain shovel, a Hilton at the col. The work was an interesting exercise in human relations. Ours was by now a confirmed leaderless expedition which meant nothing much except that it took roughly three times longer than usual to reach a decision — and there was a fair chance of it being the wrong one. There was much social interaction, each digging when his turn came, according to his own preconceived architecture — and even the two Veggies couldn't agree on that. The result was a huge hole of indeterminate shape, an uncertain door somewhere in the roof and a choice of sleeping places. As an ex-military man I found this open-plan freedom all very confusing.

But we had our home, our base from which to launch at the mountain. It had taken a week but it had been fun and improved our fitness, and we were getting used to that ridge.

There still being time that day for a recce, we tip-i-toed along as far as the first steepening — a couple of hundred yards or so. I think none of us much liked what he saw. Ribbons on edges of ribbons, great meringues of snow and crevasses where no crevasses should have been. Where else was it possible to fall into a crevasse when *à cheval* a knife-edge ridge? But this was Alaska and Roger might have said 'I told you so', but he didn't. But we'd tangled with it, tangled in it, felt the better for it. Back at the cave we discussed tactics. Do we fix? was the question. We decided that we would — at least to start with.

Then for four days we paid the price to the mountain gods for our fixed-rope sacrilege. It blew and snowed and snowed. The first day was great: we rested, snoozed and slowly screwed the courage to some sort of sticking place. But after three more days of jokes, stories and desert island anything — discs, rock climbs, ice climbs, mountains — desert island everything, we'd had enough of rest. The sticking place was slipping and I was becoming increasingly depressed at how every conversation revealed new depths of ignorance. My Rolling Stones were outgunned by Rob's Brahms and Beethoven, crotchet by crotchet, quaver by quaver; my Kipling was knocked for six by a glitterati of greats; my fail at the University of Life cruelly exposed by the bright light of Cambridge culture. (Not that Rob intended, or indeed is capable of, cruelty. No, these were self-inflicted wounds, the most painful kind of all.) Roger knew about I Ching, and could have explained it had I been able (or willing) to understand; he knew about Yin and Yang, I knew they weren't pandas or words for scrabble. 'Drink deep or taste not the Pierian Spring', it was the old message. We got to know each other better but I'm not sure that was necessarily a good thing. Soul-baring may be inelegantly fashionable, especially amongst Americans, but there is more than rhyme to the Englishman's reserve.

I kept a diary. The entries reflect the growing boredom. On the 4th day I wrote 'Snowing again. No change. Level out bed space. Cold.'

And then we started climbing. Looking back I'm tempted to write the story afresh, add some wishful thinking, essay a fancy interpretation or two; adorn, embellish, polish. But that is not the way of climbs, and might result in cant or something more than the truth. It would be wrong for this climb which was a straightforward, stern affair with a nag never far behind and a hope just ahead; a decent sort of struggle for which sparse diary notes tell the tale as well as it needs to be told (where I cannot resist comment, or where I dare open a window to my thoughts I have added them in parenthesis). Of course there's idleness too: diary notes are easy, not strained, the truth doesn't have to be squeezed out. Writing is hard work. Like climbing, to do it well you go slowly, backwards even, and some days nothing happens. So the diary takes up the tale.

6th May. (Rob explains in my diary — the cultural conquest complete.) Apparently still snowing or drifting and still in pits after breakfast when galvanised into action by sound of aircraft. Made several low runs over us and retrieved five boxes of food — but not for us. Note saying Dave and Carl are headed for Hess West Ridge. Later saw him skiing up the glacier and by evening nearing upper seracs of our approach route. Weather good, cloud coming and going but plenty of sun too. Set off along the ridge, John breaking trail at a great rate but a bit close to the edge for comfort — foot through cornice fracture line four or five times. Reached foot of first rock buttress and trace of old fixed rope, bit of sacking and a peg. Immediately hard climbing — over an ice bulge then up steep shattered rock, covered with snow, for 30 ft. Then snow, steep in places for two rope-lengths to next buttress. Another buttress, difficult climbing, wide bridging, John's crampon fell off. (I experience endless problems with my crampon bindings. My embarrassment matched my incompetence.) Fragile knife-edge of snow, then good to just short of next buttress. Abseiled down, having fixed 900 ft of rope.

6th May (By self). Abseiled home feeling satisfied to have tangled with the ridge at last. Still plenty to come. The two fellows rolled up. One American, one South African. (Carl Tobin and Dave Cheesemond, respectively.) Friendly. Going for same ridge. We give them a cup of tea. Rob disappointed to have company — me not so much.

240

7th May. Sunny, warm. Leave at 9 am after discussing tactics with others. No conflict — then set out to find air drops. We pack six days' food. Move off up fixed ropes. Swing leads. Roger leads a very hard rock pitch which I fail on when crampons come off (again!). Staggering cornices. As we abseil down to bivouac we pass the others (who have come up our ropes) setting up the tiniest of tents on the most improbable of cornices. We abseil about 500 ft and spend 20 minutes brushing (with a small polythene brush bought at Safeways for just this job) every last snow-flake from clothes and boots — 'from tiny snow-flakes do bloody great puddles grow' — before squeezing three into a two-man bivouac bag on a ledge scraped from the cornice: Roger's the necessary disciplinarian in these things.

8th May. Snowed all night. (In the middle of it Roger and Rob had an argument about some disputed leg space — it was badly cramped three in that bag. Rob solved the problem by quitting its co-mingling heat and sleeping *al fresco*. A noble gesture worthy of the man — two was cosy — thanks Rob.)

8th May. 2 ft of snow or so over tent by morning. Lie-in wondering what to do. After much dithering get going about 11-ish — more to avoid being suffocated than desire to climb. Jumar up to high point passing the American team who stay ensconced in their tent all day, occasionally shouting encouragement, 'yeah man, everything's gonna be all right', through half an inch of unzipped door. They must have been possessed of some sort of psychological sixth sense for their cry — it was always the same — came floating up just when we were convinced everything was far from all right — and it's difficult to be frightened with so joyous a battle-cry snapping at your heels.

Some fantastic climbing (with a traverse that made the 'Traverse of the Gods' look like a garden path) to within 100 ft of the rock band. (The one that so impressed Roberts.) Cornices, steep ice, rotten rock, incredible exposure; the lot. Back to same bivvy site. Big brew by Rob. Had snowed all day. Weather good at evening. Brief parlez with other team on way down. They are going early tomorrow, about 3 am weather allowing.

9th May. Up at 5 am. Within two minutes it's snowing, not hard but annoying. Jumar, exciting enough with 'sacks. Dave and Carl only one pitch above our high point. Snow steep and soft. (Steeper than I would have believed possible when that soft.) Began a big traverse to north toward a snow cone and gully system we hoped would lead through the rock band (it did). Moving very slowly — in each other's way a bit. Snow atrocious in places. Several hundred, trying and insecure feet lead to a hard rock pitch led by Dave. I get the chimney/gully between snow cone and mountain. Superb pitch — real Scottish winter stuff. Belayed to a snarg at the top of a steep gully. Roger jumared up and led through on what looked in the gloom (it was about 10 pm) to the easy ground. But the snow was awful, showering down. The whole slope threatening to slide off the ice beneath. Dave jumared with his own 'sack and mine — two 'sacks (for full 150 ft). Getting dark, already cold. I'm three-quarters covered in snow. Ropes in a mess, have to cut to sort. 2½ hours later when others have climbed on into the night Rob comes up. Very tired under a mountain of gear — seems to be carrying all we own — both teams. Rob and I jumar to ledge someone had cut in the snow from where others have fixed a long traverse into the obscurity. (I shouted to Roger whom we had lost in the darkness above. 'How's it look up there Rog?' 'I've found a bivvy site', his silver answer rang — the silverest I ever heard.) We dump most of the gear and cross several hundred feet to Roger who has done great work finding bivvy site. Feel insecure in the dark — now midnight. Rog cooks. Rob and I chop a notch for three. Dave and Carl erect tent on briefest of camp sites. Hard day but all in good spirits. Mighty brew, sardines, cheese. To sleep at 3 am — it's daylight! Sleep the sleep of the innocent.

10th May. Awake to sun. Sun! Sun like a bishop's bum. (From Hayward Asquith's 'The sun like a bishop's bottom, rosy and round and hot'.) We are east facing — warm. Sun dries bags and boots, warms the soul. Brew and snooze, snooze and brew. The best morning of my life. Rob and Dave go back to collect gear. Rog sleeps. Move off at 11 am. Rob leads easy slopes to a huge (70 ft) overhanging serac. Animated discussion about the best way. (I arrived to find

242

the two Americans tackling the serac direct, Rob several hundred feet down the north side of the mountain ploughing the lonely furrow he loves so much and Rog casually tending both sets of ropes while brewing tea!) Tour de force by Carl climbing 70 ft of overhanging ice on horizontally driven snow stakes, all the while he dangling in space with 5000 ft free beneath him. (What frightened me most was the way he could withdraw each stake by hand as an arrow from a quiver. It was as spectacular a feat of mountaineering as I ever hope to witness.) Rob returns from his detour. Carl gets up; we jumar. I make a real balls of jumaring with a 'sack. Then long slopes to top, some steep bits, heavily corniced. Rob ploughs two more lonely furrows, happy as a lark, going like a train. (I made a note to take a look at this vegetarian business — I too felt almost disappointingly good; I'd been looking forward to a good whinge about the imposed diet.) The summit in evening sun, 9.30. Grand views. Shake hands. Bivvy. (Oh yes we so wonderfully forgot ourselves.)

That will do with the diary.

We set up our bivvy bag as the light fell short. The Americans disappeared into their amazing little yellow tent. Rob opted for the open sky again; it was our nearest neighbour. Roger prepared for entry to our bivvy bag. This meant meticulous brushing away of every flake of snow from clothing and footwear with a tiny plastic hearth brush we had bought for the purpose back in Anchorage. Failure to do this simple chore well, meant snow inside the bivvy bag and that soon meant water and wetness. As Roger assiduously brushed I looked north to earth's last horizon; and for a moment I held eternity in heart and hand. Then the bitter cold drove me inside with Roger and soon we were asleep.

The next morning the sun was up well before us; with it came warmth, light and lightness. In the last hours of the previous day, as we neared the top, the cold clamp of seriousness had begun to melt away. But the dark, cold and sleep came before it had melted full away so that a brewing contentedness never quite bubbled its full promise that night. But it boiled busily in the morning when released by the sun's rays, a great inner joy burst, enough for some to spill over to the outside. In the cold clamp we had worked well as a team. Now as a team we were happy. On

243

that day on that mountain it would have been impossible to be anything else.

Often, on the way up we would stand amazed at Roberts' efforts. All those years ago. Now, at the top, we were able to smile at those words he had written; a smile of relief that the job he had started so well was now well done. There was no smugness, no sense of victory. Just a good honest feeling of relief. I like to think that Dave Roberts would also be pleased. His was the first effort, his photograph the inspiration, his book a reference, his words a spur.

I had a few regrets. We fixed ropes on the first third. But our style improved as we gained height, as we got to know our mountain and its secrets. Two strangers turned up at the last minute to steal some of the climb. But we joined forces — after some sparring — and climbed the thing together. Now we are friends.

I no longer regret. It was a great adventure and memory of it is unblemished; a perfect reflection.

But it wasn't over. We had still to get down — back to Base Camp — and back to civilisation. There was some way to go.

The descent. We went down to the west; the Beckey/Harrer route. It was indeed spectacular and it demanded care but there was no stopping us now. Almost immediately we had to rig an abseil. We chopped a biggish mushroom from the snow and ice, reinforced it with paper, card, anything we could spare — we'd carried all our rubbish with us and now we felt justified in leaving a little as insurance. We carefully checked everything; would the rope cut through the mushroom bollard? No, we reckoned it would hold. Would the rope run when we wanted to retrieve it? Quick test. We hoped it would. And so on. I think we all felt we had taken all the risks that we wanted to take this week — though there was plenty of excitement to come. The snow formations continued to surprise, to dazzle; the climbing remained interesting — all just about right for a sunny May day going home with a new route in the bag.

In a few hours we gained easy snow slopes that led to the foot of the West Face of Deborah at the Yannert Glacier. These slopes were heavily crevassed but gave us no great toil. Three hours later we all stood one *bergschrund* away from a deliciously flat Yannert. I have never been a lover of flat places but this one looked fine, dandy, and I was impatient to reach its relaxing

244

flatness. While the others foraged for a crossing point I found a narrowing that I reckoned I could jump. I threw my rucksack across first — it landed heavily — then followed easily after. Then a few yards to the flatness. The others arrived a minute later having found an easier crossing place, and someone suggested a brew. I delved into my rucksack to get the petrol stove to find that in my last act on the mountain I had smashed my camera to smithereens. I had finished and removed my last film on the summit — a camera — it mattered not at all on that day in that place. Yet had I done the same thing back at home I would have been furious.

Then something jarred the day. Roger and I had an argument. A silly argument, the quibbling of tired men relieved of anxiety, returning to pettiness. It was about the rope. We had been climbing on two 300-foot lengths. The theory was that they would allow longer abseils going down whilst going up we hoped to entwine them in the snow formations to afford some protection — or at least a feeling of security. It had worked quite well until I had had to cut one to escape my belay the night I was buried — the night before the 'bishops bum' morning. Since then one of our ropes had been somewhat longer than the other and now it seemed sensible to cut the 300-foot one in two so that its load could be split. We would have done this in any case some time later — 150 being the usual length for a climbing rope. Here I have to admit that since it looked as if I might be carrying the full 300 feet I had interest other than purely functional. Rob agreed. I took a knife but Roger snapped,

'If the rope is to be cut, it should be done properly — I'll do it.'

I threw all 300 foot of the thing into my rucksack and stomped off after Dave and Carl who were trudging ahead, down the Yannert. I was angry and hurt but, uncharacteristically said nothing. All the way up I had found Roger's querulousness annoying. When it was grim he said so or wore it plain upon his face; I could see no point in that. When I was miserable with cold and discomfort I assumed everyone else was too and that they would not be very interested in my condition. Rob, from the same sort of background as my old friend Dave Nicholls, never complained. I thought Roger was being selfish and thoughtless, which he was. But so, I realised later, was I.

For the moment we trudged along in silence. Something had

come between us. Usually I am quick to the apology; this time I couldn't bring myself to say those melting words. I was so angry that he had been so unfair. Back on the flat again, the excitement went from the adventure and only the hard work poked through. The snow was half crusted; it promised to support me, promised then let me down, six inches at a time; a thousand times, ten thousand. It was exhausting. I switched off and trudged. Carl and I found the same speed and went together. Dave and Rob sped ahead, their longer legs and lighter weight a great asset on this terrain. Poor Roger fell behind. His knee, a knee that had been bared by the surgeon's scalpel at Oswestry less than a month before, that had borne the climbing so well was complaining at last at all this hard work. Roger did not complain.

Later we faced each other and the obstacle that had grown between us. I told him that I thought he had been thoughtless and selfish, particularly in what he'd said about the rope. The damn silly rope! He told me he thought I had been thoughtless and selfish. 'What?' I was staggered. 'What about your crampons? What about the day you went through the cornice half a dozen times?' That shook me. He was right. A badly fitting crampon is not just mechanical ineptitude — it would be if the wearer were the only one likely to suffer — but when he is one of a team of three it is at least as selfish as complaining about the cold. And there was I all smug with my borrowed stoicism while Roger worried about my carelessness. I should have left the charging in New Zealand. He was right. Months later a bottle of whisky put it all to rights. We drank it between us till we fell over and we lay shouting to the stars and moon of an alpine sky. 'It's Alaska man, if you don't like it, you can go.' We both said we were sorry, which we were. We said it again and again, and we were. Next morning, through a terrible hangover, it was all right, Deborah was a perfect memory, perfectly and invisibly repaired, Roger and I better mates for it. And if all that sounds silly I won't argue with you.

After a few miles we swung south off the Yannert and began the long gentle climb up to the col where we had pre-dumped our snow shoes seventeen days before.

It was late, about 1 am. We were all very tired. My eyes were playing strange tricks. Carl's too, when I asked him. All at once

246

the senselessness of flogging on occurred to us all and we flopped down where we were for a huge brew and another bivouac — an indiscriminate jumble of a bivouac, a far cry from the tight, disciplined affairs on the climb. But it didn't matter here, nothing could happen to us or our gear. I took perverse pleasure from the acres I occupied with bag and 'sack and kit.

The next morning, the 12th May, we awoke to a cold blustery wind. A short plod led to the Col where Rob and I were delighted to find the snow-shoes and food exactly as we had left them — I'm not sure what we expected. There followed a brew and a great eating of cheese and chocolate. Then we fitted the snow shoes, Malc's pair were spare for Carl, Dave volunteered to go without — not that he had much choice. He had the advantage of being well over 6 feet tall, weighing well under 10 stones and having size twelve feet. I am no mathematician but his pressure per square inch must have been about half that of mine; he could scitter across the surface of snow that would claim me to my knees. On we went, following the route that Rob and I had skied, around the south side of Deborah in a great duck-like waddle, the snow shoes comically effective, resting and chatting and head-down plodding, Cheesemond hanging on to Carl's hips and scampering in our partly-padded trail, all the way round to the arm of the West Fork Glacier where our Base Camp lay. We rounded a corner through another little col and — there it was. Malc saw us half a mile away and skied down with a can of beer each — Carl's beer, Dave's beer, we hadn't planned such a luxury.

That night in the igloo we drank beer and whisky and talked nonsense, wonderful carefree, harmless, drivelling nonsense. Much later in the tent I lay awake, couldn't sleep. Rob sensing that I was awake asked me what was wrong. It was nothing. I was trying to make sense of it all. I was happy with the adventure but I couldn't shake off thoughts about some moments of near surrender that I had experienced, moments that had been carried by the psychological strength of three, then five. In my language it was not so much a victory as a draw; but I was happy, content to draw with Deborah; she had been good to us. I told Rob that somewhere on the climb I had decided that I had no intention of dying on this mountain. I was half embarrassed with the melodrama of my words and half at the confessed weakness. But I had made that conscious decision then, and now with the whisky I said

247

so. To my surprise Rob said that he had been of the same mind. That made me feel better. I tried to read from *Other Men's Flowers*

'I have gathered a posie of other men's flowers
and nothing but the thread that
binds them is my own.'

but got not much further than those lines by Montaigne. I couldn't concentrate. Dark thought prowled the conscious. I was 'climbing, climbing up the back of my mind'. I blasted away the rest of the night and all those struggling thoughts reaching for reason I couldn't grasp, with Springsteen, Vivaldi, Dylan, Brahms, Albinoni, The Silver Bullet Band. Blasted it all away in the headphones until the simple sanity of breakfast and work rescued a troubled mind. I never thought so hard upon it again; but I had learnt that mountaineering was as much to do with weakness as with strengths.

We dossed disconsolately all the next day. The following day four of us agreed to go back up to Col Cave to retrieve the food and equipment we had left there. It mostly belonged to Carl and Dave but Rob and I saw it as a way to while away the time. Our pilot wasn't due for another two days. It was fun to be on skis again, strange to be back at the Col. We found the cave exactly as we had left it. The weather looked as if it was worsening so we hurried away with huge loads. Going back down the glacier, a rope of four, I found myself appointed front man. I found a crevasse and fell in. And again, and again. Five times, once by twenty feet or so. There was no real danger; the other three held me easily, but it was annoying and unnerving. Every time it happened I crawled out angrier than the last, shouting that it was time someone else took a turn at the front — and stomping off again before anyone could do so.

I didn't know it at the time but the other three were enjoying it all enormously. When we regained the place we had left our skis Carl came up with a huge grin and said in his drawl, a drawl so slow you wondered if the sentence would escape his mouth,

'John, you're really beautiful when you're angry.' The anger vanished, fled in an instant. We all laughed uproariously.

The next morning Rob and I lay chatting in our tent when the febrile energy of a Cheesemond monologue silenced us from the tent next door.

'Carl, tell you what I reckon we oughta do today. (They were

248

staying for another climb.) I reckon we oughta ski here . . . oughta carry loads there . . . oughta fix ropes here . . . oughta bivvy there . . . oughta do this . . . oughta do that . . . oughta do the other. Whadya think of that?'

It was a formidable programme even by Cheesemond's standards. Rob and I were staggered and listened in silence for the reply. It was a long time coming and when it came it came very slowly, only just, spare, laconic,

'Waall I-reckon-we-oughta-give-a-lot-of-thought-to-what-we're-gonna-have-for-breakfast.'

The 16th May. Our plane was due. It didn't arrive. The next day there was a storm. No plane. On the 18th we decided that Roger and I should ski and walk out to try to raise the pilot. Malc and Rob were to wait in case he arrived while we were on our way out. Carl and Dave skied away to their next mountain. Roger and I set off towards the main West Fork Glacier. The days were warm now and the snow as rotten as any I have experienced. Even on skis we were sinking up to our knees. It was hard and unpleasant work. We skied south to the snout of the glacier where we camped for the night. We were off by five the next morning. Leaving the glacier and the arctic behind we passed through the moraine, crossing a hundred streams, trying to pick a sure way out of the delta. I slipped in to an icy glacial stream up to my neck and was swept away. Roger thrust a ski stick at me, held me while I struggled out. Suddenly there were birds, plants, beaver and moose,

'The naked earth is warm with spring.'

Tundra; the Monahan Flat. Dave had warned us of it — he'd trudged the same weary miles years before. It was miserable going: tripping, falling, sinking, swimming, tufts, scrub, logs, bark, ponds, streams, the Susitna river. We stopped at midnight, exhausted. Five miles in twelve hours. Somewhere ahead in that featureless tundra was the Denali Highway, a dirt road. Surely it could be no more than a few miles. We worried that it might not have been opened for the spring. That would leave us with a forty-mile walk to Cantwell on the Alaska Highway.

I lay cold and damp and worrying about bears — bears! In the bag I was using as a pillow there was a pot of honey. I threw it as far as I could, pot, bag and all. There had been a stuffed giant of a grizzly bear at Anchorage airport, full ten feet tall and I spent the rest of the night trying to forget him.

Early morning, the 20th May, I heard a drone. Was it? It was. There was a vehicle on the Highway. It couldn't be far away, we could hear it. The road was open.

Two hours later we were sitting happily in the dirt of the road, brewing, in ambush for the first vehicle along. It was a vast pick-up truck full of huge tartan-jacketed, bristling, bearded men, all with faces two sizes too big and fearsome-looking rifles. They stopped while I tried to look brave and a bit bigger.

'Any chance of a lift?' I asked politely.

They looked, stared. Then,

'Where dya wanna go?' — a growl from behind which beard I couldn't see.

'Anywhere — we're trying to get to Cantwell.'

'Where ya bin?'

'Climbing. Over there.' I pointed to the Hayes Range 25 miles away.

'How long?'

'A month.' I wondered what they were after.

'Seen any grizz?'

'No, thank God.'

'We're huntin' grizz. Get in. Say why dya talk like a goddam fairy?'

What could I say?

That evening, after coffee and eggs in every café on the way, we hitched to Talkeetna. To our surprise Malc and Rob were already there. The plane had managed to get in the day after we left. The misery of that walk! Ah well it didn't matter now — in a way it was a good finish — and Talkeetna was in spring. I had never before been so abruptly aware of that good season as after this a month of unremitting winter white, and 'no-one thinks of winter when the grass is green!' A festival was planned in town that night. Roger and I showered, for hours; soaking in the benison of warm water, washing away the winter grub, left us spruce for spring outside — and that festival.

The festival was terrific. Kathy had often said, knowing my pre-diliction for third-rate bars and honky-tonk, that I was born 100 years too late. She saw me fit for the Wild West — at least the west of films. And here it was; the Talkeetna Spring Festival had it all — bar girls with trussed-up waists and thrust-up bosoms, swing-door bars, cowboy boots, jeans, square dancing — the lot, all gone

West. I loved it and went West too. In no time I was hundreds of years and thousands of miles from Deborah, drifting on another dream, another game.

Later on I got the notion to phone Kathy. She could hear the revelry and the pianos.

'What on earth's going on?' she wanted to know.

'I've found it, I've found it; listen. . . it's the Wild West, I've gone back that 100 years.'

She said, 'Come home you silly bugger.' I trotted happily off to sleep in a shed, feet back on the ground, though none too firmly, post-expedition blues blown away by the Spring Festival and Kath's good common sense. I lay on a mattress I'd salvaged from a tip, dreaming of Chaste Deborah and Honky Tonk Woman, bivouacs and broncos, ice fights and gun fights and all those silly things, and reflected — I was just able — that it was the wives and girlfriends that were the real heroes of the climbing game.

And that is near where I came in. I have run some risks, found many climbs hard; but writing this book was harder than any of them; and the biggest risk of all. If I have taken longer to tell the tale than I should, then I am sorry. I had the time to tell them shorter (though perhaps not the strength, nor the courage), but rather than tell them less I would rather not have told them at all.

If you have found it too light, then wish it more earnest; if too earnest wish it lighter. If too quick, read it slow; if too slow read it quick. Whatever it is, it is. I may be the first to wish it wasn't. What author, I wonder, hasn't lived to rue the permanency of the the written word?

'I hardly ever ope my lips' one cries;
"Simonides, what think you of my rule?"
"If you're a fool, I think you're very wise;
If you are wise, I think you are a fool." '
Who knows, how do you tell?

Where's the next adventure? The Himalayas — there's room enough there — and I have still to get up one of them; New Zealand, room enough there too. Of Patagonia, the Andes, Kenya, Alaska again, Karakorum, Hindu Kush, South Georgia, Greenland — hills on hills, crying out to the climber; saying. . . well, you know what they're saying.